EDMUND SPENSER: PRINCE OF POETS

English Literature

———

Editor

JOHN LAWLOR

Professor of English Language and Literature
in the University of Keele

EDMUND SPENSER:
PRINCE OF POETS

Peter Bayley
Fellow of University College, Oxford

HUTCHINSON UNIVERSITY LIBRARY
LONDON

HUTCHINSON & CO (*Publishers*) LTD
3 Fitzroy Square, London W1

London Melbourne Sydney Auckland
Wellington Johannesburg Cape Town
and agencies throughout the world

First published 1971

The late sixteenth-century bed valance on the cover of
the paperback edition is reproduced by courtesy of
the Trustees of the Victoria and Albert Museum

This book has been set in Fournier type, printed in Great Britain
on smooth wove paper by Anchor Press, and
bound by Wm. Brendon, both of Tiptree, Essex

ISBN 0 09 109390 2 (cased)
0 09 109391 0 (paper)

To my family
and to my colleges old and new:
University College Oxford
and
Collingwood College Durham

CONTENTS

AUTHOR'S NOTE

The 'Prince of Poets'—as he is proclaimed on his monument in Westminster Abbey—has, since Charles Lamb's time, often been thought of as the 'poets' poet'. Spenser is now in some danger of becoming the 'professors' poet', so elaborate and learned has been the scholarly investigation of his work in the last twenty years. I hope I may to some extent counteract what I think of as an over-emphasis on Spenser as intellectual and *philosophe*: I look at him chiefly as poet, story-teller and teacher of marvellous imaginative gifts.

This book has been slumbering for longer than I like to admit. I was introduced to Spenser by my original tutor, C. S. Lewis, at the beginning of the 1939–45 war. I first studied him six years later at the end of the war with my then tutor Hugo Dyson, who stimulated my interest in him as he did in everything he taught. I formed at this time the general view of Spenser's achievement which I advance in this book. I first lectured on Spenser in 1949, and I have lectured on him in almost every year since. A first draft of a book was written in 1950–1 and laid aside.

I have used the Oxford text, *The Faerie Queene* edited by J. C. Smith and the *Minor Poems* edited by E. de Selincourt, the three volumes of the Oxford English Texts edition which forms also the text of the one-volume Oxford Standard Authors edition, slightly modernising it by giving 'v' for 'u', 'j' for 'i'. I have glossed difficult words and modernised the spelling of prose.

Professor Dame Helen Gardner has probably forgotten that in 1949 she generously decided not to prepare lectures on Spenser when she heard that a new member of the Faculty was proposing to do so. Instead she lectured on Dryden. Dryden's gain was Spenser's loss, and I feel some guilt at having inadvertently deprived the Oxford English School and Spenserian studies of the benefit of her scholarship and insight. I am deeply indebted to John Lawlor who encouraged, indeed compelled me to write the book. He has been an exemplary editor, whose instinct tells him surely when to push an author and when to leave him alone. I am also grateful to Ann Douglas of Hutchinson's for her patience, encouragement and scrupulous editorial care.

I acknowledge with gratitude the generosity of the Delegates of the Oxford University Press for permission to make a little use of material in my editions for them of *The Faerie Queene*, Book I (1966) and Book II (1965); and to Edward Arnold for permission to quote from my chapter 'Order, Grace and Courtesy in Spenser's World' in *Patterns of Love and Courtesy; Essays in Memory of C. S. Lewis*, edited by John Lawlor in 1966.

University College, Oxford   P.C.B.
January 1971

LIST OF DATES

1552(?)Edmund Spenser born in London

(1558 Accession of Queen Elizabeth, on the death of the Catholic Queen Mary)

1561–9 Spenser at the Merchant Taylors' School in London

1569 *Spenser contributed verse translations to 'A Theatre' by J. van der Noodt*

1569 May: Spenser matriculated as a sizar of Pembroke Hall, Cambridge

1578 Spenser secretary to John Young (ex-Master of Pembroke Hall), Bishop of Rochester

1579 *'The Faerie Queene' probably begun*
Spenser possibly married to 'Machabyas Chylde'

1580 *'The Shepheardes Calender' published by Hugh Singleton*
Spenser-Harvey letters published
Spenser appointed secretary to the Lord Deputy of Ireland, Lord Grey de Wilton
August: Spenser probably sailed for Ireland
November: Spenser present at the siege of Smerwick, in Munster, and the defeat of the Spanish and Italian invading forces

(1581 Publication of Tasso's *Gerusalemme Liberata*)

1583 Spenser appointed a Commissioner of Musters in County Kildare

1586 Spenser took over the 'plantation' of Kilcolman, of 3000 acres in Munster

(1588 The Armada)

How does it have its life—which must be in the present or not at all? . . . if
you eliminate the past from the present—that is, if you break that continuity
which of its nature is unceasingly creative—you destroy the essential human
achievement, that which makes civilisation a spiritual reality.

F. R. LEAVIS

Poetic writing can be understood and misunderstood in many ways. In most
cases the author is not the right authority to decide on where the reader
ceases to understand and the misunderstanding begins. Many an author has
found readers to whom his work seemed more lucid than it was to himself.
Moreover, misunderstandings may be fruitful . . . frequently it is actually the
affirmative and enthusiastic readers, rather than those who rejected the book,
who have reacted to it oddly. . . . This book (*Steppenwolf*), no doubt tells of
griefs and needs; still it is not a book of a man despairing but, of a man
believing. HERMAN HESSE

. . . what the poet dreams is of the strenuous effort, physical, mental, and
moral, of waking up to one's true humanity.

NORTHROP FRYE on The Faerie Queene

To read him is to grow in mental health.

C. S. LEWIS on The Faerie Queene

I

INTRODUCTORY

'Why is it not good to have every part of the body: and every power of the soul to be fined (refined) to his best? . . . the end of education . . . is to help nature unto her perfection, which is, when all her abilities be perfected in their habit.' The writer was Richard Mulcaster, the first headmaster of the Merchant Taylors' School, at which Spenser was one of the first pupils, in his treatise on education, but it is not an inadequate description of the theme and aim of his pupil's great poem. As in all grammar schools the chief subjects studied were Latin and Greek (which largely accounts for the dissemination of classical ideas and their influence on the developing English literary tradition in the sixteenth century), but Mulcaster was significantly modern. Almost certainly he also transmitted to the young Spenser his belief in the potentialities of the English language, and his awareness of the need to enrich it into a language that could rival the classical tongues and the vernaculars of Italy and France, and so make possible the creation of a new literature, comparable to the new literatures of Italy and France, to the honour of the English nation. 'No one tongue is more fine than other naturally, but by industry of the speaker.'* 'I love *Rome*, but *London* better, I favour *Italy*, but England more, I honour the Latin, but I worship the English.' The English language he thought 'a tongue of it self both deep in conceit, and frank in delivery . . . [it] will strain with the strongest, and stretch with the furthest . . . not any whit behind either the subtle *Greek* for couching close, or the stately

* Mulcaster, *Elementarie*, Ed., E. T. Campagnac, Oxford 1925, part I, ch. 7.

Latin for spreading fair. . . . But ye will say it is uncouth. In deed being unused. And so it was in *Latin*, and so it is in each language. . . .'*

In Italy and in France writers like Dante, Boccaccio, Boiardo, Ariosto, and Ronsard, Marot and du Bellay had already shown that great literature could be created in the vernacular. No one tongue, not even perhaps a classical one, was 'more fine than other naturally, but by industry of the speaker'. Speroni in Italy in his *Dialogo delle Lingue* (1543) long before Mulcaster declared 'The tongues of every country, Arabian and Indian as Roman and Athenian, are of equal value . . . they are made and regulated by the artifice of the peoples after their own will, not planted or sown'.† Joachim du Bellay, something of whose work Spenser was early to translate, closely followed Speroni in his *La Deffence et Illustration de la Langue Francoyse* (1549). It was a general European movement, which England joined, as usual, rather late in the day. Spenser was to be the first great English vernacular poet, indeed the only great one, since Chaucer. He loved and admired Chaucer, whose influence upon him was profound, but, like Chaucer, his indebtedness to France and Italy was great, and the influence from the continent is more conspicuous than his debt to old English 'Tityrus'.

That Spenser dedicated himself to the high purpose of creating a poetic language fit for great poetry and a great heroic poem in English cannot be questioned, although he wrote no apologia like Milton's digression about his dedication to this purpose in *The Reason of Church Government*, or the great personal passages in *Paradise Lost*. His apologia is to be found in the sequence of poems he wrote. In *The Shepheardes Calender* by 'Immerito', published anonymously in 1579, the unidentified commentator E.K. (now only by a few assumed to be the mock-modest poet himself) presented the author as 'the new Poet' and spoke chiefly of his mastery of decorum, and his use of a special language, style and syntax, pointing to his belief 'that our Mother tonge, which truly of it self is both full enough for prose and stately enough for verse, hath long time been counted most barren and bare of both'. He wrote too of the author beginning with pastoral 'doubting perhaps his ability, which he little needed, or minding to furnish our tongue with this kind, wherein it faulteth, or following the example of the best and most ancient Poets . . . as young birds, that be

---

* ibid., 'The Peroration'.
† Quoted W. L. Renwick, *Edmund Spenser*, London 1925, p. 14.

newly crept out of the nest, by little first to prove their tender wings, before they make a greater flight. So flew Theocritus . . . Virgil, as not yet well feeling his wings . . . Mantuan . . . Petrarch . . . Boccaccio . . . Marot, Sannazaro and also divers other excellent both Italian and French Poets . . .' *The Shepheardes Calender*, which has the feel of deliberateness not spontaneity, derivativeness not originality, is frankly the work of a dedicated apprentice.

Ten years later Spenser himself introduced the first three parts of *The Faerie Queene*, declaring that he has followed 'all the antique Poets historical, first Homer, who in the Person of Agamemnon and Ulysses hath ensampled a good governor and a virtuous man, the one in his Iliad, the other in his Odysseis: then Virgil, whose like intention was to do in the person of Aeneas: after him Ariostos comprised them both in his Orlando: and lately Tasso dissevered them again, and formed both parts in two persons. . . .'

Between the writing of *The Shepheardes Calender* and *The Faerie Queene*, although not published until after both of them, Spenser wrote a number of poems of varied kinds most of which suggest either deliberate dependence on or imitation or emulation of the new kinds of poetry and the new poets of the century, especially in France. They were brought together in the volume *Complaints*, published in 1591. 'The Ruines of Time' is an English cousin of du Bellay's *Antiquitez de Rome*. The themes of 'The Teares of the Muses'—the poet's power to confer immortality on his patrons, on whom he in return depended entirely for his livelihood, the 'divine gift and heavenly instinct' of poetry, the poet's function as custodian and celebrator of virtue—are all commonplaces of the French poets and commentators of the Pléiade, especially of Ronsard and du Bellay. 'The Ruines of Rome' is a translation of du Bellay's *Antiquitez*, as 'The Visions of Bellay' is a translation of the French poet's *Songe*, and 'The Visions of Petrarch' of a translation by another French poet, Marot, of a *canzone* from Petrarch's *Morte di Madonna Laura*.

The other poems in the *Complaints* volume look back to older authorities: 'Virgil's Gnat', a version of an epyllion or little epic then thought to be by Virgil; 'Muiopotmos' or 'The Fate of the Butterflie', another but an original epyllion with Ovid in its ancestry; and 'Mother Hubberds Tale,' an original satire relying for the persons of its fable on the medieval French Renard cycle but Chaucerian in its energy, humour, colloquialism and couplet form.

Yet Spenser was no mere copier. Plagiarism did not become certainly a pejorative word until late in the seventeenth century and imitation has always been a valid activity for artists, and one by which most of them have learned their craft and often discovered their *métier* and subject-matter. England needed literary models, and Spenser was frankly a deliberate imitator, which is another way of saying he was a dedicated pioneer determined to naturalise in English Italian and French literary developments.

He introduced into English literature a surprising number of new metrical forms, but he also introduced a number of 'kinds' of poetry. Before him there was no pastoral worthy of the name, only Barclay's oafish clumping and his crude adaptation of Renaissance satirical pastoral into heavy-handed pretended-peasant dialogues, and George Turberville's and Barnaby Googe's more fluent but even more bathetic jingles. He introduced and acclimatised the classical ode, and those forms in which it often most happily functions, panegyric, elegiac and epithalamic. He wrote the first mock-epic ('Mother Hubberds Tale') and further anticipated the later masters of the form by writing it in couplets. 'Virgil's Gnat' and 'Muiopotmos' are pioneer English *epyllia*, playful mock-epic fancies, 'Colin Clouts Come Home Again' a unique use of pastoral for a combination of autobiographical, eulogistic and satirical purposes. Of his complaints, three are translations, from du Bellay and Petrarch, and others ('The Vision of the Worlds Vanitie' and parts of 'The Ruines of Time') imitations of the *genre*, the first, and pretty nearly the last, for it is not an important or productive *genre*, in English. His 'Astrophel' was the first true English pastoral elegy, and if not a surpassing example at least it made the way for 'Lycidas' and later for 'Adonais' and 'Thyrsis'. In the *Four Hymnes* he brought into English poetry, with Ronsard as unsuspecting midwife, a fine classical form related to the ode, just as in the two marriage-hymns he had, with far more originality, brilliance and success, acclimatised the Latin form and put it into an English version of the structure of the Italian *canzone*. Above all he gave England its first epic poem, and its only romantic epic, *The Faerie Queene*. The greatest, almost the only significant poet between Chaucer and Shakespeare, he gave to English literature achievement, example and incentive in almost all the poetic forms of the European Renaissance. He made England a great literary power, as his Queen was making it great through trade, conquest and order.

But none of these 'kinds', pastoral, ode, elegy, epithalamium, mock-epic, epic, or complaint survives. No poet now would attempt to write in any one of them. Nor would anyone emulate his styles or diction. His language is to many a real stumbling-block, not only the deliberately rude dialect of parts of *The Shepheardes Calender* intended to give the effect of rustic debate, but, in *The Faerie Queene* particularly, the seemingly archaic words and defunct forms. Ben Jonson has not been alone in thinking that 'in affecting the ancients he writ no language'. The extent of this archaism has been exaggerated. Not everything that looks archaic to us was archaic to the Elizabethans, and some archaisms, chiefly from Chaucer, had some literary vogue at the time. Spenser needed to create an entire, different and self-consistent imaginary world, and to create the glamour and imaginative force and sense of a reality more than human appropriate to his fabled land of 'Faerie'. Borrowings, adaptings and enrichings from Chaucer, like *warray*, to make war or to harass, or *encheason* for occasion or cause, or like Chaucer's *chevisaunce* quite arbitrarily (and charmingly) recruited for the name of a flower; and from French, Italian or Malorian Romance, such as *amenage* and *portaunce* for to control and for demeanour or bearing, *belgard* for a loving look, *paravaunt* for before, bring with them the glamour of their distant heritage and context. They also give invaluable help in rhyming to a poet in English, a language notoriously deficient in rhyme words. Many others, which I suspect sound for many modern readers as jejune as the 'Quoths' and 'Gramercies' of minor historical novelists, were in fact not obsolete but at the most only obsolescent in Spenser's day, and are to be found fairly easily in other Elizabethan writers: *eftsoons*, *whilom*, *uncouth* for example. One authority* estimates that in the whole of *The Faerie Queene* there are 'not over one hundred' archaic nouns and verbs, and another† puts the total for all archaisms at about 320. Spenser's free handling of words to suit his rhyme or emphasis—*dreriment*, or *drerihed* or *drerinesse*—his casual way with forms—the verb *throb* as a noun, *embrave*, compounds like *nectar-dewed* and *sea-shouldering*, and dialect words in the epic—*mickle*, *carle*, *stound*, have all been disliked by purists but admired by poets and enjoyed by readers.

The *y-* prefix on verbs and the *-en* ending on the infinitive and present participle—*ycladd*, *ydrad* for clad and dreaded, *woxen* for waxed (grown), *dispredden* for spread and *wonnen* for dwelt or,

---

* H. Sugden, *The Grammar of The Faerie Queene*, Philadelphia 1936.
† B. R. McElderry, 'Archaism and Innovation in Spenser's Poetic Diction', in *Publications of the Modern Languages Association of America*, 47 (1932).

alternatively, fought—are probably the more annoying of Spenser's archaising forms. As obtrusive, and perhaps therefore as off-putting, is his alliteration. This is also used to give an impression of an old fashion of writing because of the surviving strength of the old alliterative metre, but it also contributes valuably to the sound and to emphasis and therefore to the vividness of the poetry, its power to move us suitably.

All these characteristics of Spenser's diction and style have been attacked, as have some characteristics of his syntax, notably his masterfulness about word-order, and his determined imitation of Latin constructions, in both of which he was followed by our other great epic poet Milton. He is the first positive creator of a deliberate poetic diction and epic style in our language. The more intense the criticism of it by modern writers, the more successful we may assume the poet was. His is an absolutely unique style in a new and expressive stanza-form (both of which have proved fatal to would-be imitators). Criticism of it usually ignores a vital factor, the certainty with which any Elizabethan poet or reader would demand what is called *decorum*, or the art of writing in forms, style, language and diction appropriate to the subject-matter and 'kind' of poem. E.K.'s praise of the Spenser of *The Shepheardes Calender* in his commendatory letter for 'his complaints of love so lovely, his discourses of pleasure so pleasantly, his pastoral rudenesse', was incidental praise for his *decorum*. Contemporary readers of this poem, despite Sidney's criticism (odd in one who acknowledged and indeed advocated the principle of *decorum*) of 'that same framing of his style to an old rustic language', would have taken it for granted that the shepherds of *The Shepheardes Calender* should use rustic terms. They would not have been troubled, either, by the elaboration and learning of 'The Teares of The Muses', or the fancy and artifice of 'Muiopotmos', or the plain forcefulness of 'Mother Hubberds Tale', or by the mixture of the simple and the courtly in 'Colin Clouts Come Home Again', or by the melancholy iterations of 'Daphnaida'. And in *The Faerie Queene* they would not have found it matter for surprise or complaint that Spenser's style, diction, vocabulary and presentation vary, according to whether the matter in hand is pastoral, chivalric, courtly, epic and romantic, religious or doctrinal, apocalyptic, or of contemporary reference.

Difficulties such as these are however only contingent. They are easily overcome and need not deter a resolute reader. The real charge against Spenser is more profound: that in *The Faerie Queene* he wrote

in a dying form about a world that never was, and one which, where it
is not merely fanciful, is used for didactic purposes. Further, he uses
allegory. The combination makes a powerful deterrent in the mid-
twentieth century. Yet, when we look at these objections, we see that
they are, individually, negligible. Didacticism in literature, which
seemed to die out after the death of Ruskin and Matthew Arnold,
except for sports like Wells and Shaw whose art was always seen as
limited by their dialectic, has in the 1950s and '60s re-asserted itself.
In the theatre in particular non-plays or dramas poorly constructed
and with inadequate characterisation get by on grounds of relevance
to general or particular problems. And allegory itself, though detached
completely from its medieval and religious origins, is a device more
in vogue, especially in the theatre (*Waiting for Godot*, the plays
of Pinter) than it has ever been and, often in the novel, especially
in the work of William Golding, as ineluctable as ever it was in
Spenser.

A special aura, or miasma, of the unreal and too perfect hangs about
the poetry of Spenser. It originated with the Romantic critics, whose
loving misunderstanding of his poetry has influenced all subsequent
readers. They told readers not to worry about the story, above all
not to worry about the allegory. They recommended looking at the
pictures, surrendering to the sounds, delighting in the colour. Their
constant emphasis on the 'golden-tongued' luxuriance, the dreamlike
quality of *The Faerie Queene*, and the sort of words they used about
it—sweetness, fancy, charm, richness, grace, enchantment, harmony,
luxury, languor, delicious, drowsy, smooth, bewitching, sensuous—
are seriously misleading. In fact, of course, one could produce a rival
list—sourness, realism, repulsion, starkness, ugliness, disharmony,
energy, violence, repellent, vigorous, rough, plain, actual, harsh—
which would be more appropriate to many sequences in *The Faerie
Queene*. Hazlitt's 'the love of beauty . . . and not of truth is the moving
principle of his mind' would be truer the other way round, though
Spenser would not have made the distinction. Leigh Hunt wrote 'If
you go to him for a story, you will be disappointed' and 'Spenser is
the farthest removed from the ordinary cares and haunts of the world
of all the poets that ever wrote, except perhaps Ovid'. On the contrary,
he is a story-teller of great narrative skill and appeal, and it is increasingly realised by critics and commentators that *The Faerie Queene*
is most intimately concerned with the ordinary cares of the world.
He is far more concerned than Milton, Pope, Wordsworth, Keats,

Tennyson, Yeats or Eliot, almost as much as Chaucer, Shakespeare and the great novelists. That is my first claim for him, and one of the main themes of this book.

The leisured length of his poems, which admittedly are often repetitive and occasionally pleonastic, is another barrier for readers. In addition, I do not think Spenser 'reads' well. The more lyrical, elegiac, celebratory poems, and especially of course 'Epithalamion', are indeed fluent and musical, but *The Faerie Queene* does not on the whole read aloud well, despite many lyrical and dramatic passages of great beauty or power, and many effective conversations and speeches. It is not an oral epic, like Milton's. This is not to deny the splendour of the Spenserian stanza, in which what are in effect two quatrains are subtly linked by rhyme and then associated with the alexandrine, there being only three rhymes altogether. So it effectively combines variation and continuity, amplitude and conciseness, leisure and speed, contributing to the poem an almost tidal feeling of things happening, of life going on. The break after the long alexandrine which concludes each stanza, like the brief calm after the tumult of the ninth wave on the beach, which temporarily disturbs the even rhythm of the tide, gives us time to reflect upon, even to digest the significance while we are actually reading the lines.

There are a number of other difficulties which it would seem sensible to discuss briefly at the outset. Pastoral, a mode dear to Spenser, has almost completely lost its appeal and effect. Spenser frequented the pastoral world throughout his writing career, from the deliberate and, some may think, mechanical way of *The Shepheardes Calender*, to the triumph of its symbolic use in Book VI of *The Faerie Queene*. In almost everything he wrote between these two works, pastoral plays a part, sometimes diffident, sometimes confident, sometimes exclusive. The noble induction to 'The Ruines of Time', the shepherd-hero of 'Virgil's Gnat', Chaucer's knight in black turned into the mourning shepherd Alcyon in 'Daphnaida', in 'Astrophel' Sir Philip Sidney mourned as

A Gentle Shepherd borne in *Arcady*,
of gentlest race that ever shepheard bore:

the poet's own journey to London and back to Ireland and his experiences and reflections upon them allegorised in what he called a 'simple pastorall', though it is not the epithet I would use of 'Colin Clouts Come Home Again'; these testify to the especial attraction of pastoral for Spenser and to his varied employment of it. Elsewhere, his poetry is full of pastoral imagery and evocation. Not a nature poet in any sense, however vivid his realisation of natural scenes and of the seasons and country life, the world he describes or conjures up in his poetry (and in his poetry he is ever *creating* a world) is often seen through the filter of the pastoral convention.

He is a pastoralist in the way of Theocritus, conscious of the early days of the world as innocent, serene and happy; in the way of the Greek Romances and of Ovid where the early shepherds have been largely replaced by fauns and nymphs in a world still sunny and leafy but now governed by capricious gods; and in the way of early Christian writers in which the first and greatest shepherd, saviour of his flock, is Jesus Christ. The actual world which lay about all these writers was in truth a pastoral world; pre-industrial, not by any means innocent but not ugly; small populations and small areas of cultivation amid vast empty spaces of forest, plain or hill. Exile, and sense of loss, physical or spiritual, seem to have been elements in the idealisation characteristic of pastoral writing, whether by the Syracusan Theocritus in Alexandria or by Ovid in his Black Sea exile, or by Virgil. The biblical writers, too, were always conscious of the long exiles of the Jews and of man's banishment from the perfect pastoral garden of Eden. But Spenser is also a pastoralist in the Renaissance way. The new poets of Italy and France, seeking to establish all the classical forms in their vernaculars, wrote pastorals because Theocritus, Bion, Moschus and Virgil had, but they soon isolated an element in them, that of regret or nostalgia, and exaggerated it into complaint. So the idyllic or ideal element in pastoral became first twisted into and then overcome by sharp tones of censure. This is not as surprising as it seems. Although pastoral and satire seem to be poles apart, the impulse behind both is the same. The satirist attacks the vices, follies and abuses of his day. However violent his onslaught may be, however savage his indignation, his motivation comes from an ambition for the good. So does that of the pastoralist. The satirist attacks his age for its imperfections and corruptions; the pastoralist celebrates the perfection of an age long past, an imagined age of simplicity and piety, of simple pleasure and contentment. It is a short step from nostalgic love of the past to bitter rejection of the present. While the classical pastoralists indulged in nostalgia but only by implication condemned their own time, the Renaissance pastoralist concerned himself much more roughly and openly to express his hatred of his own times. For a time pastoral became the form in which one wrote satire. The shepherd's cloak and classical name, and the implied remoteness of the time described gave useful concealment to the satirical aim of the writer, who could disclaim any specific, libellous or politically dangerous intention.

Spenser's first collection of poems was the pastoral *Shepheardes Calender*, 'following the example of the best and most ancient Poets', but also 'minding to furnish our tongue with this kind, wherein it faulteth'. It marks a great advance on the crude pastorals of Barclay and Googe, but some of it is sorry stuff, and the poet was obviously not yet fully aware of the tremendous imaginative potentiality of pastoral.

Johnson's measured praise of idyllic pastoral,* because 'it exhibits a life, to which we have always been accustomed to associate peace, and leisure, and innocence; and therefore we readily set open the heart for the admission of its images, which contribute to drive away cares and perturbations', is qualified by a sense of the narrowness of its range. He defined pastoral poetry as that '*in which any action or passion is represented by its effects upon a country life*'.† The noble process of rendering the pastoral convention available as symbol had already happened, and Johnson did not perceive it. Most readers however would endorse his dismissal of 'September' in *The Shepheardes Calender*, which begins, he said, 'with studied barbarity:

> "*Diggon Davie*, I bid her good-day:
> Or, Diggon her is, or I missay.
> *Dig.* Her was her while it was day-light,
> But now her is a most wretched wight."‡

What will the reader imagine to be the subject on which speakers like these exercise their eloquence? Will he not be somewhat disappointed, when he finds them met together to condemn the corruptions of the church of Rome. Surely, at the same time that a shepherd learns theology, he may gain some acquaintance with his native language.' The heavy irony is two-handled, scorning at once the satire on an ecclesiastical subject, and the rude dialect. I would

* *Rambler*, no. 36.
† ibid., no. 37.
‡ Which Professor Wrenn in *Word and Symbol*, London 1967, p. 107, found 'read aloud in a resonant south-western accent . . . delightfully effective'.

not wish to defend Spenser here, though it is a brave, or foolhardy, attempt at a difficult craft, dialect in rhyme; and as a Renaissance pastoralist he would have evaded his role of naturalising all the forms into English if he had not written satirically. The subject-matter, too, concerned him. It was not only because of the convention that Spenser included satirical eclogues in *The Shepheardes Calender*.

Always a moralist, although generally concealing his moral purpose in the richness of his conjurations of imaginary worlds, it is only to be expected that he will sometimes be a satirist as well as a pastoralist. 'Mother Hubberds Tale', his most ambitious satirical work, reviews in its serio-comic form of a beast-fable many of the abuses of Elizabethan England, political, social and ecclesiastical. The satire in the ecclesiastical eclogues of *The Shepheardes Calender*, 'May', 'July', and 'September' is narrower and cruder. Spenser has gone to school to Alexander Barclay, some of whose eclogues first appeared in about 1514. They were in the tradition of the satirical eclogues (1498) of Baptista Spagnuoli, known as the Mantuan, though their matter was sometimes derived from a prose satire on the miseries of courtiers, *Miseriae Curialium*, by Aeneas Sylvius who became Pope Pius II in 1458. They contained debates between classically-named shepherds, Coridon, Cornix, Codrus, Minalcas, who are presented as simple English shepherds, speaking in jog-trot couplets on such subjects as the miseries and evil of court life, the neglect of poets by patrons, and the respective merits of town and country life. What is chiefly wrong about them, apart from their intrinsic unpoeticalness, is what is wrong with Mantuan, cogently expressed by C. S. Lewis: 'the extraordinary spectacle of a literary impulse almost exactly like that of Juvenal expressing itself through a medium originally devised for the purposes of refreshment and escape.'*

Spenser's shepherds in his three satirical eclogues do not express Juvenalian themes directly. When he writes, as in 'October', of the neglect of patrons, it is not in a satirical eclogue, and this topic is subservient to a larger comment about his faith in the poetical vocation. His satire is limited to discussion about the state of the church in the England of his time. It is unlike Barclay's, and like the great English satires of Dryden and Pope, in being directly related to actual events that concerned the poet. The three eclogues belong to and reflect his period after leaving Cambridge, when he was employed as secretary to a bishop, John Young, who had been Master of Spenser's college

* *Oxford History of English Literature*, vol. III, 1954, p. 131.

of Pembroke Hall throughout his time there. Young became Bishop
of Rochester in 1577, the same year that the Archbishop of Canterbury,
Edmund Grindal, incurred the Queen's displeasure and was suspended
for his sympathy with the ecclesiastical left wing. Grindal had also
been Master of Pembroke Hall. It was a college with a tradition of
liberal churchmanship in a Cambridge that provided the stage for the
first struggles of the Puritans, as they were soon to be called, with the
authority of Elizabeth's established church.

The period at the beginning of her reign when it seemed that the
English church would move gradually further away from the old
church, when the Marian exiles—such as Grindal—on their return had
found their views, impregnated by the European Reformation, in
some favour and had thought them likely to prevail, was beginning to
wane. Elizabeth's view of a state church came to seem to the advanced
reformers almost as reactionary and deplorable as Rome itself. The
open struggle began at Cambridge.

Spenser's Pembroke connexions biassed him to the left, a bias which
appears in the satirical religious eclogues of *The Shepheardes Calender*.
There have been many interpretations of these crude allegories,
some arguing that they are simply anti-Catholic, some that they are
puritan in slant and attack the Anglican establishment for its continued
contamination by Roman practices, vestments and rituals. It is always
difficult and usually mistaken to try to be too precise in interpretation
of allegory. Spenser was not, as far as we can tell from his writings,
doctrinally a Puritan but he moved in reformist circles.* It is unlikely
in the light of his generally conventional views on order and of his
convinced support of the monarchy and of aristocratic ideals, that he
would have favoured the abolition of the established church and its
replacement by a Presbyterian system. Although there is in these
ecclesiastical eclogues considerable contemporary colouring, with a
left-wing Protestant bias, Spenser is more concerned with what is
after all more appropriate in pastoral, even in satirical pastoral, the
contrast between the great opposites, virtue and evil, simplicity and
sophistication, humility and pride, austerity and indulgence. Here
they are crudely contrasted, dully drawn, but they lie at the heart of
the pastoral ideal, and are the concern of all moralists and most satirists.

So, raw as they are in *The Shepheardes Calender* they presage the

* At Cambridge, at Rochester and in London, particularly with the Leicester
circle. Also the publisher of *The Shepheardes Calender*, Hugh Singleton, was a
prominent Puritan publisher.

great preoccupations of *The Faerie Queene*. In that work, too, while innocence and simplicity are everywhere celebrated, there is little if any allegorical reference to Puritanism as such although several important episodes clearly expose the corruptions of Catholicism and the dangers of Rome.

2

'THE NEW POET'

Spenser's poetry is unusually homogeneous. The subjects that concerned him, and the attitudes he expressed to them at the beginning of his career were the subjects and attitudes of all his poetry to the very end, however different the forms in which he wrote. His first published poems were translations which appeared in 1569, without attribution. They are assumed to have been Spenser's because in 1591 most of them appeared in slightly different form under his name in his collection *Complaints*. Were this not so, they are so characteristic of Spenser, and so clearly anticipated much of his later work that it would be an easy claim to make with confidence.

The work must have been done while Spenser was still at school, yet the verse is as fluent and melodious as anything written in the sixteenth century in English except the songs of Wyatt and Surrey and Sackville's 'Induction' to *The Mirror for Magistrates*. There are early examples of effective blank verse, and a clever use of assonance and consonantal rhyming to induce an atmosphere of strange doom appropriate to the subjects. The volume's title, *A Theatre wherein be represented as wel the miseries and calamities that follow the voluptuous worldlings, as also the great joyes and pleasures which the faithful do enjoy. An argument both profitable and delectable to all that sincerely love the Word of God*, advertises its moralising nature but not the vehement and crude anti-Catholic tone of much of it. John van der Noodt of Antwerp, the compiler, was a Protestant refugee in London from Spanish persecution in the Netherlands. Spenser was perhaps permanently influenced by the fervour of his attack on the pomp, vanity, cruelty and evil of Rome in the prose treatise of which the volume is chiefly composed, and also by his four apocalyptic sonnets.

The words of that long title happen to summarise Spenser's lifelong triple preoccupations as a poet: with virtue, and with the imperfections and the transitoriness of human life. He wrote no poem, long or short, which did not express one or more of these preoccupations. He trafficked in them with the utmost versatility, of 'kind' of poem, of verse-form, of imaginative scale and range, of emotional depth and of intellectuality, most marvellously and subtly of course in *The Faerie Queene*, most clumsily and tentatively in *A Theatre for Worldlings*, to which he contributed translations of twenty-one epigrams and sonnets from the French: six 'Epigrams', translations from Marot's French versions of Petrarch, eleven 'Sonets' from du Bellay, and four more sonnets dealing with the Apocalypse, translated from the French of van der Noodt. All of them are near kin to the popular 'vision' and 'emblem' poetry of the time: moralising verses, accompanying copper or wood engravings which present simple allegories, or summarise classical stories, or are derived from folk lore, while they commend some moral action, behaviour or attitude. Characteristic 'Epigrams' show, both in verse and picture, such episodes as a ship overwhelmed in a storm, a laurel tree struck by lightning, a spring that vanishes into the earth with its muses and nymphs. The 'Sonets' show a great building thrown down by an earthquake, a triumphal arch broken all to dust, a woodland spring with a hundred nymphs about it who are driven to flight by a rout of fauns. All are images of the transitoriness of human life or human glory. Van der Noodt provides some specific interpretations: the ship represents Petrarch's Laura and all her beauty and virtues, the laurel tree is Laura and the singing birds her fair speech and singing, the lightning and the storm her death. His own apocalyptic sonnets, presenting the beast of Revelation, the woman on the beast, the Word of God and the New Jerusalem, contrast cosmic transitoriness—the two apocalyptic visions of Antichrist—with the promise of redemption.

Allegory may be interpreted in several ways, and often the less specifically the more satisfactorily. The examples mentioned treat of the vicissitudes of fortune, and the sudden loss of beauty, security, joy or life itself. This is a commonplace enough poetic theme, and the young Spenser took it up because it was a commonplace, but it became a major preoccupation of his creative imagination.

He thus began his poetical apprenticeship translating the most celebrated of the new poets of Italy and France. And he began also with a *genre*—the vision or emblem-poem—and a sequence of *themes*, the vanity of human wishes and aspirations, the transience of earthly glory and human life, the precariousness of virtue, which were congenial to him, and which dominated his imagination and dictated the subjects of his poetry for the rest of his life. Furthermore, he frequented from the very beginning of his poetic career, the strange, intriguing world of allegory. Admittedly it was allegory at its most simple and static, but it was still allegory, and the young poet thus began in yet another way at the centre of the intellectual and artistic fashion of the day. It was a fashion that admirably combined the two functions of literature, as they were seen by the Elizabethans: profit and delight, teaching and pleasing. To take an example from the 'Epigrams':

> Within this wood, out of the rocke did rise
> A Spring of Water mildely romblyng downe,
> Whereto approched not in any wise
> The homely Shepherde, nor the ruder cloune,
> But many Muses, and the Nymphes withall,
> That sweetly in accorde did tune their voice
> Unto the gentle sounding of the waters fall.
> The sight whereof dyd make my heart rejoyce.
> But while I take herein my chiefe delight,
> I sawe (alas) the gaping earth devoure
> The Spring, the place, and all cleane out of sight.
> Which yet agreves my heart even to this hour.

A reader of *A Theatre for Worldlings*, coming to this epigram, would receive a number of minor pleasures: a woodcut showing four admittedly rather massive nymphs singing by a spring in a wood; the poem itself, quite an assured piece of versification for a schoolboy of sixteen or seventeen, melodious and vivid; and then the pleasure of recognising the allegorical moral, which dawns on the reader as the poem closes— beauty passes, happiness may not endure. There is another incidental pleasure: that of recognising and frequenting an imaginative world, the world of clasical belief. It was the classical world seen through the enhancing and prettifying filter of the Renaissance imagination. Elizabethan writers were naturalised inhabitants of that imaginative world, and Spenser of them all the most at home in it.

This early piece of translation, tentative and slight though it is, gives a small key to the understanding and enjoyment of much

Elizabethan literature, and particularly to the poetry of 'the prince of
poets in his time'. The pictorial interest, the imagining of a classical
world, the fascination of emblem and allegory, the moral concern,
and the aphoristic moral comment are all to be found almost everywhere in Spenser, reaching their fulfilment in *The Faerie Queene*. It
is worth noticing that this imagined world, in this little poem, is
already as it were a part of the world of *The Faerie Queene*, that
unsurveyed territory of woods and glades and springs, muse-haunted,
peopled with nymphs, fairies and satyrs which lay still in embryo in
Spenser's imagination. It is also worth noticing the first appearance
of one of Spenser's favourite figures:

> That sweetely in accorde did tune their voice
> Unto the gentle sounding of the waters fall;

and, already, his command over feeling, shown in the change from the
sweet calm of the first eight lines to the shock and sadness of the last
quatrain.

The 'Epigrams' are translations of a French version by Clément
Marot of Canzone VI in *Morte di Madonna Laura*; the 'Sonets' are
taken from the *Songe* or 'Dream' of du Bellay, inspired by Petrarch's
24th canzone, which had already also been translated into French
by Marot, under the title of *Des Visions de Petrarch*. They are introduced by a sonnet which tells of a ghost appearing to the poet on the
banks of the Tiber:

> And calling me then by my propre name,
> He bade me upward into heaven looke.
> He cride to me, and loe (quod he) beholde,
> What under this great Temple[1] is containde,
> Loe all is nought but flying vanitie.
> So I knowing the worldes unstedfastnesse,
> Sith onely God surmounts the force of tyme,
> In God alone do stay my confidence.

This again might well stand for a statement of Spenser's faith, both
as a man and as poet. All his poetry declares that in the end 'all is
nought but flying vanitie', and the concluding lines are echoed in
what are probably the last lines Spenser ever wrote, in the Mutabilitie
Cantos. Here Spenser declared that he loathed

[1] *this great Temple* the heavens

> This state of life so tickle
> And love of things so vaine to cast away;
> Whose flowering pride, so fading and so fickle,
> Short *Time* shall soon cut down with his consuming sickle.

But by the time of the Mutabilitie Cantos, Spenser was able to refute this overpowering sense of the transitoriness and vanity of human life, and the second of the two stanzas which are subjoined to the Mutabilitie Cantos continues:

> Then gin I think on that which Nature sayd
> Of that same time when no more Change shall be
> But steadfast rest of all things firmely stayd
> Upon the pillours of Eternity . . .
>
> .   .   .
>
> . . . thenceforth all shall rest eternally
> With him that is the God of Sabbaoth hight:

Spenser progressed from translation of poetry which expressed a conventional poetic commonplace, through a number of original writings on the same theme, to a full discussion of the ways in which living according to the precepts of God will give the lie to the pessimistic view of the vanity and instability of human life. *The Faerie Queene* does not altogether confidently refute it, in the end, although that is what it set out to do; but it remains the most morally *convinced* work in our language, as well as the most imaginative.

Later, Spenser spent a little more time on the sonnets and epigrams, when he prepared them for publication in *Complaints* (1591). He then wisely omitted from the 'Sonets' the four apocalyptic poems, replacing them by four new emblems, giving them all rhyme and entitling them 'The Visions of Bellay'; and polished the 'Epigrams' making them all true sonnets, adding another about 'vaine worlds glorie', and calling them 'The Visions of Petrarch', but the roughness of the original translation had an uncouth force, and the need to amplify the twelve-line stanza—his version of the twelve-line stanzas of the original Petrarchan canzone and of Marot's French version—into the sonnet's fourteen lines has led to some dilution of strength. For example, the addition

> And wounds my soule with rufull memorie,
> To see such pleasures gon so suddenly.

weakens, not strengthens the force of the 'epigram' quoted on page 30.

But these versions, whether as they originally appeared in *A Theatre* or as they appeared in *Complaints*, are of little originality or intrinsic value. Their interest lies in their promise, and in their anticipation of Spenserian themes, moods and worlds to come.

Between 1569 and 1591 Spenser wrote much other poetry, most of it conventional or traditional, or having a literary ancestry rather than springing from his own imagination or experience. The next work of his to be published, again without mention of his name, *The Shepheardes Calender* (1579), has many difficulties for the modern reader, difficulties which often look more like blemishes. Spenser's version of pastoral has little of the idyllic charm of Theocritan pastoral; the language is sometimes deliberately crude, the metres often intentionally stumbling or banal, and the subject-matter often simple or tedious. Further, while it is ostensibly a collection of twelve pieces unified by the device of the twelve months and by the pastoral convention, it is in fact heterogeneous enough for the claim of unity to seem specious. Most damning of all, it undeniably seems manufactured, even to those who admire it. One does not often feel that the creator is genuinely and excitedly involved in his creation. A final difficulty is that *The Shepheardes Calender* is accompanied by an elaborate apparatus of gloss and comment, and treated as if it were a great addition to the glories of world literature. It is not that, but the learned apparatus is perhaps justified in that it gave the collection a larger splash, made it more clearly a manifesto of new directions in English poetry and new achievements by a 'new poet'.

There have been many interpretations of *The Shepheardes Calender*. One sees its argument as about the rejection of the pastoral life for the truly dedicated life of the world, which for Spenser is that of the heroic poet whose high religious calling is to serve the Queen and to inspire this countrymen to virtuous action. 'Within this structure Spenser explores the role of the poet and pastor in society. The subject of the eclogues alternates from poet to pastor regularly (three and four being taken as one) until October where the poet aspires to fulfil the pastor's role in society.'* Another, finding it based upon three topics, love, religion and poetry, thinks that its governing subject is the contrast between good shepherds (Hobbinol, Thenot, Piers) and bad ones (Palinode, Cuddie, Morrell), and between the Spirit and the

* A. C. Hamilton, 'The Argument of *The Shepheardes Calender*', *Journal of English Literary History*, XXIII (1956), pp. 177ff.

B

Flesh, but reaches a similar conclusion, that '*the Shepheardes Calender* is the young Spenser's declaration . . . that he knows to what heights he is called, to what purpose he has been graced, and that he is ready to undertake the task

> 'To teach the ruder shepherd how to feede his sheep . . .'

Colin is not Spenser; at most he is what Spenser or any other gifted poet, or pastor, might become.'* This is clearly an important element in the poem, but I do not believe this derivative and deliberately eclectic work is so decisively stated a manifesto of future purpose. Spenser took its name from the French *Le Compost et Kalendrier des Bergiers* (originally 1493), a sort of popular almanac, encyclopaedia and handbook of devotion, but of course changed its Romish into Protestant polemic. He also took the idea of comparing the course of human life with the passing of the year from Marot's *Eclogue au Roy* (to which 'December' is especially indebted). *Piers Plowman* and Skelton's anti-prelatical satire *The Boke of Colin Clout* suggested names, and point to strong elements in the poem. Conventional Renaissance topics for satire, especially on niggardly patrons, on the importance of the poet's role and on the evils and miseries of court life are more than balanced by Spenser's piety to classical pastoral, with its shepherds' singing-contests, elegies, eulogies and discussions of love. Many themes as well as many forms and metres are brought together and many writers are under levy from England's 'new poet'. It is not helpful to seek to impose too definite a statement of aim or theme, and I doubt whether anything written on *The Shepheardes Calender* is as just and helpful as E.K.'s dedicatory accounts which preface the collection, and which emphasise the poet's practical desire to learn his trade, exercise the language and introduce into it his imitations of the great classical and Renaissance poets.

What Spenser did in *The Shepheardes Calender* was to combine in one collection of twelve eclogues much idyllic pastoral in most of its modes, some satirical-pastoral and contemporary allegory, some verse which was neither specifically satirical nor pastoral, many general reflections on conventional topics or truisms, some comment on the poet's trade and vocation, some conventional flattery of the Queen, and probably some deliberate autobiographical references. He linked

---

* R. A. Durr, 'Spenser's Calender of Christian Time', *ELH*, XXIV (1957), pp. 270 ff.

this variety of subject-matter by creating a *dramatis persona* and by the device of the passing of the months.

'January' begins the year, and the eclogue for that month is a brief pastoral lament for lost love. The season of the year corresponds with the season in the life of the shepherd poet, Colin Clout, who is shown as unhappy as the season and the landscape in which he appears. He is forlorn and miserable like the month, and sees in his surroundings a complete metaphor of his grief. The sheep, like their shepherd, are pale and wan. He 'pynes' with mourning, they 'with pyning mourne'. The barren ground mirrors his plight. Such rage as winter's reigns in his heart; his life-blood freezes like the ground, and from his eyes 'the drizzling tears descend' as on the boughs 'the ycicles depend'. In every respect his miserable state echoes and balances the sad season of the year, but there is also antithesis, first in the fact that the shepherd in his spring of life is likened to winter, secondly in that this particular January day, which is 'a sunneshine day', presages recovery, warmth and renewal, but there is no such hope for Colin:

> And yet alas, but now my spring begonne,
> And yet alas, yt is already donne. (29–30)

The poem is a subtle exercise in balance and antithesis, of structure as of matter.

It is also a poem of a rare formal perfection. The stanza is a light one, admirable in size and weight for its purpose: a spare six-line stanza with alternate rhyme in the quatrain and a concluding rhymed couplet. The stanza though a unity in itself falls naturally into its two parts, and the emphasis, whether on quatrain or couplet, varies through-out the poem. The balance or proportion of the 'January' stanza, a proportion of four to two, holds also for the poem as a whole. The 'quatrain' section, the first two-thirds, shows the shepherd as unhappy as the season and the landscape in which he appears. At the end of it, at the proper point of balance, in stanza 9 comes for the first time a broken couplet—

> Yet all for naught: such sight hath bred my bane,
> Ah, God, that love should breede both joy and payne— (53–4)

making an emphatic general observation and relating the particular, Colin's unhappy love, to a general statement about love. After it comes the 'couplet' section, the concluding one-third, which provides a marked *dénouement*. The particular cause of the previously generalised pain and sorrow is revealed: Rosalind's rejection of him is the particular cause of Colin's seasonable melancholy.

The poem is built on a firm rhetorical structure. The pastoral framework (the first two stanzas and the last stanza) encloses a formal 'complaint' with a standard rhetorical scheme: *apostrophe* ('Ye Gods of love, that pitie lovers payne') plus *narratio* plus *lament*. But Spenser further breaks down the standard rhetorical scheme into smaller components so that six of the ten stanzas that comprise the complaint are themselves stock complaints in miniature, though the pattern is not uniform. Stanzas 3 and 4 are each complete in their rhetorical form, but stanza 5 does not begin with *apostrophe* but continues the *narratio* and *then* the *lament*. Stanzas 6 and 7 repeat the pattern of stanzas 4 and 5. The *apostrophe* of stanza 8 is followed by *narratio* which occupies the rest of the stanza and most of the next, but stanza 9 *ends* with a further *apostrophe*, the important 'Ah God, that love should breede both joy and payne', as does stanza 10.

It needs assurance as well as great technical control thus to adopt a discipline and to diverge from it. Lesser poets could not and did not so break and counterpoint their rhetorical pattern, and in them the uniformity of the pattern makes for tedium. Spenser as always varies considerably within his rule, and is always aware of the need for some freedom within a discipline. The repetition of a rhetorical formula obviously gives weight and emphasis as well as echo to a poem, and is especially efficacious in elegy or complaint. Repetition with variation is an added intellectual and musical pleasure. Much of Spenser's much-lauded harmony is due to the strong rhetorical framework on which his poems, particularly formal ones, complaints, elegies, wedding-odes, are built, and his poetic mastery is revealed in the ease and grace and the effect of spontaneity even these most rigidly assembled poems possess. Discipline here increases delight. This is not only evidenced in Spenser's poetic practice; it is one of his chief poetic themes.

Perhaps I have given the 'January' eclogue disproportionate attention. This discussion of it is meant to show the technical skill of the 'new poet' and to serve as an introduction to some of Spenser's predilections and poetic methods. It should also declare that although this is a poet who seems in the effortless flow of his verse and the apparently superficial nature of his thought to be an unsubtle, unintellectual poet, a painter of pictures and a maker of music, in fact the texture is dense and his poetry demands as careful reading and thought as that of poets more obviously complex.

Colin Clout, the poet himself, is the chief character of the *Calender*.
He figures in 'June' and 'November', as well as opening and closing
the collection in 'January' and 'December', and he is a subject for
discussion by other shepherds in 'April', 'August' and 'October', in
two of which a lay of his is sung by another shepherd. In 'April'
a discussion between two shepherds Thenot and Hobbinol about
Colin Clout's unhappiness in love, is followed by Colin's lay 'of
faire Eliza, Queene of shepheardes all',

> Which once he made, as by a spring he laye,
> And tuned it unto the Waters fall. (36–7)

The discussion is carried on rather clumsily in decasyllabic quatrains
with clumping alternate rhyme, and some interlacing of rhyme between stanzas. They are clumsy by design (though there are clumsier
elsewhere in the collection) to suggest rustic wits and also to emphasise by contrast Colin's 'more excellencie and skill in poetrie', referred
to in the Argument to the eclogue. This skill is certainly demonstrated
in the lay in 'April', the first of Spenser's many poetic celebrations of
Queen Elizabeth. It is one of Spenser's own original verse-forms,
a nine-line stanza with lines of varying length, which proclaims its
musical affinities and its musical nature. C. H. Herford hit off its
quality nicely when he wrote of its 'wayward and wanton buoyancy'
and its 'rapturous tone'. The lay or ode in praise of the Queen has
antecedents in Virgilian eclogues in praise of Caesar, and in Italy and
France there had been a renaissance of panegyric, but there was
nothing quite like this. Spenser's originality has been underprized.
He completely acclimatised here a number of disparate elements. The
Queen is flattered and praised, presented as a virgin of surpassing
beauty sitting on 'the grassie greene' garlanded with English flowers;
but she is also daughter of Syrinx and Pan, Phoebus and Cynthia, the
sun and moon, are abashed at her beauty, the Muses play and sing to
her, the Graces dance before her and the nymphs attend. Spenser
creates this Botticellian idyll in a free ode which has yet the simplicity
and insouciance of an English country song. Spenser's lightness and
informality here, the freshness and seemingly random ease of versification, diction and vocabulary, make the words 'ode' and 'panegyric'
seem too portentous. The form and intention may have the highest
literary ancestry, but the result is nearer to song and to the spirit of
the pageants and shows devised for entertaining the Queen when she
visited cities and great houses, than it is to Virgil, or Italian or

French pastoralists and panegyrists of the Renaissance.

The 'June' eclogue continues the tale of a lover's woe begun in 'January'. Hobbinol, content with his state—

> The simple ayre, the gentle warbling wynde,
> So calme, so coole, as no where else I fynde:
> The grassye ground with daintye Daysies dight,
> The Bramble bush, where Byrds of every kynde
> To the waters fall their tunes attemper right— (4–8)

is contrasted with the hapless Colin Clout rejected by his Lady, Rosalind. Hobbinol urges Colin to leave those hills where he dwells and resort to the dales where, instead of night ravens, elvish ghosts and 'ghostly owles' he will encounter 'friendly Faeries', many Graces, 'lightfote Nymphes', the Muses and Pan himself. As Colin Clout always stands for Spenser himself, so Hobbinol, first mentioned by Colin himself in 'January', stands for Gabriel Harvey, and is so identified in E.K.'s *glosse* to 'September'. Harvey, a young Fellow of Spenser's college, Pembroke Hall, later a Fellow of Trinity Hall and a great personal friend, remained in Cambridge. Spenser did not. Hobbinol may well be speaking of Cambridge, haunt of the Graces and Muses; Colin had left Cambridge and may have been in the North, unsuccessfully wooing Rosalind, but certainly he is shown as restless and unhappy. The love-plaint itself, examples of which begin, end and form the pivot ('January', 'December', 'June') of the collection of eclogues, may or may not be autobiographical, though complaint of love is a conventional topic in this kind of pastoral writing. But beneath the autobiographical element of this eclogue, often found beneath the pastoral convention, lies another element, in which 'shepherd' stands for 'poet', and 'June' is related also to 'October' in its discussion of the poetic vocation. Colin envies Hobbinol his dwelling and the circumstances of his life which are conducive to literary endeavour, and remembers that when he was younger and lived there he was able to sing and write. Hobbinol recalls Colin's 'rymes and roundelayes' of those days, which taught the birds to hold their peace 'for shame of thy swete layes' and which made Calliope with the other Muses

> ... from the fountaine, where they sat around,
> Renne after hastely thy silver sound.
> But when they came, where thou thy skill didst showe,
> They drewe abacke, as halfe with shame confound,
> Shepheard to see, them in theyr art outgoe. (60–4)

Colin rejects such hyperbole, and protests that as it was presumption of Pan to strive with Apollo (as recounted in Ovid, *Metamorphoses* XI) so he himself never presumed 'to Parnasse hyll'—that is, to write in any but the humblest and simplest of poetic forms. These, he asserts, are in any case, appropriate to his subject-matter, his own misery at rejected love.

Rosalind's cruelty is again bewailed in 'August', in the 'heavy laye', a repetitive hyperbole of woe, which the shepherd Cuddie sings—it is Colin Clout's 'doolefull verse of Rosalend'—after a tripping duet between the shepherds Willye and Perigot. This eclogue shows as clearly as any Spenser trying out his wings in conventional forms. Willye and Perigot challenge each other to a singing-match, like the shepherds in Theocritus (*Idylls* 4 and 5), Virgil (*Eclogues* 3 and 5), and Ronsard (4) and others, in the same six-line stanza (*ababcc*) as is used in 'January' and 'December'; here it is continually broken up into couplets, quatrains and once enlarged into a double-stanza so that the two shepherds do not speak only in formal stanzas. The singing-match is not at all like the decorous antiphony of Virgil's third eclogue, or the separate grand virtuoso performance of his fifth, and is closer to the more informal work of the Pléiade. Spenser's is really a roundelay in which Perigot leads and Willye chimes the 'undersong'; sometimes merely echoing Perigot, sometimes amplifying his line. Simple and rough in diction, it really sings. Perhaps it sings too jollily for its subject-matter, the smarts of love. Again Spenser gives us the distinct feeling of country life and country song. But the 'doolefull verse' which Cuddie then sings—

> Ye wastefull woodes beare witnesse of my woe—

is a version of the—originally Provençal—elaborate Petrarchan *sestina*, a poem of six stanzas of six lines each (plus an *envoi*), worked upon six rhyme-sounds only. Spenser's scheme is even more elaborate. It is played on the words *woe, sound, cryes, part, sleepe, augment*, which come always in that order, each new stanza repeating the rhyme-word at the end of its predecessor; so it rhymes *abcdef, fabcde, efabcd, defabc, cdefab, bcdefa*; and the three-line *envoi* uses internal rhyme to repeat the sequence in half the time! Commentators have been contemptuous of this lay—'dull', 'fustian', 'unsubstantial' and 'conventional'; I find it a skilful rhetorical construction, with some power to move:

> Thus all the night in plaints, the daye in woe
> I vowed have to wayst, till safe and sound
> She home returne, whose voyces silver sound
>   To cheerefull songs can chaunge my cherelesse cryes.
> Hence with the Nightingale will I take part,
> That blessed byrd, that spends her time of sleepe
> In songs and plaintive pleas, the more taugment
> The memory of hys misdeede, that bred her woe:
> And you that feele no woe, when as the sound
>   Of these my nightly cryes ye heare apart
>   Let breake your sounder sleepe and pitie augment.   (178–89)

What other poet writing in 1577 or 1578, or what poet of the preceding thirty years, except perhaps Sackville, could write like this? The repetitiveness and hyperbole, and the insistent alliteration, of which critics have complained, powerfully impose Spenser's mood on the reader's or listener's response. This is an aspect of his writing which has been under-regarded. Spenser so fills the reader's imagination that he can think of nothing else and feel nothing else, except the mood the poet wills: here, lifeless misery and despair.

Colin does not appear in 'October' but Piers and Cuddie pay tribute to him as poet, and through them Spenser allows himself to ruminate a little on the poetic vocation. In 'Lycidas' Milton's paragraph on the ill-rewards of poetry which ends with Phoebus's rebuke descends from Piers's—

> Cuddie, the prayse is better, than the price,
> The glory eke much greater than the gayne— (19–20)

as Cuddie's complaint in 'October' about the neglect of poets by patrons descends from Theocritus (*Idyll* XVI) through a host of other poets including Mantuan (*Eclogue* 5) and through him the rude English pastoralist Barclay (*Eclogue* 4). It is a common theme, too, in du Bellay and Ronsard. But Spenser in 'October' goes beyond simple grievance, and has Piers and Cuddie discuss poetic ambition and the moral power of poetry. We would not be surprised if this were openly a discussion between Hobbinol (Gabriel Harvey) and Colin Clout (Spenser) rather than Piers and Cuddie, but the poet modestly has Piers encourage, not Colin, but Cuddie, to

> Abandon then the base & viler clowne,
> Lyft up thy selfe out of the lowly dust:
> And sing of bloody Mars, of wars, of giusts,[1]

[1] *giusts* jousts

> Turne thee to those, that weld the awful crowne.
> To doubted[1] Knights, whose woundlesse armour rusts,
> And helmes unbruzed waxen dayly browne.   (37–42)

This advertises by implication Spenser's readiness to move on from pastoral verse and concern with lowly subjects to epic poetry, the romantic epic dominant for a hundred years since Boiardo prepared the way for Ariosto and Tasso. Cuddie is reminded of Virgil ('Romish *Tityrus*') who 'left his Oaten reede' (the *Eclogues*) and 'laboured lands to yield the timely care' (wrote the *Georgics*) before going on to

> . . . sing of warres and deadly drede,
> So as the Heavens did quake his verse to here

(the master-work of the *Aeneid*). Spenser thus early in his career marks out his future path and his ambitions for future greatness. But he is also aware of the inadequacies of patrons. When Piers suggests that Cuddie should continue to write high verse to celebrate the Queen, or, if he pleases, to celebrate

> . . . the worthy whome she loveth best,
> That first the white beare to the stake did bring— (47–8)

that is, Robert Dudley, Earl of Leicester, whose arms portray a white bear and ragged staff (still familiar on many an inn-sign in the Midlands), Cuddie complains that Maecœnas and Augustus are long dead and there are none in the present age to encourage poets to high endeavour. He goes on to say that he is too weak and wan for noble writing, but that Colin is fit to mount high, 'were he not with love so ill bedight'. So Spenser returns again to the hapless lover *motif* in the *Calender*, but with a difference, for Piers now preaches the Platonic doctrine of the ennobling power of love, which, he says, teaches Colin how to climb up, out of the loathsome mire. Cuddie does not agree, and speaks of love as a fell tyrant.

Although most critics and commentators think it the noblest and most interesting of the poems in *The Shepheardes Calender*, it seems to me rather synthetic, 'assembled', but it is an interesting declaration of faith in the vocation of poetry, and it appropriately introduces its successor.

In the 'November' eclogue Thenot asks Colin Clout for a joyful song, either of love or in honour of Pan. Colin replies that November

---

[1] *doubted* redoubted

is no time for a song of merry-making; sad winter, the sullen season, calls for a sad song, and he therefore provides a dirge for Dido. It is modelled on Clément Marot's *Complainct de Madame Loyse de Savoye* (1531), although both derive ultimately from Greek elegy, and especially from Moschus's elegy for Bion. It contains the standard *motifs* of lament: statement of the cause of grief, the questioning why Fate has removed a worthy soul, and the finding of consolation in religion, or philosophy, or in belief in immortality or the after-life, and it makes full use of the pathetic fallacy, all nature mourning the loss. Spenser's is the first classical elegy in English, as his lyrical panegyric of Elizabeth in 'April' was the first classical panegyric ode in English. The verse-form is original. Each stanza begins with an alexandrine, continues in four decasyllables, followed by an octosyllabic couplet (except stanza three), a four-syllabled refrain 'O heavie herse' broken by a decasyllabic line before the four-syllabled refrain is completed with 'O carefull verse' (in the last third of the poem, stanzas 12–15, the refrain lifts to 'O happy herse . . . O joyfull verse'). It is astonishingly and successfully elaborate: there has been no more resourceful inventor or adaptor of metres and verse-forms than Spenser in our language. Although the change of mood from despair to hope in an elegy is common, few have handled it so triumphantly. In his twelfth stanza the transition from grief to triumph is heralded by three heavy stresses and strengthened by heavy weighting and by insistent alliteration:

> But maugre death, and dreaded sisters deadly spight,
> And gates of hel, and fyrie furies forse:
> She hath the bonds broke of eternall night.   (163–5)

The opening of this stanza, the turning-point of the poem, sounds forth like trumpets. There is one stanza in the elegy, stanza 11, which is not in Marot and owes little to other elegists, although it is a poetic commonplace elsewhere in post-Christian poetry:

> O trustlesse state of earthly things, and slipper[1] hope
> Of mortal men, that swincke[2] and sweate for nought,
> And shooting wide, doe misse the marked scope[3]:
> Now have I learnd (a lesson derely bought)
> That nys[4] on earth assurance to be sought.   (153–62)

It is, of course, perfectly appropriate in an elegy. I draw attention to

[1] *slipper* slippery   [2] *swincke* work   [3] *scope* target   [4] *nys* is not

it because it expresses that lifelong preoccupation, not to say obsession, of Spenser's, first noted in the sonnets he contributed to *A Theatre*.*

'Colin Clout' was always particularly apt at the elegiac mode. The mood, the music, the repetition, the emphasis, the hyperbole, the cadences, the dying fall—these he was peculiarly master of. Though he wrote much elegiac poetry, from the artificiality of 'Daphnaida' to the simple perfection of 'Astrophell', as well as the 'January', 'August', 'November' and 'December' eclogues of *The Shepheardes Calender*, he seems never to have wearied of this mood. It was evidently congenial to his temperament, and he always brought to it some new and different poetic device, of inversion, of refrain, of stanzaic pattern, of refrain with variation, making an extraordinary contribution to English poetic techniques, and encouraging innovation and experiment in others. In him English letters gained a voice of its own, through his understanding and use of the methods and practices as well as the subject-matter of the European Renaissance, added to a profound understanding of the native inheritance, especially from Chaucer, 'God of shepheards *Tityrus*', whose praises he sang in 'June'.

The *Calender* ends as it began with its lamenting chief figure, Colin Clout. 'December' in all ways admirably balances 'January'. Again it is chiefly in monologue, written in the six-line stanza but more surely controlled; again the poem contains love-lament; again the poet sees his state as mirrored in the season. The shepherd-poet-lover in the winter of his days looks back over his life and sees the lapse of seasons as emblematic of his own life. He recounts the heedless joys and pleasures of the spring-time of his life (with oddly strong if fleeting anticipations of the Wordsworth of 'Tintern Abbey' and the first two books of *The Prelude*). He tells how when he was first 'ybent to song and musicks mirth' a 'good olde shephearde, Wrenock' made him 'by arte more cunning in the same' (most probably a tribute to his old headmaster Richard Mulcaster), and how Hobbinol (Gabriel Harvey) encouraged him and led him to believe that he need not yield to Pan himself in piping skill. But then summer's heat kindled the raging fire of love within him, and his summer was 'worne away and wasted':

> The eare that budded faire, is burnt and blasted,
> And all my hoped gaine is turnd to scathe.
>   Of all the seede, that in my youth was sowne,
>   Was nought but brakes and brambles to be mowne. (99–102)

* See p. 29.

Now winter is upon him, a winter of the spirit as well as of age and season:

> Winter is come, that blowes the balefull breath,
> And after Winter commeth timely death.   (149–50)

This is a poem of authority and high skill. It affords an instructive example of Spenser's tact and originality in handling a source. In his *Eclogue au Roy*, in decasyllabic couplets, Marot, 'maintenant, que je suis en l'automme', lamented his autumnal gloom after surveying his happy spring and summer with many a charming instance of happy country activity. But Marot was a middle-aged man, one looking back on the lost favour of a king. In any case, after offering confident prayer to Pan (the King) to stay the fate which will quell his song, his plea is heard and granted. The royal relief comes and he takes up his pipe again. Spenser's poem is not an allegory of actual events in his own life. Marot seems to be writing about real activities in youth in the country: Spenser's scenes are more imagined, more mythical. Even in small details—Marot's 'en la forêt' becomes 'the wasteful woodes and forest wyde'—Spenser enlarges into a deliberately vague unconfined imaginative world, in a small way foreshadowing his creation in *The Faerie Queene* of that whole new imaginary world of Faerie. And yet, as always in Spenser, the detail he gives is firm, clear, vivid, palpable, as well as instantly metaphoric:

> And thus of all my harvest hope I have
> Nought reaped but a weedye crop of care:
> Which, when I thought have thresht in swelling sheave,
> Cockel for corne, and chaffe for barley bare.
>   Soon as the chaffe should in the fan be fynd,
>   All was blowne away of the wavering wynd.   (121–6)

(In the final couplet, notice the strong onomatopoeic effect of the irregular and wavering stress and the alliteration of the last line.) 'December', if not an allegory of actual events in the poet's own life, is in a humble way metaphorical of human life in general. The observation may be obvious, yet this metaphorising is so fundamental an activity in Spenser, *The Faerie Queene* affording the most powerful example, that it should be recognised as soon as it appears. And yet, having said this, one must return to the poem and adjust the scale of comment again: what 'December' is, after all, is a fanciful pastoral

complaint to Pan of a shepherd's ill-success in love, of the unhappiness
it brought, and of his sad decline into old age:

> Delight is layd abedde, and pleasure past,
> No sonne now shines, cloudes han all overcast. (137–8)

The material in *The Shepheardes Calender* is so varied that the
poem has been classified and arranged by commentators in many
different ways. I have chosen to look first at the seven eclogues which
are either devoted to Colin Clout ('January', 'April', 'June', 'November', and 'December') or in which another shepherd sings a song of
Colin's ('August') or in which he is prominently a subject for discussion by fellow-shepherds ('October'). The 'generall argument' which
is part of the elaborate introductory matter to the collection divides the
eclogues into Plaintive ('January', 'June', November' and 'December',
four of the 'Colin Clout' eclogues); Recreative, 'such as al those be,
which conceive matter of love, or commendation of special personages', which would obviously include the remaining Colin Clout
eclogues: and Moral 'which for the most part be mixed with some
satyrical bitternesse' ('February', 'May', 'July', 'September' and
'October'). If the seven Colin Clout eclogues are taken together, of
the remaining five, 'February', 'March', 'May', 'July' and 'September',
the last three clearly belong to the same category (Moral and Satyricall).
They are concerned with abuses of religion presented in simple
allegory, and in rather stilted verse deploy their argument in a standard
form: a discussion between two shepherds who represent contrasting
views, followed by an illustrative fable. 'February' has also been taken
to be allegorical but I think it is not so certainly allegorical that it
should be classified with the satirical religious allegories. To the
complaints of Cuddie, a young herdsman's boy, about the February
cold, an old shepherd Thenot retorts stoically about season's change
and its reflection of the way the world wends:

> From good to badd, and from badde to worse,
> From worse unto that is worst of all,
> And then returne to his former fall, (12–14)

and he goes on to speak of his own lifelong acceptance of whatever
Fortune brings. Cuddie rejoins that winter is the appropriate season for
an old man, but that his own 'flowring youth is foe to frost'. Thenot
warns him not to think that if the sun 'laugheth once' spring is come
and he may scorn the cold and think himself Lord of the year, for

winter weather may well follow; the reference is to life itself as well
as to the seasons. Cuddie scorns him, an old tree compared to a
'budding branch', and contrasts his herd of bullocks with Thenot's
old ewes, worn-out ram and their pitiful offspring. Thenot describes
Youth in the most powerful—and medieval-sounding—lines in the
poem as

> . . . a bubble blown up with breath,
> Whose witt is weakenesse, whose wage is death,
> Whose way is wildernesse, whose ynne Penaunce,
> And stoopegallaunt Age the hoste of Greevaunce.   (87–90)

He goes on to tell an appropriate moral fable of youth and age, the
fable of the Oak and the Briar, said to have been learned of Chaucer,
though it is not in fact Chaucerian and might well have been (though
it is not exactly) a fable of Aesop..An insolent briar, growing near an
ancient oak, complains that the old tree only cumbers the ground and
calls on the husbandman to cut it down. This done, the briar briefly
enjoys his freedom

> . . . like a Lord alone,
> Puffed up with pryde and vaine pleasaunce;   (222–3)

but when winter comes, no longer protected by the great oak, it
is nipped dead by frost, bowed down by rain, held down by snow and
finally trampled by cattle.

It is Spenser's fate, as an allegorist, to be assumed to be writing
allegory all the time, and commentators will not let him alone. Even
when, as in the Argument to 'February', E.K. writes 'This Aeglogue
is rather moral and general, than bent to any secret or particular
purpose', commentators readily assume that it is all the more bent to
a secret or particular purpose because of the disclaimer. Some have
seen it as an allegory of the execution of the Duke of Norfolk (the
oak) in 1572 by the upstart briar (Lord Burleigh) and the husbandman
(Queen Elizabeth). Others have seen it as an allegory of 'the true
spirit of Christianity degenerated under the influence of Romish
superstition' (the oak) and of 'the irreverent and godless temper of the
new clergy' (the briar). Recently it has been claimed that the oak
represents Leicester and his fall from favour, the briar the Earl of
Oxford, Burleigh's son-in-law, and the husbandman, the Queen: it
is pointed out that in the woodcut the husbandman in dress and stance
looks like a woman with an axe. But 'February' is innocent of the

obvious pointers—anagrammatic or otherwise meaningful names for characters, a story so cumbrous (as in 'July') that it has clearly been constructed or perverted for ends other than simple story-telling; above all it is free from clear clues or interpretations offered in the Argument. More important, its appropriateness to its month, its relationship to general Spenserian themes of time, man, change and impermanence, suggest a general rather than any particular significance.

No one has found contemporary allegorical significance in 'March', a 'recreative' eclogue deriving ultimately from Bion's fourth Idyll. Like 'February' it comments on youth and age. Willye and Thomalin console themselves out of a woeful mood with the thought that the joyous season of spring, the time of love, is drawing near. So far so good. Then, in an unusually clumsy way, Spenser introduces Greek idyll 'matter'. Thomalin says he saw Cupid hiding in a bush, and would have been able to show him to Willye but that his sheep strayed away. Willye calls on him to forget the past and tell of what is to come as a consequence of what he saw, whereupon Thomalin tells of his encounter with Cupid. It is one of the rare instances of Spenser failing to harmonise disparate elements. The detail of a shepherd's job which follows is grotesquely dissonant with the light fancy of the encounter with Cupid. The metre remains the same throughout, basically six syllable lines rhyming *aabccb*, but it is happily varied so that sometimes a six-line stanza is devoted to one speech by Thomalin or Willye, sometimes it is split between them, and sometimes a speech occupies two, sometimes two and a half, once as many as seven stanzas (Thomalin's description of his meeting with Cupid). But the shepherd dialogue provides an awkwardly plain setting for the rather exotic little tale, and Spenser makes little of the potentialities of the fable, whether he was using Bion, or a Latin version of Bion, or Ronsard's version 'L'Amour oyseau' of 1560. The point of Bion's 'Idyll' is that the young should stay away from the evil bird of love, which may hop and flee away now but will, when they are older, come suddenly upon them. Ronsard goes further, seeing Eros 'comme oyseau de mauvais augure' and in doing so typifies the Renaissance interpretation of Cupid as a cruel bringer of unhappiness. This idea exists in Spenser's version, in which Thomalin, after failing to hit Cupid as he leaped from bough to bough, is himself hit in the ankle by one of Cupid's shafts. The wound

> . . . ranckleth more and more,
> And inwardly it festreth sore,
> Ne wote I, how to cease it.   (100–2)

E.K. adds an elaborate gloss explaining that 'by wounding in the hele, is meant lustful love' because of a supposed connexion between the heel and the genitals, and further explains that the eclogue means 'that all the delights of Love, wherein wanton youth walloweth, be but follye mixt with bitternesse, and sorrow sawced with repentance' and that in course of time when youth's flower is withered we shall find that the things we most liked will seem loathsome and breed us annoyance. So 'March' adds its bit to that theme in the *Calender* which assumes that love is pain as well as folly; '*The Honye is much, but the Gaule is more*' is Thomalin's *Embleme*, and Willye's is

> *To be wise and eke to love,*
> *Is graunted scarce to God above.*

Much in *The Faerie Queene* is concerned with this *motif*, but the mature Spenser moves far beyond the narrow conception of the ills of love which he makes a constant theme in the *Calender* and especially in the Colin eclogues, and his celebration of the happiness of virtuous love in his great poem is one of the grandest, most moving (and wholly convincing) elements in it. I do not think we need to find personal autobiography in the *Calender's motif* of Colin's unhappy rejection by Rosalind. Spenser is adopting a conventional Renaissance attitude, and is, albeit in the chosen lowly form of pastoral, as Petrarchan as his courtly predecessors in the mode, Wyatt and Surrey. In 'March', in any case, the tone is light; we are not meant to feel grief or woe, although despite Spenser's use of Chaucer's 'Sir Thopas' metre, I do not agree with Hallett Smith* that it is a comic eclogue.

This account has so far dealt only with those eclogues which belong to the classical pastoral tradition, bucolic, concerned with shepherds in love, in conversation, in singing-contests, singing praises or dirges, discussing love, discussing poetry. In them the tradition was modified by Renaissance Italy, by the poets of the Pléiade and most of all by Spenser's own temperament and Englishing vision. There was no need for these to appear anonymously. 'Immerito' was modest, or affected modesty, or used the appearance of it to increase public curiosity; and the unknown introducer E.K. laid several clues to identity in his prefatory letter to Gabriel Harvey and

* *Elizabethan Poetry*, Harvard 1952.

in his 'generall argument of the whole book'. But the three remaining eclogues, belonging firmly to that part of the Renaissance pastoral convention which deals in outright complaint and criticism, probably demanded for their author the shelter of anonymity.

In 'May' the debating shepherds are Palinode and Piers. Although the Argument declares that they represent 'two formes of pastours or Ministers, or the protestant and the Catholique', their debate is really between a Palinode defending and advocating the pleasures of life, and a Piers commenting on the folly of those priests who let 'their sheepe runne at large'.

> Passen their time, that should be sparely spent,
> In lustihede and wanton meryment.   (41–2)

Palinode anticipates Milton's Comus when he says

> Good is no good, but if it be spend:
> God giveth good for none other end.   (71–2)

and Piers in reply advocates the good priestly life of simplicity, renunciation of the world's pleasures, and husbandry of the world's good and God's gifts. There is nothing of doctrine here, and nothing overtly of Catholicism versus Protestantism, but there is praise of simple virtue and the early church, and the beginning of an attack on selfish and neglectful priests.

In the fable of the Fox and the Kid which follows ('May', 'July' and 'September' have in common, as does 'February', the pattern of a debate between two shepherds followed by an illustrative fable), the eclogue moves nearer to ecclesiastical satire as the heedless kid is seized by the false fox, whom it has admitted in its mother's absence neglectful of her warnings. Spenser turns the traditional wolf of this fable into a fox because the fox was a common symbol for the Catholic Church. What he seems to mean by thus juxtaposing a fable and an argument not very obviously related to it, is that if the church is not served by a faithful and devoted clergy the enemy (of Rome) will creep back into power. Spenser's sympathies are obviously with Piers, named no doubt partly from *Piers Plowman*, now again since the Reformation extraordinarily popular, so that the name of Piers is common in the religious tracts of the time for virtuous and humble priests who resist corruption, pride and laxity in the church. Probably also Spenser means to praise Dr John Piers, who as Dean of Salisbury in 1573 had set about abolishing papistical statutes and practices there.

But Palinode does not crudely represent Catholicism and Piers Puritanism, and the eclogue ends with them, still in perfect friendship, going home together as dewy night draws on. Spenser is preserving a characteristic balance, one which informs the whole of his writing and is most strongly evident in *The Faerie Queene*, between love of the pleasures of life and the beauties of the world, and a firm belief, puritanical in a general sense if you like, of the importance and attractions of restraint, simplicity and dutifulness. Here, while Palinode, like Comus, has the better of the poetry in his description of the merry May festivities, Piers has the better of the argument.

'July' is often thought the worst poem in the whole collection. It is written in the divided fourteener or eight and six, which to modern ears falls so easily into jog-trot and banality, though it was to the Elizabethans not only the old ballad measure but also that of the versified psalms. It admittedly conveys some sense of the rustic. In addition, the alliteration is prodigal, and the handling of the argument and the telling of the illustrative fable which follows seem inexpertly done. Partly based on Mantuan's eighth eclogue on rustic religion, it continues the same Protestant argument as 'May', though rather more clearly distinguishing, as the Argument says, 'good shepheardes' from 'proude and ambitious Pastours'. A goat-herd, Morrell, sitting on a high hill discusses with Thomalin, a lowly shepherd in the vale, the superiority of hills to dales. It is an awkward and confused debate, and it would be more natural (as in Mantuan) for humility to be represented by a bare hill and pride by the fat dale. Now, Thomalin says, the clergy are clad 'in purple and pall':

> They reigne and rulen over all,
>   And lord it, as they list: (175–6)

> .   .   .

> Theyr sheepe have crustes, and they the bread:
>   The chippes, and they the chere:
> They have the fleece, and eke the flesh,
>   (O seely sheepe the while)
> The corne is theyrs, let other thresh,
> Their hands they may not file[1]. (187–92)

This attack, while explicitly directed against Rome, has force against Anglican prelates, too, who neglect their duties in advancing their own material interests, but in the brief fable that concludes the eclogue Thomalin pays tribute to a good prelate, Grindal, who had recently

[1] *file* defile

fallen out of favour and been punished by the Queen. Spenser here, with unwonted clumsiness, uses the grotesque little story of the she-eagle dropping a shell fish on to what she took to be an outcrop of chalk in order to break it, but in fact dropping it on to the bald head of a good shepherd, to stand for Elizabeth's suspension of Archbishop Grindal (anagrammatised into Algrind) in June 1577, not long before Spenser became secretary to the Bishop of Rochester*. Spenser certainly took a risk in thus honouring one who had incurred the Queen's strong displeasure, but Grindal was to the poet of the ecclesiastical eclogues the very type of the faithful and dutiful shepherd-priest, also exemplified here in Thomalin. Probably Piers stands for no single actual pastor, simply representing a pastoral ideal; it should not be forgotten that the very origins of pastoral poetry lie in recognition and approval of an ideal of simple virtue, so that the transition from classical shepherd to Renaissance good pastor is an obvious and easy one. Morrell has always been taken to be an anagrammatic reference to Aylmer, Bishop of London—Morrell, Elmor, Aylmer—but it is a mistake to read 'July' as a disguised attack on him as a proud, wealthy and acquisitive prelate. Certainly the eclogue is about the pride and wealth of prelates, especially Roman ones, contrasted with simple poor virtuous pastors, of whom Algrin is shown to be one. But Thomalin and Morrell both agree about the virtue of Algrin at the end and go off amicably together, and although Morrell presents the opposite point of view to Thomalin, we are not meant to think of him as a proud and lordly prelate. He was in fact, if not one of the lowly ones of the earth (nor was Thomas Cooper, nor Thomas Cartwright who is sometimes assumed to be presented in Thomalin), a sound and effective bishop, and no sparer either of Puritan or Papist. That he was a friend of Bishop Young makes it less probable that the picture of Aylmer is satirical. Further, there is a light, almost railing or bantering tone, partly induced by the jaunty 8–6, 8–6 metre, and Spenser contrives to include, along with his reference to Biblical and classical shepherds, several pleasing references to Kent, and the country near where he lived as secretary to the Bishop of Rochester:

> The salt Medway that trickling streims
>   Adowne the dales of Kent:
> Till with his older brother Themis,
>   his brackish waves be maynt.[1] (81–4)

* See pp. 25–6.
[1] *maynt* mingled

This is not a harsh Juvenalian satire; Spenser has his slippers on, presenting in shepherd guise, but not really disguised, for their names are obviously deliberately revealing, two friends, probably known to him, indulging quite light-heartedly in a *débat*. One can imagine their pleasure in reading or having it read, and the pleasure of Spenser's employer, Bishop Young of Rochester, who of course knew them both, as well as Grindal who is presented as a pattern of simple virtue, and shown as punished for it.

'September' comes much nearer to satire, and here Spenser is much more clear in presenting the subjects of his attack. The discussion is between Hobbinol—presumably as usual Spenser's old friend Gabriel Harvey—and Diggon Davie, who probably stands for Richard Davies, Bishop of St David's. It is roughly based on Virgil's first eclogue in which a wandering shepherd driven from his home into exile discourses with a more fortunate friend, and on Mantuan's ninth eclogue. But clearly it refers to the state of the church with complaints about the traffic in livings (32–46), and the oppression of the lower clergy; the idleness and corruption of many clergy (80–101); the pride and corruption of bishops, and the rapacity of courtiers in getting hold of church lands and revenues (104–35); and the consequent slackness and degradation of the laity (141–9). E.K. in his Argument to 'September' refers to the 'abuses' and 'loose living of Popish prelates' but it seems not significantly or especially anti-Papist, and here as often Spenser seems to be thinking of church corruption and the pride and worthlessness of prelates in the Anglican church, though this does not make him a Puritan. As usual, he is contrasting simple virtue with pomp, pride, vanity, self-indulgence and sophistication. But Diggon Davie goes on to say that because of the corruption of the clergy and the consequent laxity and lack of direction of the laity, there is great and dangerous opportunity for wolves to get in among the flocks—for Papists, that is, to infiltrate, corrupt and proselytise. And this is illustrated in the fable of the Wolf in Sheep's Clothing, which Diggon says is the story of what happened to Roffyn not long ago. (Roffyn of course stands for Roffensis, the Latin name used by the Bishops of Rochester to this day.)

Again, this eclogue would clearly have been of great interest to Spenser's employer Bishop Young, and to other clergy in the diocese and elsewhere. It is the closest Spenser comes in *The Shepheardes Calender* to real people and real events; and for us, I suppose, the less rewarding, yet the general relevance of the collection is clear and behind the simple shepherds with their often petty concerns can dimly be descried the great antitheses in human life: innocence and worldliness, simplicity and sophistication, humility and pride, discipline and licence, idealism and materialism. They appear unmistakable and vivid behind the personages of *The Faerie Queene*, but already in *The Shepheardes Calender* their presence may be felt, however faintly or clumsily.

3

'FEELING HIS WINGS'

In the dedicatory epistle E.K. hoped that the publication of *The Shepheardes Calender* 'will the rather occasion him, to put forth divers other excellent works of his, which sleep in silence'. The sleep of silence lasted over ten years, during which Spenser was writing *The Faerie Queene* whenever he could in the course of active duty in responsible government service in Ireland. The works E.K. had named 'his Dreames, his Legendes, his Court of Cupide' were never published unless the 'Dreames' became the vision poems 'Vision of the World's Vanitie', 'Bellays Visions' and 'Petrarches Visions' which eventually appeared in the volume, *Complaints*, in 1591; it is probable, too, that the 'Legendes' and 'Court of Cupide' were incorporated in *The Faerie Queene*.

But Spenser was writing other poems as well as developing *The Faerie Queene*, and the reception accorded the first three books of his epic in 1590 stimulated him to assemble a collection of poems, some perhaps new but most I think revisions and re-workings of earlier poems, called *Complaints, Containing Sundrie Small Poemes of the World's Vanitie*. One of these, 'Muiopotmos' has a separate title page dated 1590, but the volume itself appeared in 1591. It is a varied collection, including visions, translations of vision poems by Petrarch and du Bellay, an epyllion ('Virgil's Gnat'), elegy, a satire in the form of a beast-epic ('Mother Hubberds Tale'), and another epyllion which is also mock-epic ('Muiopotmos'). All in some way are poems which lament the fall of the great, the languishing and precariousness of virtue, the mutability of the world, or the vulnerability of beauty. They extend with sophistication and subtlety the themes and subjects of the poems he first published, those translations of Petrarch, Marot and du Bellay contributed to van der Noodt's *A Theatre*. They were published clearly as part of Spenser's campaign for patronage. *The Faerie Queene*, though of course dedicated to the Queen, was also accompanied in print by sonnets addressed originally to Sir Christopher Hatton the Lord Chancellor, to Essex the Queen's new favourite, the Earls of Oxford, Northumberland and Ormond and Ossory, to the Lord High Admiral, Victor of the Armada Lord Howard, Lord Grey de Wilton, Sir Walter Raleigh, and to Lady Carew, a member of the noble family of Spencers with which Spenser claimed kinship; further sonnets were added addressed to very important people such as Lord Burleigh Lord High Treasurer, Sir Francis Walsingham, the Queen's principal secretary, and Lords Hunsdon and Buckhurst. It is a comprehensive list. With it Spenser bade for the favour of the great and influential, and he continued the campaign by dedicating many of the poems in the *Complaints* volume to ladies of the court.

First of these is 'The Ruines of Time', dedicated to the Countess of Pembroke. She was not only a poet herself and a patron of poets but a member of two noble families and related to many more. She was the sister of Sir Philip Sidney and the niece of Robert Dudley Earl of Leicester. A sister-in-law, Philip's widow, was a Walsingham, and the Russells, Earls of Bedford, as well as the Northumberland family were close kin. Many of these relationships are noted in 'The Ruines of Time', which is a splendid patchwork piece in *rime royal*, composed of allegory, lament, elegy, emblem and vision-poetry, and owing much to du Bellay's *Antiquitez de Rome* for the opening 170 lines or so and to his *Songe* for the last two hundred. Possibly several existing poems or parts of poems were carpentered together here. The first section (to about line 175), in which the poet encounters a sorrowing woman, the Genius of Verulamium (St Albans), on the shore of the Thames, as in du Bellay the poet encountered the Spirit of Rome beside the Tiber, is a lament for the fall of a great city and civilisation, which is not only in ruins but forgotten. It is implied that the forgetting is almost as lamentable as the fall, and said that only one man remembers or bewails. This is William Camden,

> . . . the nourice[1] of antiquitie
> And lanterne unto late succeeding age. (169–70)

[1] *nourice* nurse

whose *Britannia* had been published (in Latin) in 1586. Possibly
this imitation of du Bellay may also have been intended at one stage
to be a commendatory poem in praise of the great antiquarian and his-
torian. The second part of the poem (176–344) consists of Verulam's
elegiac celebration of Leicester, recently dead, and of other members
of his family, including his brother Ambrose, his sister (Sir Philip
Sidney's mother), his father Northumberland, concluding with a
passionate lament for Sir Philip Sidney. Spenser then for a while
seems to forget the figure of Verulam, and goes on (345–483) in a
characteristic Renaissance *topos* to admonish Princes to provide for
poets in their lifetimes,

> That of the *Muses* ye may friended bee,
> Which unto Men eternitie do give;

and reinforces the claim:

> For deeds do die, how ever noblie donne,
> And thoughts of men do as themselves decay,
> But wise wordes taught in numbers for to runne,
> Recorded by the Muses, live for ay:
> Ne may with storming showers be washt away,
> Ne bitter breathing windes with harmfull blast,
> Nor age, nor envie shall them ever wast.   (400–7)

Conceivably parts of this section may bear some relation to Spenser's
Stemmata Dudleiana referred to in the postscript of his letter of
April 1580 to Gabriel Harvey, evidently a poem or poems honouring
the Dudley family. At the end of this section Spenser remembers
Verulam, and has her speak with scarcely concealed criticism of
Burleigh who

> now welds all things at his will,

as she had earlier spoken of him as the Fox which had

> crept
> Into the hole, the which the Badger swept

(after Leicester's death).

Now for the final section of the poem (485 ff) the *rime royal* becomes
a sort of sonnet form, clamped in coupled stanzas, which present a
series of visions of the world's vanity, some of them exactly like those
Spenser translated for *A Theatre* in 1569 and later adapted as the

'Vision' poems for this *Complaints* volume. He introduces them as
'strange sights . . . Like tragicke Pageants', and it may be that they
are part of, or are related to, the *Dreames* mentioned by E.K. in his
preface to *The Shepheardes Calender* and referred to by Spenser in his
letter to Harvey of April 1580, and the Pageaunts referred to in
E.K.'s *glosse* to the 'June' eclogue of *The Shepheardes Calender*.
First come a golden image which falls from the altar upon which it is
set because of poor foundations, like that in Daniel ii, 31–3, and
then some of the Wonders of the World: the Pharos of Alexander
built on sand, the Gardens of Semiramis in Babylon that are laid waste,
and the Colossus of Rhodes who slipped and fell. This sequence concludes with one not technically a Wonder of the World, a great bridge
spanning the sea in one single arch without supports, greater than
Trajan's bridge over the Danube, but which has 'one foote not fastened
well'.

These fairly conventional objects, which might well have been
illustrated by crude woodcuts like those in *A Theatre*, express in an
elementary way the conventional theme, dear to Spenser,

> . . . What can long abide above this ground
> In state of blis, or stedfast happinesse? (568–9)

and show

> That all is vanitie and griefe of minde,
> Ne other comfort in this world can be,
> But hope of heaven, and heart to God inclinde. (582–5)

The last of them is of a different and incongruous kind, introducing
another and different series. The two white bears 'of milde aspect'
that are killed when their cave falls in upon them may perhaps allude
heraldically to the Dudleys. Its successors, a series of emblems which
are symbolic of poetic creativity, certainly all apply to the rarest of
the Dudleys and the truest poet, Sir Philip Sidney. Spenser sees a
swan singing before its death, symbol of a poet dying untimely, and
being taken up to heaven where it becomes the constellation Cygnus, the
harp of Orpheus, now called the Harp of Philisides ('lover of the star',
a name invented by Sidney for himself), borne up to heaven, making

> . . . all the way most heavenly noyse . . .
> Of the strings, stirred with the warbling wind,
> That wrought both joy and sorrow in my mind: (612–15)

and becoming in the skies the constellation Lyra.

The unusual clumsiness of parts of this poem extends to the next vision, of an ebony coffer rescued from a flood by two angels and borne up to heaven. It presumably stands for Sidney's coffin—'That in it did most precious treasure hide'. Its successor is no more felicitous, save in its gentle, lively diction which momentarily anticipates the festal sublimity of 'Epithalamion'; it pictures a rich and stately bed containing a sleeping virgin who is summoned to her bridegroom and starts up joyfully at the summons and disappears: a simple image of the soul of Sidney going to God. Spenser evokes another conventional symbol for poetry, after the swan and the lyre, in his next image, of a knight on a winged horse which bears him straight to heaven. Because of Sidney's mortal wound at Zutphen, the knight seen in the vision, although garlanded for his victories, is mortally wounded. Spenser's imagination hovered, in these two last visions, between the constellations associated with Perseus: Cassiopeia and her daughter Andromeda. Finally the poet sees a golden ark containing the ashes of a great prince, which is borne to heaven by Mercury, who is, of course, not only the messenger of the gods but also the inventor of the lyre (which he gave to Apollo, god of light and of music and poetry).

The poem is an uneven one. Often when Spenser is most ingenious he is least successful, and something like this may be said of 'The Ruines of Time'. Yet in some of the visions the emblem is exalted into symbol by the completeness and aptness of his imaginative vision. Some of the astronomical conceits to recall and honour Sir Philip Sidney are sublimely felicitous: they are not so much conceits as the concepts of genius. And the poem as a whole is a remarkable assemblage. Spenser contrived in less than seven hundred lines to debate the transitoriness of life and the immortality conferred by poetry, to celebrate a noble household and to lament some of its deceased members, to pay special tribute to one of them, and to perform the very function of immortalisation which in the poem he has once again claimed for poetry, in a series of allegories, complaints, apostrophes, elegies and visions. They are admittedly only loosely held together by the figure of Verulam, which fades, returns and then disappears before the end of the poem, but Spenser relies here, as he so often does, more on harmony of tone, mood and theme, than on the mechanics of structure for his unity.

It has been plausibly suggested that 'The Teares of the Muses' owes something to Erasmus's Colloquy, *Conflictus Thaliae et Barbariae*, having as its subject the same conflict between Barbarism and the

Muses deployed with many similar details. It is one of Spenser's most laboured and repetitive works. The youngest of the three daughters of Sir John Spencer, with which family Spenser claimed, in the dedication here to Alice, Lady Strange, 'private bands of affinitie', might well have felt she came off worst, for her two older sisters were honoured respectively with the much more interesting and successful 'Muiopotmos' and 'Mother Hubberds Tale'. It is repetitive by its very nature and form: the nine Muses one by one complain of the lamentable state of the times. The springs of Helicon are now the scene of 'Hart-breaking mone';

> The joyous Nymphes and lightfoote Faeries
> Which thether came to heare their musick sweet,
> And to the measure of their melodies
> Did learne to move their nimble shifting feete;
> Now hearing them so heavily lament,
> Like heavily lamenting from them went. (31–6)

One by one they complain: wisdom, learning, nobility, virtue, heroism, reason are all overthrown or devalued, and ignorance, baseness, indulgence and barbarity reign in their stead. Clio, the Muse of History, begins with a general picture of the times in which 'The foes of learning, and each gentle thought' are in the ascendant, despising learning and wisdom and concerned only to

> ... strive themselves to raise
> Through pompous pride, and foolish vanite. (91–2)

The general barbarism is reflected in the state of poetry, and the Muses of Tragedy (Melpomene), Comedy (Thalia), Lyric (Erato), Epic (Calliope) and Rhetoric (Polyhymnia), in turn show the sad state of affairs. There is no tragic art, only the actual tragedy 'of men depriv'd of sense and minde'. In comedy

> Fine Counterfesaunce and unhurtfull Sport,
> Delight and Laughter deckt in seemly sort, (197–8)

are ousted by

> ... scoffing Scurrilitie,
> And scornful Follie with Contempt is crept,
> Rolling in rymes of shameles ribaudrie
> Without regard, or due Decorum kept. (211–14)

The poetry of love is debased into lewdness by a 'base-born brood'
with 'dunghill thoughts'. Epic is dead for there are no worthy deeds
to celebrate, and

> . . . noble Peeres whom I was wont to raise,
> Now onely seeke for pleasure, nought for praise.   (467–8)

The 'hidden mysterie' of 'goodly Poesie', that used to be

> . . . held in soveraigne dignitie,
> And made the noursling of Nobilitie,   (563–4)

is profaned by 'the base vulgar'. Only Queen Elizabeth

> Supports the praise of noble Poësie

with some few beside who also 'this sacred skill esteeme'. If this
wholesale depreciation of literature is sincere, it must point to an
early date for 'The Teares of the Muses', and one would think that
the dullness of much of the writing and its rather monotonously used
six-line stanza (like that of 'January' and 'December' less sensitively
employed) supports this view. In 1580 or so the Muses of Comedy,
Tragedy and Lyric could well have complained, but they could not
as justifiably do so in 1590. Perhaps again it is basically an early poem
a little worked up for publication. The final passage of characteristic
hyperbolical praise of the Queen particularly sounds like the mature
Spenser. The poem is chiefly remarkable as an example of that emphasis
and repetition with which the poet customarily induces a mood in his
reader or establishes a dominating point of view; and it is perhaps
worth pointing out that it is meticulously constructed: a nine-stanza
apostrophe to the Muses introduces nine sections each of ten stanzas
(except Euterpe's section which has eleven stanzas) making a total
of exactly one hundred stanzas. Perhaps complying with this strict
formula accounts for a feeling that some of Spenser's material has been
spread as thinly as it could go. Like other poems in the collection, it
is too long.

The next poem in *Complaints* is by contrast a deft and assured piece
of work, Spenser's version of the 'Culex', then still thought to be by
Virgil. It is an epyllion or little decorated epic, of marvellous *tone*.
From its carefully casual beginning,

> We now have playde (Augustus) wantonly,
> Tuning our song unto a tender Muse,
> And like a cobweb weaving slenderly,
> Have onely playde:

it moves imperceptibly into invocation in a tone of high mock-heroic, and then, still in an assured *ottava-rima* that begins to suggest the flowing amplitude of *The Faerie Queene* stanza, into epic-sounding narrative. It reads wonderfully like an original poem, for Spenser has re-minted it in his own metal and enlarged upon the model. The idyllic description of the pastoral life, for example, in lines 89–152, is half as long again as the original and twice as joyous. Spenser's imagination seems often closely kin to that of Virgil and Virgil's imitator, but often he develops an idea in the original into something that we readily recognise as peculiarly Spenserian. For example, he develops a brief reference to the frogs' response to the voice of birds in 'Culex' into the following stanza:

> But the small Birds in their wide boughs embowring,
> Chaunted their sundrie tunes with sweete consent,
> And under them a silver Spring forth powring
> His trickling streames, a gentle murmure sent;
> Thereto the frogs, bred in the slimie scowring
> Of the moist moores, their jarring voyces bent:
> And shrill grasshoppers chirped them around:
> All which the ayrie Echo did resound.   (225–32)

Not only is that stanza peculiarly Spenserian in its juxtaposing of beauty and ugliness, but it seems to have in it the germ of something that in *The Faerie Queene* is often even more characteristic of his mastery of mood and suggestion, a deliberate warning or premonition: the shepherd casts himself down to sleep in this seemingly pleasant place where the croaking frogs and shrill grasshoppers jar on the sweet sounds of the birds, and within three stanzas, as the shepherd sleeps, the vile serpent comes. Characteristically Spenserian too is the impression given of delight in depicting horrid beauty or power, in the description, actually very faithful to the original, of the serpent. If we weary of the long lament, with all its innumerable classical references, by the spirit of the gnat that was killed by the shepherd for stinging him on the eye to warn him of his danger from the snake, we may absolve Spenser who is in this, as he is throughout his version, fundamentally faithful to his original.

'Virgil's Gnat' has a dedicatory sonnet to the Earl of Leicester, *late deceased*, which suggests that the poet had in some sense performed for Leicester 'the causer of my care' a warning function similar to that performed by the gnat for the shepherd in the poem. If so, the implication is that he suffered as a result of giving a warning to Leicester which in fact saved him from some disaster. Commentators have seized on this to prove that another work of Spenser's, 'Mother Hubberds Tale', was originally written in about 1579 to warn Leicester of the dangers of the proposed marriage of Queen Elizabeth to the Duke of Alençon, for which service Spenser (the gnat) was killed by Leicester (that is, not rewarded by some employment about the court but sent into virtual exile in Ireland). The theory rests upon two very wobbly stilts: one, that there really is a close connexion between 'Virgil's Gnat' and 'Mother Hubberds Tale', for which there is no evidence at all; and two, that in an original version 'Mother Hubberds Tale' was a satire specifically about the design of Burleigh (the fox) to forward a marriage between the Queen and Alençon with the aid of the Duke's representative Simier (*simia* a monkey). I think if we bear heavily enough on either of these stilts it will give way and bring both theories tumbling. As often in reading Spenser it is dangerous to attempt too precise interpretation of things Spenser has not made unarguably clear; and we would do well to follow his advice in the sonnet dedicating 'Virgil's Gnat': 'Ne further seeke to glose upon the text'.

'Mother Hubberds Tale' has proved particularly tempting to commentators intent on detecting specific satirical design. There have been many precise interpretations of this beast-fable and many inferences have been drawn from these differing accounts to date the writing of the poem either in the late 1570s or in 1590. (In the dedication, to Anne Lady Compton and Mounteagle, second daughter of Sir John Spencer, Spenser declares that it was 'long sithens composed in the raw conceipt of my youth'.) It is pretty obvious that this is one of the poems in *Complaints* that Spenser had a second go at, changing the satirical focus, but I am not convinced that it ever had any of the extremely specific satirical aims that have been claimed for it. There is an obvious break, indeed an obvious weakness in the design. The tale told to the sick poet in a time of plague by Mother Hubberd (like Sir Thomas More's 'mother Mawde' who in *A Dialogue of Comfort* 'told us once, that the Asse and the Wolfe came upon a time to confession to the Foxe') presents for five hundred and eighty lines

an account of a fox and an ape seeking their fortunes far abroad in a
world of men. After much discussion they decide that the best disguise
to choose is that of soldier, with the ape playing the part as most
like 'For manly semblance, and small skill in warre' and the fox as
his cur. Their first encounter is with an honest husbandman, whom they
serve in shepherding but whose flock they ultimately kill and eat.
Next they disguise themselves as clerks, and get advice from a priest,
who is as corrupt as he is illiterate, about how to obtain a benefice.
That advice is to procure a patron, either a nobleman

> That hath a zealous disposition
> To God, and so to his religion:
>
> .   .   .
>
> Fast much, pray oft, looke lowly on the ground,
> And unto everie one doo curtesie meeke: (490ff.)

or by going to Court:

> Then must thou thee dispose another way:
> For there thou needs must learne, to laugh, to lie,
> To face, to forge, to scoffe, to companie,
> To crouche, to please, to be a beetle stock
> Of thy great Masters will, to scorne, or mock: (504ff.)

The benefice is obtained and Reynold the fox is ordained with the
ape as his parish clerk. So far Spenser has contrasted the duplicity
and self-seeking of the ape and fox with the honour and decency of
the simple husbandman, and shown them in much more appropriate
company with the illiterate and ignoble priest. He satirises the church
particularly by means of the account the priest gives of his view of his
work and of the present state of affairs: the clergy have only to 'lay
the meate before' the people; 'Eate they that list';

> Ne is the paines so great, but beare ye may:
> For not so great as it was wont of yore,
> It's now a dayes, ne halfe so streight and sore:
> They whilom used duly everie day
> Their service and their holie things to say,
> At morne and even, besides their Anthemes sweete,
> Their penie Masses, and their Complynes meete,
> Their Diriges, their Trentals, and their shrifts,
> Their memories, their singings, and their gifts.
> Now all those needlesse works are laid away:

> Now once a weeke upon the Sabbath day,
> It is enough to doo our small devotion,
> And then to follow any merrie motion. (446ff.)

(This extract gives a reasonable idea of how Spenser made 'Mother Hubberds Tale' at once Chaucerian and Drydenesque.) The priest tells them too of the pleasures and rewards of priesthood:

> . . . with the finest silkes us to aray,
> That before God we may appeare more gay. (461–2)

> •   •   •

> Beside we may have lying by our sides
> Our lovely lasses, or bright shining Brides:
> We be not tyde to wilfull chastitie,
> But have the Gospell of free libertie. (475–8)

and then advises them how to get on in the church by trickery, bribery and corruption. This section of the poem ends—at line 580— with the flight of the fox and ape when their greed, abuses, crimes and heresies have eventually forced the threat of action against them. It seems very likely that this part of the poem was devised during Spenser's period as secretary to the Bishop of Rochester; the relationship with the ecclesiastical satires of *The Shepheardes Calender* is clear.

Immediately after line 580 the poem changes: it is now concerned with satire of court life, introduced by the ape and fox meeting a mule, 'all deckt in goodly rich aray', straight from Court. For a time it depicts a world of animals, for the mule replies to the ape's question

> Who now in Court doth beare the greatest sway:

> •   •   •

> Marie (said he) the highest now in grace,
> Be the wilde beasts, that swiftest are in chace. (616ff.)

Spenser makes marvellous fun out of the mule's advice about how to get on at Court, and out of the ape's successful counterfeiting of a courtier. You are to get on, advises the mule,

> . . . with a good bold face,
> And with big words, and with a stately pace,
> That men may thinke of you in generall,
> That to be in you, which is not at all:
> For not by that which is, the world now deemeth,
> (As it was wont) but by that same that seemeth. (645ff.)

When they come to Court, the ape as gentleman, the fox as his groom,

> ... the fond Ape himselfe uprearing hy
> Upon his tiptoes, stalketh stately by,
> As if he were some great *Magnifico*,
> And boldlie doth amongst the boldest go.
>
> .   .   .
>
> Then gan the Courtiers gaze on everie side,
> And stare on him, with big lookes basen wide,
> Wondring what mister wight he was, and whence:
>
> .   .   .
>
> But his behaviour altogether was
> *Alla Turchesca*, much the more admyr'd,
> And his lookes loftie, as if he aspyr'd
> To dignitie, and sdeign'd the low degree;
>
> .   .   .
>
> For he could play, and daunce, and vaute, and spring,
> And all that els pertaines to reveling,
> Onely through kindly aptnes of his joynts.   (663ff.)

In contrast, Spenser then draws a detailed and moving picture of the virtuous gentleman with 'all his minde on honour fixed', and then an even more emotional one, seeming almost personal in its complaint of the woes of being a suitor at Court:

> What hell it is, in suing long to bide:
> To loose good dayes, that might be better spent;
> To wast long nights in pensive discontent;
> To speed to day, to be put back to morrow;
> To feed on hope, to pine with feare and sorrow;
> To have thy Princes grace, yet want her Peeres;
> To have thy asking, yet waite manie yeeres;
> To fret thy soule with crosses and with cares;
> To eate thy heart through comfortlesse dispaires;
> To fawne, to crowche, to waite, to ride, to ronne,
> To spend, to give, to want, to be undonne.   (896ff.)

The contrast between potentiality and actuality at Court, even at the Court of Queen Elizabeth, Gloriana the Faerie Queene herself, is one that often recurs rankling to Spenser's mind, notably in *The Faerie Queene* and in 'Colin Clouts Come Home Again'.

By the time Spenser has reached this point in 'Mother Hubberds Tale', he has moved into an anthropomorphic world, but seems to

C

recall himself and moves the fable on with a swift account of the fox's banishment, after being found out in a series of trickeries in disguise, and of the ape's inability to keep up his role without the fox,

> Like as a Puppit placed in a play,
> Whose part once past all men bid take away. (930–1)

The poem changes direction yet again now, from about line 942, and from this point becomes an animal-fable indeed; ape and fox come upon the sleeping lion, steal the lion's crown and mace, quarrel about who shall be 'lord of lords', resolve it by deciding that the ape shall have the crown and apparent rule but that the fox will in fact rule him in all matters, and so they enter tyrannously and rapaciously upon their kingdom. It seems very likely that this section of the poem, which is powerful concentrated satire against great statesmen and rulers who gather power into their hands and terribly abuse it, was added in about 1590 as the *Complaints* volume was being prepared, perhaps as a slightly concealed attack on Lord Burleigh, but certainly as an expression, however lightly and amusingly presented, of Spenser's disgust at corruption in high places. It is almost certain that *Complaints*, or some parts of the collection, were 'called in' or suppressed, and certain that 'Mother Hubberds Tale' did not reappear in 1611 when *Complaints* was re-published, but only came out again in 1612 after the death of Burleigh's son Robert Cecil. The satire seems to have reached its target, but the matter remains a perplexing one, for it is difficult to reconcile Spenser's elaborate campaign to win patronage with his temerity as a satirist apparently attacking the most powerful of Elizabeth's ministers. I would not confidently claim that any more than glancing blows are struck.

As always in reading Spenser it is wiser not to attempt to define too precisely. Sometimes, briefly, he allows a particular reference to emerge from a general account, but it is likely to have merged or changed into another and then expanded again into a generality before we have spotted it clearly. Spenser's poetry is generally *cursive* and critics who think of it as primarily *uncial*—understandably, as he is a definite moralist and one who uses a method, allegory, which in most other writers is static—are liable to misinterpret his work through expecting it to be too categorical in meaning. He does not insist, normally, on very precisely defined actions and meanings for his larger strategy, though he makes considerable tactical use of them.

The method seems to be intuitive, however carefully worked out. This is one reason why *The Faerie Queene* seems so living, seems to be growing as we read it, and is, in the end, so life-like.

A disadvantage is that often a poem will seem not merely to turn to a quite different subject but to become a quite different poem. 'Mother Hubberds Tale', as I have pointed out, fluctuates between beast-fable and a fable of a world inhabited by men as well as animals, as if Spenser changed his purpose or his method when he took up again an earlier version. Towards the end the poem changes again, moving, at about line 1225, towards epic, or, at the least, epyllion:

> . . . high *Jove*, in whose almightie hand
> The care of Kings, and power of Empires stand,
> Sitting one day within his turret hye,
> From whence he vewes with his blacklidded eye,
> Whatso the heaven in his wide vawte containes,
> And all that in the deepest earth remaines,
> The troubled kingdome of wilde beastes behelde.   (1225–31)

So Spenser achieves the *dénouement* of his satirical beast-fable of the fox and the ape, told by old Mother Hubberd, by introducing, in a cool Virgilian way, the god Jupiter. Angered by the evils and corruption of 'the troubled kingdome of wilde beastes', Jupiter sends Mercury to unseat and punish the usurping fox and ape, and to re-establish the lion on the throne. (Incidentally, those who interpret 'Mother Hubberds Tale' as specific contemporary satirical allegory tend to ignore the difficulties posed by the fact that if they are right the heedless sleeping lion *must* be a figure for the Queen.) Naturally the tone of the poem has completely changed. Few readers, presented anonymously with lines 1257–65, which describe the arrival of Mercury on earth, would guess they came from a satirical beast-epic:

> The sonne of *Maia* soone as he receiv'd
> That word, streight with his azure wings he cleav'd
> The liquid clowdes, and lucid firmament;
> Ne staid, till that he came with steep descent
> Unto the place, where his prescript did showe.
> There stouping like an arrowe from a bowe,
> He soft arrived on the grassie plaine,
> And fairly paced forth with easie paine,
> Till that unto the Pallace nigh he came.

It is well done, and something of the majesty of *The Faerie Queene*

seems to have extended and ennobled the couplet form here. At
times, appropriately, the verse becomes demotic again, and we catch
an anticipatory whiff of Dryden, as when Mercury awakens the
sluggish and dishonoured Lion:

> But when his Crowne and scepter both he wanted,
> Lord how he fum'd, and sweld, and rag'd, and panted;
> And threatned death, and thousand deadly dolours
> To them that had purloyn'd his Princely honours.   (1339–42)

Admirers of Spenser will speak of this poem's variety, urbanity
and humour, others of its unclear purpose and sense of direction.
There seems little doubt that this was one of the pieces put together
perhaps rather hurriedly for William Ponsonby, and probably it was
an adaptation, extension or inflation of a fairly simple early satire on
abuses in the church. It is to be esteemed for those qualities of variety
and humour, and for its originality (it is easily the most imaginative
and the most deft of English satires before Dryden). The romantic
idolaters did not have much to say about 'Mother Hubberds Tale'.
It is the least 'Spenserian' of his poems. Some characteristic attributes
of Spenser should be noticed: his two-armed power in fabling and
world-creating so that we are engrossed in his world and his story;
his eye for detail of all kinds, the way a monkey walks, a sycophant
behaves, a suitor feels; his constant celebration of virtue and his longing for the Golden Age. And, as with all successful satirical fabling,
the reader feels a little cheated. The poet's powers, especially those of
fabling and world-creating, seem too great, his vision too wide and
his imagination too large for satire's comparatively small and limited
scope. Who, admiring, has not sadly regretted that Pope did not live
in an age that could write and receive epic?

Spenser, of course, lived in an age that esteemed the heroic poem
above all other kinds. He had set himself to furnish England with an
example of it, and by 1590 he had published the first three books of
The Faerie Queene. Many other things that he had written or that he
was writing at the same time seem occasionally to be struggling to
become epic, even when they are avowedly mock-epic, like 'Mother
Hubberds Tale', or a decorative 'little epic' or epyllion, like 'Muiopotmos: or the Fate of the Butterflie'.

> I sing of deadly dolorous debate,
> Stir'd up through wrathfull Nemesis despight,
> Betwixt two mightie ones of great estate,

> Drawne into armes, and proofe of mortall fight,
> Through prowd ambition, and hartswelling hate,
> Whilest neither could the others greater might
> And sdeignfull scorne endure; that from small jarre
> Their wraths at length broke into open warre.

If this opening stanza were all that survived of 'Muiopotmos' could
we be sure, could we even guess, that it was not the introductory
stanza to an epic poem? It certainly could not be guessed that the
'mortall fight' and the 'open warre' were to be between a spider and
a butterfly. Later in the poem, in explaining the malice of the spider,
Spenser describes the contest between his mother Arachne and Minerva
to prove which was 'the most fine-fingred workwoman' with the
needle in passionate terms and with as much fine and emotive detail
as he gave to similar descriptions of contests and of tapestries in
The Faerie Queene. Minerva made in her tapestry a butterfly

> Fluttring among the Olives wantonly,
> That seem'd to live, so like it was in sight:
> The velvet nap which on his wings doth lie,
> The silken downe with which his back is dight,
> His broad outstretched hornes, his hayrie thies,
> His glorious colours, and his glistering eies. (331–6)

Arachne, defeated in the contest, turns hideously into a spider before
our eyes:

> Eftsoones her white streight legs were altered
> To crooked crawling shankes, of marrowe empted,
> And her faire face to fowle and loathsome hewe,
> And her fine corpes to a bag of venim grewe. (349–52)

And the poem concludes with a deliberate echo of the death of Turnus
in the *Aeneid* and of the death of the great Saracen Rodomont in
Ariosto's *Orlando Furioso:*

> Which when the greisly tyrant did espie,
> Like a grimme Lyon rushing with fierce might
> Out of his den, he seized greedelie
> On the resistles pray, and with fell spight,
> Under the left wing stroke his weapon slie
> Into his heart, that his deepe groning spright
> In bloodie streames foorth fled into the aire,
> His bodie left the spectacle of care. (433–40)

Spenser maintains a remarkable balance in this poem, keeping it light despite the epic gravity, so that the reader can be moved as well as delighted, and instructed as well as entertained. It has, like everything of Spenser's, been interpreted in terms of contemporary personalities. The butterfly Clarion has been seen as Sir Walter Raleigh, as Sir Philip Sidney and as the Earl of Essex,* and more recently as the rational soul wandering into error and so caught in the eternal war between reason and sensuality.† I will again plead for a light rein, and that the reader should look at Spenser as poet not propagandist or *philosophe*. Clearly he enjoyed the imaginative, allusive and serio-comic possibilities of this Ovid-like fable, and as always got carried away at times in the delight of his own invention. He is as concerned to make us believe in the cruising butterfly and the lurking spider as he is to make us believe in the world and the people of the land of Faerie. He does not reserve his world-making capacity or his imaginative powers for his most important poems. The most prominent impression 'Muiopotmos' leaves is of the vivid contrast between the butterfly, so young, so joyous and so beautiful, and the cursed spider, full of 'enfestred grudge' and 'vengefull malice'. If Spenser here, as often in *The Faerie Queene*, seems to write of evil and ugliness with as much relish as he does of virtue and beauty, and almost to delight in the depiction of beauty spoiled, we are not entitled to find aberration or psychological twist in him. In life beauty is often spoiled, virtue overcome, and Spenser was obsessed by his sense of the precariousness of the good in a fallen and mutable world. The constant pressure of evil upon good dominated his mind, and he always presented their unceasing struggle with a vivid power impartially applied. 'Muiopotmos', like *The Faerie Queene* in innumerable places, shows Spenser's preoccupation with the transitoriness of beauty or virtue. The effect is the more poignant because of the power with which evil is presented. In a collection of *Complaints*, 'sundrie small Poemes of the Worlds Vanitie', a poem like 'Muiopotmos', for all its fancy and decoration and the slightness of its subject-matter, makes a contribution as significant as it is unorthodox. It is not at all surprising that William Ponsonby should have included this poem, originally published separately in 1590, in the *Complaints* volume of 1591.

The three pieces that follow are slighter, duller and more conventional. 'The Visions of Bellay' and 'The Visions of Petrarch' are slightly

---

* See Variorum edn., *Minor Poems*, vol. II, Appendix V.
† Don Cameron Allen, 'On Spenser's *Muiopotmos*', *Studies in Philology*, 53 (1956).

altered versions of those that had appeared, entitled 'Sonets' and
'Epigrams' respectively, in 1569 in *A Theatre*, the former unchanged
save by skilful conversion to rhyme, and the latter in some places
lengthened so that all are now sonnets.* 'The Visions of the Worlds
Vanitie' is original, in that there is no direct source, but it is the same
kind of visionary and emblematic poetry on the subject of mutability,
shown in the vicissitudes of fortune, the transitoriness of the works of
man, and the fall of the great and the proud. The general moral is
most clearly expressed in the lines

> Lo all is nought but flying vanitee.
> So I that know this worlds inconstancies,
>   Sith onely God surmounts all times decay,
>   In God alone my confidence do stay.
> ('The Visions of Bellay', 11–14)

These 'Visions' and another translation from du Bellay, 'The Ruines
of Rome', are only occasionally enlivened or made melodious and it
is likely that they date from Spenser's early versifying at Cambridge
or even at school. But they fit appropriately into the *Complaints*
volume, demonstrating as they do

> ... this tickle trustles state
> Of vaine worldes glorie, flitting to and fro.
> And mortal men tossed by troublous fate
> In restles seas of wretchedness and woe.
> ('The Visions of Petrarch', 85–8)

Ponsonby published another poem of Spenser's in 1591. It did not
appear in *Complaints* though in some respects it could have qualified
for inclusion as it is a complaint about mutability and transitoriness.
This was 'Daphnaida', written in memory of Douglas Howard the
young wife of Sir Arthur Gorges. It is a highly artificial composition,
begotten by Spenser's taste for elegy and nostalgia and by his practice
in pastoral on his admiration for Chaucer, for it is *The Boke of the
Duchesse* made more plaintive, more melodious, more artificial and
less dramatic and homely. It provides an interesting and instructive
example of what the Renaissance could do in the way of formalising
the informal and classicising the indigenous. Chaucer's Man in Black
becomes the shepherd Alcyon, Sir Arthur Gorges; the lost lady,
Blanche, is Daphne, Gorges's young wife Douglas. The naturalness

* See p. 32.

and humanity of Chaucer's poem and its sense of immediacy are
lost in Spenser's more formal lament. In pastoral elegy Spenser evidently does not seek Chaucerian effects of variety. There is no May
morning, no jolly rout of huntsmen, no dream, no placing of the
melancholy situation in a world in which life goes gaily on in
order to isolate and emphasise the sorrow. Instead Spenser follows his
customary practice and seeks to submerge the reader in an appropriate
mood, summoning not the Muses but the Fates and 'the Queene of
darknesse and grisly ghosts' to hear the poet tell how he walked abroad,
not on a spring morning but in 'gloomie evening',

> In open fields, whose flowring pride opprest
> With early frosts, had lost their beautie faire.   (27–8)

and, musing there on the misery in which men live in this fallen
world, met Alcyon 'clad all in black'. Alcyon tells of his grief and
bereavement not with Chaucer's analogy of the chessboard but in
armorial terms; his Daphne whom he has loved and lost is first described as

> . . . a faire young Lionesse,
> White as the native Rose before the chaunge.   (107–8)

a reference to the heraldic lion of the Howard family. But it is an
unusually lifeless personification for Spenser, and much of the dirge
which follows is also lifeless and mechanical. It is a formal dirge in
seven-line stanzas grouped in seven sections of seven stanzas each;
six sections end with the refrain

> Weepe Shepheard weepe, to make my undersong

and the last ends with a dismissory variation of it:

> Cease Shepheard, cease, and end thy undersong.

It is clearly much too long, occupying forty-nine of the poem's
eighty-one stanzas, but at its best, in such stanzas as

> She fell away in her first ages spring,
> Whil'st yet her leafe was greene, and fresh her rinde,
> And whil'st her braunch faire blossomes foorth did bring,
> She fell away against all course of kinde:
> For age to dye is right, but youth is wrong;

> She fel away like fruit blowne downe with winde:
> Weepe Shepheard weepe, to make my undersong. (239–46)

or as

> Yet fell she not, as one enforst to dye,
> Ne dyde with dread and grudging discontent,
> But as one toyled with travaile downe doth lye,
> So lay she downe, as if to sleepe she went,
> And closde her eyes with carelesse quietnesse;
> The whiles soft death away her spirit hent,
> And soule assoyled from sinfull fleshlinesse. (253–9)

there are pregnant ideas to justify the weight of repetition and emphasis, as well as a harmony of sound and a control of cadence which make them moving and appropriately narcotic without blurring the meaning. It is worth noting, in this justifiably rather neglected poem, some Spenserian characteristics: in the first of the two stanzas the paradox or antithesis inherent in the idea of untimeliness; the easy appropriation of a suggestion from an ancient myth, that of Daphne, in the peculiarly apposite use of a tree in the pathetic fallacy, by means of which he creates potent symbol out of metaphor; and in the second stanza a further use of paradox: although Daphne lies dead like a stricken tree, she is not to be thought of as decayed or deformed by death; it is as if she sleeps, having closed her eyes 'with carelesse quietnesse' for 'soft death' to attend her. So the sad picture of beauty broken in one stanza is dissolved into the picture of death as a quiet and beneficent attendant in the other. Here, as always when he is at his best, Spenser's meaning has depth and complexity however easy and superficial the writing seems to be. But as a whole, 'Daphnaida' achieves only a precarious success.

This is true of the poems in the *Complaints* volume as well. It is all minor poetry, interesting chiefly as examples of sustained and varied effort in one mood. Spenser had worked the seam out, and did not return to it, although the same sense of mutability permeates *The Faerie Queene*, receiving its final consideration (and in fact resolution) in the so-called 'Mutabilitie Cantos'. In all these early poems the voice of the mature Spenser, all this time also engaged upon *The Faerie Queene*, is heard only above the babel of his other voices, lamenting, complaining, flattering, condemning, satirising, hyperbolical, occasionally inflated and strained. But *Complaints* and 'Daphnaida' in a hundred places presage Spenser at his best: in the use of emphasis and repetition to create and sustain a mood or an emotion; in paradox and antithesis; in preoccupation with mutability and the vulnerability of virtue in a fallen world; in complexity or subtlety of meaning in passages apparently merely descriptive or superficial; and in the myth-making and world-making powers, which all reach triumphant fulfilment in *The Faerie Queene*. What they mostly lack, which the great romantic epic does not, is a fully communicated sense of the human.

4

'A GREATER FLIGHT'

Four other works of Spenser, all published by William Ponsonby, to whom he entrusted everything after *The Shepheardes Calender*, appeared in 1595 and in the year of the publication of the second instalment of the romantic epic, 1596, but some of it was originally written earlier. 'Colin Clouts Come Home Again' (1595) was dedicated to Sir Walter Raleigh in a letter 'From my house of Kilcolman' in Ireland, 27 December 1591. Although some references* are certainly later, the main matter of the poem seems certainly to be Spenser's visit to England with Raleigh in 1589–91. If 'Astrophel' was only written shortly before its publication in 1595 it was tardy, for Sir Philip Sidney whom it commemorates had died after the battle of Zutphen nearly ten years before (and, in dedicating to Sidney's sister 'The Ruines of Time' in 1590, in which also he eulogised and elegised Sidney, he apologised for having not hitherto 'shewed any thankful remembrance' to him). In any case it has the feel of an earlier work, and may perhaps have originally been a first shot at commemorating the dead Sidney fairly soon after his death in 1586.† And Spenser wrote in the dedicatory epistle to the *Four Hymnes* that the first two, 'Of Love' and 'Of Beautie', were composed 'in the greener times' of his youth. While one doesn't necessarily believe Elizabethan authors' or publishers' statements in dedications or prefaces, it seems likely that

* See Variorum edn.
† The elegy by his friend Lodowick Bryskett, included in the collection, was entered in the Stationers' Register as early as August 1587.

these were in fact earlier works, revised or adapted. After Spenser's posting to Ireland in 1580, his works were published in two bursts, when he returned to England on leave in 1589–91 (*The Faerie Queene* I–III, *Complaints* and 'Daphnaida'), and in 1595–6 (*The Faerie Queene* in two volumes including the second part—Books IV–VI then published for the first time, and the poems mentioned above).

They all in various ways celebrate love, sometimes while ostensibly doing other things. All Spenser's earlier poetry was moral, most often pastoral and regretful; its tone was rather distant and unengaged, except perhaps when it touched on Colin's love for Rosalind. The unhappy love for Rosalind may have been a fiction. He almost certainly married in 1579–80, possibly a girl with the intriguing name of Machabyas Chylde.* She seems to have died in about 1590 (as line 64 of 'Daphnaida' in which the narrator tells the bereaved Man in Black of his own 'like wofulnesse' suggests). Within a few years he enjoyed the rapturous love of Elizabeth Boyle, who was almost certainly the subject of *Amoretti* and whose epithalamium probably celebrates his marriage on 11 June 1594. There is no disputing the fact that his second outpouring of poetry is marked by a warmth and sense of personal involvement missing, on the whole, from the poems published in 1590–1. But his chief poetic energies, in the course of a life of responsible public service, must always have been directed into the writing of *The Faerie Queene*.

'Astrophel' is vastly superior to the other elegies in the collection which it introduced. It flows sweetly and successfully, conveying a true sense of grief at the loss of Sidney, yet its elements and design are more conventional. Spenser's mastery is clear, especially in the assimilation of classical myth and in the music of lament. It is peculiarly appropriate that Sir Philip Sidney should be mourned and celebrated in a pastoral elegy, not only because he was a pattern of virtue but also because he created the whole pastoral world of Arcadia in his prose epic Romance. Astrophel ('lover of the star', that is of Stella, the ideal lady celebrated in his sonnet sequence *Astrophel and Stella*) like Sidney 'With gentle usage and demeanure myld . . . all mens hearts with secret ravishment . . . stole away';

> His sports were faire, his joyance innocent,
> Sweet without sowre, and honny without gall:

* Harvey's letter of 23 April 1580 refers to a 'Mistress Immerito' and 'my most charming Lady Colin Clout', and his son Sylvanus must have been born later than 1582 (see Variorum edn., *Life* by A. C. Judson).

> And he himselfe seemd made for meriment,
> Merily masking both in bowre and hall. (25–9)

But was Sidney, as Astrophel is said to be, 'not so happie as the rest' of the shepherds (line 12)? And if so, was it because of his unhappy love for Penelope Devereux, the wife of Lord Rich, to whom sadly punning reference was made by Sidney in his sonnets 24, 35 and 37? And if so, what is Spenser doing in referring to this in his elegy on Sidney dedicated to Sidney's widow, Frances Walsingham? I think that the 'not so happie' reference is to the conventional unhappy love of the sonnet sequence, that the Stella of *Astrophel and Stella* is an ideal lady and if it refers at all to Lady Rich it is in conventional plaint. Spenser could not have intended reference to Lady Rich, whether or not she were in fact Sidney's ideal or actual mistress, in a poem dedicated to his widow. More important than these references in 'Astrophel' is Spenser's use of the myth of Venus and Adonis, partly from Bion's classical elegiac prototype *Lament for Adonis*, partly from Ovid (*Metamorphoses* X, 708ff.). Sidney's wounding in the thigh at Zutphen and his death are pictured as the wounding of the brave hunter by a wild beast as he hunted with boarspear and sword on 'forreine soyle', just as Adonis was also wounded in the thigh by a boar. In Ovid (and in Ronsard's *Adonis*) Venus tears her hair and rends her breast, as in Spenser Astrophel's beloved fiercely tears

> Her yellow locks that shone so bright and long,
> As Sunny beames in fairest somers day—
>
> .   .   .
>
> And her faire brest the threasury of joy,
> She spoyld thereof, and filled with annoy. (157ff).

What perspectives of association Spenser can always open out as he moves with consummate ease in the world of classical myth!

Purely native and Spenserian, though, are the musical cadences, repetitions, inversions and variations which produce the haunting sense of loss and regret in the elegy which concludes the poem of which the following stanza is the best example:

> Breake now your gyrlonds, O ye shepheards lasses,
> Sith the faire flowre, which them adornd, is gon:
> The flowre, which them adornd, is gone to ashes,
> Never againe let lasse put gyrlond on.
>   In stead of gyrlond, weare sad Cypres nowe,
>   And bitter Elder broken from the bowe. (37–42)

unrivalled for melodiously suggesting the catch in the throat and breaking voice of sorrow. I follow the commentators* who hold that this 'dolefull lay' of Clorinda must have been written by Spenser, chiefly because of the authentic 'feel' of it, partly because its rhetorical uses are so characteristic of him, and partly because in none of the few poems known to have been written by Sidney's sister—who in the poem is said to have made it—are there any resemblances to this. Yet, there are bad lines and dead patches—though their inertness resembles that of some earlier work such as 'The Ruines of Time', which also honours Sir Philip Sidney (with others of his kin) and which is dedicated to the same Mary Countess of Pembroke.

There must always be reasonable doubts about the actual 'sincerity' of much personal poetry, especially elegy and love-sonnets, but there is no reason to believe that Spenser had to heave up his heart to celebrate the paragon Sidney who seems to have had him 'in some use of familiarity'. However impersonal the conventional forms of elegy may seem, especially when conceived in the further artificiality of pastoral, we know that pastoral peculiarly affected Spenser, and released in him unusual emotional force. And there is in 'Astrophel', both in the introductory narrative (lines 1–216) and in the concluding lay, a special quality of tenderness greater than is to be found in the other great English elegies—'Lycidas', 'Adonais', 'Thyrsis'. The key to it is simplicity: the simple six-line stanza rhyming *ababcc*; the usual Spenserian choice of simple unemphatic epithets, getting effects by increment rather than by shock or surprise; in the first thirty lines alone, *piteous, gentle, dolefull, mournfull, mournfulst, softened, (rudely), nycer, gentlest, grassie, lithe, seemly, sclender, comely, faire, gentle, myld, (secret), faire, innocent, sweet, (sowre), honny, (gall,) delightfull;* above all the simplicity of the pastoral idea of gentle swain among sweet maidens and simple and true shepherds in summer hills and flowery fields, all shattered into sorrow by the savage mortal wounding which soon closed Astrophel's eyelids and made his lips 'like faded leaves of rose' or 'like lillies pale and soft'. The ideal shepherd world; the vulnerability of its virtue and contentment; the succeeding pictures of beauty spoiled or fouled (lines 152 and 162); the natural recourse to the pathetic fallacy; praise of virtue; lament for instability; faith in God—'Ah no: it is not dead, ne can it die, But lives for aie, in blisfull Paradise' (lines 67–8)—set against the background landscape of fields, hills, flowers, flocks, birds: all of these the reader will recog-

* See Variorum edn.

nise as resident features of Spenser's imagination from the very earliest
of his verses, here coming together briefly in a quiet perfection and
clarity, while, probably at this very time, they were receiving their
finest expression in *The Faerie Queene*.

'Colin Clouts Come Home Again' like 'Astrophel' affects the pastoral
manner, but now relaxed, personal and easy in tone. The antithesis
in pastoral poetry, rather mechanically utilised in *The Shepheardes
Calender*, represents for the Spenser of 'Colin Clouts Come Home
Again' a fundamental reality, and he has learned a manner comparable
to Chaucer's quiet, unemphatic, and leisurely manner, a 'middle style'
that supports the narrative with ease and while never dropping into
dullness or banality can rise surely in description or in reflection into
brilliance and power. Spenser uses the cross-rhymed quatrain as the
basic metrical form of the poem but with infinite flexibility: sometimes
repeating the rhyme in a succeeding quatrain, sometimes completely
rhyme-linking consecutive quatrains, sometimes breaking down the
impact of quatrain composition by finishing a sentence anywhere within
the quatrain, sometimes by running the sense over into one or more
quatrains. The last is comparable to a common practice in *The Faerie
Queene* and has the same advantage that it avoids monotony and gives
fluidity and ease of movement, and the metrical form is not allowed to
dominate. Here the reader may for long stretches not be aware that
the poem is in quatrains.

It is a pastoral poem of many colours and weaves. In its graceful
depiction and extolling of the simple delights of pastoral life it is
idyllic pastoral. It is Renaissance pastoral in its cloaked attack on
privilege, corruption and falseness at Court. The elegiac use of pastoral
is shown in the singing-match and in the lament for Amyntas and
Astrofell. It also sings the praises of the Queen, and bewails unre-
quited love. All the topics of pastoral, except perhaps the insistence on
the golden past, are raised in the poem, and it is at the same time a
uniquely autobiographical narrative poem, telling of an actual journey
from Ireland to London and back again. Using all the conventions
of the whole pastoral range it is yet not conventional. The shepherd
world is not, for example, purely idyllic: it (Ireland) is

> ... barrein soyle
> Where cold and care and penury do dwell.

compared with the richness and beauty of England with its 'fruitfull
corne, faire trees, fresh herbage' to which Colin had journeyed with

'the Shepheard of the Ocean'. Yet, although England is a happy land
where 'heaven and heavenly graces . . . abound', and

> . . . all happie peace and plenteous store
> Conspire in one to make contented blisse:
> No wayling there nor wretchednesse is heard,
> No bloodie issues nor no leprosies,
> No griesly famine, nor no raging sweard[1],
> No nightly bodrags[2], nor no hue and cries;
> The shepheards there abroad may safely lie,
> On hills and downes, withouten dread or daunger:
> No ravenous wolves the good mans hope destroy,
> Nor outlawes fell affray the forest raunger,   (312–19)

Spenser, with his not uncommon facility of having it both ways, goes
on to affirm that Colin chooses to leave it and to return to the 'rude
fields' of Ireland.

Conversely, the court in England is criticised as well as celebrated.
In lines 590–615 the Queen herself is duly praised, in ravishing hyperbole full of Old Testament evocation—honey, ripe grapes, the fruitful
vine, wine, beams of the morning sun, frankincense, sweet odours—
and under the name of Cynthia (the name Raleigh had chosen for his
poetic celebrations of the Queen).

Many 'shepherds'—some of them courtier-poets (probably Sackville,
Turberville, Dyer, Daniel, Gascoigne, the Earl of Derby as well as
Sidney) and some have also recognised Marlowe, Shakespeare and
Drayton—are commemorated in lines 376–455; and many 'nymphs',
some identifiable as ladies to whom Spenser was known or to whom
he dedicated poems, are celebrated in lines 485–583.

Yet the Renaissance tradition of complaint if not of satire in pastoral
enters in Colin's dispraise of the Court and the 'painted blisse' of
court life

> Where each one seeks with malice and with strife,
> To thrust downe other into foule disgrace,
> Himselfe to raise . . .   (690–2)

and where success is achieved by deceit, subtlety, slander, lies and
dissembling,

> Whiles single Truth and simple honestie
> Do wander up and downe despys'd of all.   (727–8)

[1] *sweard* sword   [2] *bodrags* raids

As Colin had necessarily exempted Cynthia from criticism, so he admits that of course there are some 'right worthie' ones at Court, of 'spotlesse honestie' and 'learned arts', but he leaves no doubt, as so often in *The Faerie Queene*, that pride, envy, idleness and wasteful pleasure together with the basest forms of 'love' predominate in that atmosphere, and this leads into praise of honest love, to which I will return.

The 'conventional' singing-match is more than conventional. Colin Clout's mythological love-tale of two rivers, a variant of the 'Escaping Lovers and Pursuing Father' folk-motif, with suggestions of Ovid's story of Alpheus and Arethusa (*Metamorphoses* V) pleasingly re-inforces the country atmosphere. At the same time it gives a definite setting to the poem, for the river Bregog which has to disguise itself, and then go underground (as indeed streams do in limestone country) in order to achieve union with the stream Mulla, flowed through Spenser's own land at Kilcolman in Munster, and Colin Clout has already 'placed' himself by telling us of his first meeting with the shepherd of the ocean as he sat piping and keeping his sheep

> . . . amongst the cooly shade
> Of the greene alders by the *Mullaes* shore.   (58–9)

The shepherd of the ocean's responding song is only summarised: it was a lamentable lay,

> Of great unkindnesse, and of usage hard,
> Of *Cynthia* the Ladie of the sea,
> Which from her presence faultlesse him debard.   (164–7)

There is no reason to disbelieve the tradition that 'Colin Clouts Come Home Again' is autobiographical and that the journey Raleigh and Spenser took to London was partly in order to plead for restoration of the former's lost favour at Court, and that *The Faerie Queene*, the first great epic poem in English and one which lavishly celebrates and honours the Queen, was hastened into print to restore the fortunes of Raleigh as well as to create the fortunes of Spenser.

Finally, the love-element in this pastoral goes far beyond the conventional. Originating in that same fiction (or was it truth?) of Colin's unhappy love for Rosalind which figured at regular intervals and acted as a unifying agent in *The Shepheardes Calender*, and so making a clear link with the earlier and cruder pastoral, the love-

subject in 'Colin Clouts Come Home Again' also anticipates the
passionate worshipping love expressed in *Amoretti*, its ultimate
triumph in 'Epithalamion', and the enraptured celebration of the creative and the divine power of love of the *Four Hymns* and *The Faerie
Queene*. The autobiographical element in 'Colin Clout' and the
narrator's impassioned expression of love together lift this unique
poem well above the conventional, whether conventional pastoral,
conventional complaint or conventional love-poetry. When one of
the shepherds asks him whether love is known at Court

> I weened sure he was our God alone:
> And only woond[1] in fields and forests here,   (773–5)

Colin Clout replies that indeed it exists there, but not the 'sacred lere'
(lore) that shepherds know,

> For with lewd speeches and licentious deeds,
> His mightie mysteries they do prophane . . .
>
>   .   .   .
>
> So him they do not serve as they professe,
> But make him serve to them for sordid uses,   (786ff.)

and the poet proceeds to a brief skilful summary of the birth of Cupid,
of his upbringing in the gardens of Adonis, and of his power in the
earth, shooting his 'shafts of gold and lead', to bring happy or unhappy love.* By one of his characteristically skilful transitions, Spenser
moves on to write of 'loves perfection' and of his nature, here assimilating Cupid into a mixed Platonic and Christian view of love's power
not only in making the world but in harmonising all the discordant
elements from which it was created—cold, heat, water, fire, the heavy
and the light and so forth—and ending with an account of man's
higher nature, endowed as he is with 'reasons might . . . to rule his
passion', so that man can use his reason to choose 'for his love the
fairest in his sight'; and then he will choose virtuously, for he will
choose 'Beautie the burning lamp of heavens light'. These are only
brief anticipations of the Hymns of Love, Beauty, Heavenly Love
and Heavenly Beauty, and of a central preoccupation of *The Faerie
Queene*. There is no reason to assume merely conventional attitudes

[1] *woond* dwelt
* As in Ovid, *Metamorphoses* I, 469–71.

here: if his master Chaucer sang spryly of love, a devotee but a worldly one, Spenser celebrates it so constantly and with such hymning and spiritual enthusiasm in these poems of 1595–6, and so often with avowed personal reference, that one is entitled to recognise a genuine personal emotion, however 'conventional'—Ovidian, Platonic, Christian, Petrarchan—much of its expression may be.

Whoever Rosalind was, and whether the Rosalind of 'Colin Clout' (referred to in lines 908ff.) was the same as she of *The Shepheardes Calender* or was the *altera Rosalindula* of the Harvey correspondence or another, and indeed whether the Rosalind of the *Calender* was Machabyas Chylde, his first wife, or someone he lost, and the Rosalind of 'Colin Clout' Elizabeth Boyle (his second wife), Spenser ends with a final tribute to her 'divine regard and heavenly hew'

> Excelling all that ever ye did see, (933–4)

and a further declaration that he will always love her, less fervent but more religious than his statement earlier (472ff.):

> To her my thoughts I daily dedicate,
> To her my heart I nightly martyrize:
> To her my love I lowly do prostrate,
> To her my life I wholly sacrifice:
> My thought, my heart, my love, my life is shee,
> And I hers ever onely, ever one.

Little or nothing can be claimed to be novel or original, yet I feel in Spenser's writing on love a truly personal wonder, love, emotion and dedication.

So out of convention and make-believe, out of the classical pastoral convention and the Renaissance extension or abuse of it (an abuse that saved it from insipidity), out of his early endeavours to assimilate the two types, out of his habit of identifying himself with the shepherd as poet, lover and virtuous man, and above all out of his natural power to create an imagined world and to express imaginatively the mind's emotions and the heart's thoughts, Spenser developed pastoral as a natural and pleasing reflective fiction able with all seriousness to convey the variety and comprehensiveness of the poet's view of the world.

'Colin Clout' is one of Spenser's must successful poems, in a minor way showing that great skill, revealed most clearly in *The Faerie Queene*, of taking old forms and making of them something

new, and wonderfully appropriate for their subject: it is the most
varied and original pastoral poem in English.

The tone of humble and religious awe which Spenser adopts in his
final praise of Rosalind—a 'thing celestiall . . . not like as the other
crew Of shepheards daughters'—whom it is some reward for him
only to admire though without hope and having endured 'long
affliction', is one of the dominant tones of his sonnet-sequence *Amoretti*. While the collection is indebted to earlier sonneteers, among them
Petrarch, Desportes, Ronsard and Tasso, though none is singly
indebted to any other single sonnet, there are features which suggest
that it has some actual personal relevance or at least that Spenser went
to more trouble than most to make it seem so, referring to his Dublin
friend Lodowick Bryskett, to *The Faerie Queene*, to his beloved's
name Elizabeth and to his age—he is forty. He also gives it a sense of
order and development by use of a time-scheme, which adds to a
sense of verisimilitude; because it is calendared, it seems more true.

The fourth sonnet is a New Year poem, and spring is celebrated
in Sonnet 19. By Sonnet 60, the poet has loved for a year, and 62
records a second New Year's Day. 68 is an Easter hymn, and 70
another celebration of spring. The finely proud and seemingly im-
movable lady and not the versifying lover is the chief character of
the sequence, and her personality and appearance are more clearly
presented than is usual. The lover is a fixed star, immutably turned
towards the lady—a changeable planet—and the main concern of
the poet is wondering contemplation of a lady certain and predictable
only in her beauty, virtue and noble pride. It is a record, convincing
and moving in the aggregate (though to read a few of the single sonnets
here and there is to gain a false impression of the quality of the sequence
as a whole, as is not the case with Sidney and Shakespeare), of fearful
adoration, humility, worship and hope. There are of course nearly all
the conventional subjects and attitudes: the lover's worthlessness;
the lady's pride though here a characteristic Spenserian originality
is that her pride is what he most admires:

> For in those lofty lookes is close implide,
> Scorn of base things, and sdeigne[1] of foule dishonour
>
> (Sonnet 5)

and

---

[1] *sdeigne* disdain

... that same lofty countenance seemes to scorne
base thing, and thinke how she to heaven may clime.   (13)

the bewitchment of her smile:

Lykest it seemeth in my simple wit
   unto the fayre sunshine in somers day:
that when a dreadfull storme away is flit,
   thrugh the broad world doth spred his goodly ray:
At sight whereof each bird that sits on spray,
   and every beast that to his den was fled
comes forth afresh out of their late dismay
   and to the light lift up theyr drouping hed.
So my storme beaten hart likewise is cheared,
   with that sunshine when cloudy looks are cleared.   (40)

the grief of separation:

So oft as homeward I from her depart,
   I goe lyke one that having lost the field,
is prisoner led away with heavy hart,
   despoyled of warlike armes and knowen shield,
So doe I now my selfe a prisoner yeeld,
   to sorrow and to solitary paine:
from presence of my dearest deare exylde,
   longwhile alone in languor to remaine.   (52)

And there are conventional descriptions and analogies—flowers,
stars, sunshine, sweet smells, spring, storm-tossed ships, caged birds,
cruel victors, steel and flint, victims suing for peace. But there is an
unusual emphasis on the lady's *virtue*, and on this as the quality which
most commands the poet's love, proclaiming the sonnets the work of
the poet whose constant subject was the praise of virtue, and especially
the poet of the *Four Hymnes* and *The Faerie Queene*. There accumu-
lates also a quite unusual sense of reality through all the conventional-
isms; I think any man who has truly loved a woman with feelings of
admiration and some kind of spiritual longing as well as with desire
for her body and company, will recognise those feelings truthfully
and movingly expressed in the course of the *Amoretti* sequence. It is a
minor instance of a dominating characteristic of Spenser's poetry,
his ability to conjure a reality out of an abstraction—there are times
when the sonneteer seems to be in love with an abstraction which
represents virtue—and to depict at once the personal and particular
and the objective and general. The sequence *is* a celebration of Virtue

in many aspects, but it is a real lady who laughs the solemn lover out of countenance:

> But when I pleade, she bids me play my part,
>   and when I weep, she sayes teares are but water:
>   and when I sigh, she sayes I know the art,
>   and when I waile she turnes her selfe to laughter.   (18)

draws the moral when the tide washes away her name which he has scratched in the sand,

> Vayne man, sayd she, that doest in vaine assay,
>   a mortall thing so to immortalize,
>   for I my selve shall lyke to this decay,
>   and eek my name bee wyped out lykewize.   (75)

and who dismisses him at the appointed hour to send him home through a sudden storm which seemed against her will to demand his stay (46), as, one feels, it was a real lady who burned his poem (48), and works woodbine and eglantine into her tapestry of herself as bee and her lover—mischievously—as spider lurking 'in close awayt to catch her unaware' (71).*

This lifelike and humorous portrayal of a worshipped goddess is rare in sonnet sequences although most of the instances have parallels elsewhere. His humour is one of the qualities—often denied Spenser—which gives a sense of human reality to *Amoretti*, as, on a much larger scale, it does to *The Faerie Queene*. A great contribution to this effect in *Amoretti* is the change which comes after Sonnet 68. That sonnet records the Easter of the second year of the lover's courtship, and jubilates over Christ's victory. (The makers of *The English Hymnal*, who included it in their collection, must have been deceived by the opening:

> Most glorious Lord of lyfe, that on this day,
>   Didst make thy triumph over death and sin:
>   and having harrowd hell, didst bring away
>   captivity thence captive us to win:
> This joyous day, deare Lord, with joy begin,
>   and grant that we for whom thou diddest dye
>   being with thy deare blood clene washt from sin,
>   may live for ever in felicity

* Louis L. Martz charmingly illumined the subject in '*The Amoretti*: Most Goodly Temperature', in W. Nelson, Ed. *Form and Convention in the Poetry of Edmund Spenser*, New York and London, 1961.

for it concludes

> So let us love, deare love, lyke as we ought
> love is the lesson which the Lord us taught.)

Spenser uses it, in a way that would be blasphemous if it were only human carnal love he were celebrating, to mark the turning-point of his sequence of sonnets, for the lady at last accepts his love in Sonnet 69, in which the lover records his 'loves conquest, peerelesse beauties prise,/adorn'd with honour, love and chastity', the 'happy purchase' of his 'glorious spoile,/gotten at last with labour and long toyle'. After this, all the remaining sonnets (69–89) except four are jubilant celebrations by the happy lover, including one (74) which happily reveals his beloved's name to be Elizabeth, like his mother's and the Queen's. The exceptions are 75 which recalls a time before his love was accepted but yet expresses faith and hope in the permanence of love even after death; 80, which makes happy reference to the completion of six books of *The Faerie Queene* (in contrast to Sonnet 33 which spoke of it as 'taedious toyle' that is also 'tost with troublous fit, of a proud love, that doth my spirite spoyle', so that Spenser marks the balance of sorrow and failure with success both as poet and as lover); and 89. This last grieves over absence with a greater sense of loss—

> Dark is my day, whyles her fayre light I mis,
> and dead my life that wants such lively blis

than the earlier sonnet (52) had lamented separation from the beloved:

> So I her absens will my penaunce make,
> that of her presens I my meed may take:

rightly so, for the absence of the truly beloved who reciprocates is weightier cause for sorrow, however temporary, than the itch of regret at separation—'the sudden dumps and drery sad disdayne' (Sonnet 52)—of a straining anguished lover uncertain of a cruel mistress. Again one feels the truth of human experience in Spenser's handling of conventional themes. I have referred to the contrast in tone between Sonnets 52 and 89. It epitomises the general contrast between the sonnets of fearful longing occasionally lightened by hope (1–63) and those of fulfilment (69–89). Spenser likes a rising close of optimism, and of course in many poems it sorts with his sense of the 'eterne in mutabilitie'. That he was able to give his sonnet-sequence an upward turn into happiness may well be because it was so in life. Certainly no other sonnet-sequence moves with such poise and assurance into radiance. The forty-year-old lover (Sonnet 60) may not have suffered in all seriousness all the Petrarchan pains, but fulfilment for him is attended by a maturer serenity than younger lovers may experience, and his reward is the greater because he always knew that what he loved virtuously was virtuous and more than worthy of a man's love.*

The real Spenser married a real Elizabeth on 11 June 1594. Whether or not *Amoretti* traced the course of his real courtship, it was surely his real marriage he celebrated in the 'Epithalamion' which Ponsonby printed with the sonnet-sequence, thereby presenting the marriage-ode as a conclusion to the love-sonnets. The usual Spenserian skill at effortlessly fusing conventional, external and literary elements with personal concerns and identification, seen all along the way from *The Shepheardes Calender* to these poems of 1595–6 ('Colin Clouts Come Home Again' and *Amoretti*), reaches apotheosis in 'Epithalamion'. Its form is closely related to that of the Italian *canzone*, but instead of the regular stanza of the *canzone*, it has 23 regularly rhymed stanzas of usually 17 lines (though there are 8 of 18 lines and 1 of 17) in all of which save one there are three short lines, followed by a *tornata* of seven lines. It is thus freer and more various than the *canzone* stanza. In this Renaissance Italian form Spenser has expressed a classical 'kind', a hymenaeal ode or epithalamion ('on the marriage-bed') including in it the chief features—procession, sacrifices to the gods, exchange of gifts, banqueting, adorning of the bride, preparation of the bridal chamber, prayer for the fruitfulness of the union—which gradually became established from Homer's account of marriage feasting (*Iliad* XVIII, 491ff.), Theocritus's Idyll 18 (the 'Epithalamion of Helen'), Catallus's Carmen 61 ('The Wedding of Manlius and Vinia') to the epithalamia of the French writers of the Pléiade, Ronsard and du Bellay. A distinction is that the 'narrator' or invoker in 'Epithalamion' is not a god or just a poet but the poet who is also the bridegroom. It is a characteristically happy Spenserian innovation, which

---

* I do not know why the publisher (or poet) added the delightful Anacreontics about Venus and Cupid ending with the poet pierced by Cupid's dart and so languishing 'till he please my pining anguish to appease'. They seem, however slight, too skilful to be pure *juvenilia*, and they provide as inappropriate a conclusion as possible to the *Amoretti* sequence.

is chiefly responsible for the feeling almost all commentators have
shared that this is a personal poem in which Spenser celebrates his real
marriage to Elizabeth Boyle in Ireland (cf. 'Ye Nymphes of Mulla'
and 'the rushy lake, Where none doo fishes take' at Kilcolman in the
fourth stanza) on the day of the summer solstice in 1594.

Yet how actually personal is it? If the sonnet offers the most, the
ode, of all lyrical verse-forms offers the least opportunities for conveying intimate personal feeling, because of its public celebratory
character (and its greater length). 'Epithalamion' is of course a
glorious musical and visual celebration, in many ways transforming
the epithalamic convention, but for once I am conscious of some filling
out: for example, the repetition of reference to the bride modestly
keeping her eyes on the ground in both stanzas 9 and 13, and such
clumsy examples of treading water (rather than swimming) as

> Ne let hob Goblins, names whose sence we see not,
> Fray us with things that be not. (343–4)

They perhaps add to the credibility of Professor Kent Hieatt's* claims
about the numerological substructures of the poem here. Briefly, he
sees the 24 stanzas and 365 long lines of the poem as symbolising the
sun's progress through the skies each day and its apparent movement
round the earth in the course of a year. The 17th stanza depicts the
coming of night, and after it the refrain changes, Spenser thus marking
the 'narrative' action by stanzaic plotting, and pointing to the fact
that the hours of day-light at the summer solstice in the south of Ireland
were about $16\frac{1}{4}$, with about $7\frac{3}{4}$ of night. (I will not pursue his further
elaborations about the sidereal hours and the paralleling of the stanzas,
despite the claim that his theory makes sense of the concluding *tornata*
of 7 lines.) I am ready to believe that Spenser could and might have so
organised a poem; it would help to account also for the feeling of
premeditation. Unusually, the sublime Spenserian spontaneity and
rambling naturalness—as if it were being written down now for the
first time, without blotting line—and the sense of the poet's personality, are absent. In its place is a classical or Miltonic almost brazen
certainty. This is partly because the singer is for much of the poem
depersonalised into 'bridegroom', and he describes the wedding-day
as if he were observing it all from outside; indeed as if what the bride

* 'The Daughters of Horus: Order in the Stanzas of Epithalamion', in W.
Nelson, Ed., *Form and Convention in the Poetry of Edmund Spenser*, New York
and London 1961.

is doing is something she does all on her own, coming alone from her
chamber, entering the temple alone, standing alone and being blessed
by the holy priest before the altar on her own, feasting among the
guests alone, brought to the bridal bower and laid in her bed alone.
It is not until stanza 18 that the poet-celebrator-bridegroom imagines
himself in his beloved's arms, calling on night:

> Spread thy broad wing over my love and me,
> That no man may us see,
> And in thy sable mantle us enwrap,
> From feare of perrill and foule horror free.
> Let no false treason seeke us to entrap,
> Nor any dread disquiet once annoy
> The safety of our joy. (319–25)

In fact, of course, the ode is not so much a celebration of an actual
wedding-day, as an imaginative anticipation by the bridegroom-to-be,
offered to his betrothed, as he declares in the *tornata* or *envoy*, 'in lieu
of many ornaments', which he has been unable through 'hasty accidents' to give. So 'Epithalamion' ends, as *Amoretti* began, with a
clear statement by the poet to his assured beloved: the sonnets,
'happy lines' and 'happy rhymes' even when they describe the lover's
'sorrowes', form a volume he presents to her after her acceptance of
him as a record of his love intended 'her to please alone', while the
marriage-ode is a poem given to her after their betrothal and before
their marriage-day as a present and an anticipatory celebration; the
one looks backward over the recent past, the other forward into the
near future. It is to be, as the last line claims,

> . . . for short time an endless moniment,

a permanent monument to a brief period—that one day of 24 hours
in the life of lover and beloved. Professor Hieatt has several arcane
interpretations, linking the 24 hours of that wedding-day with 'that
order in mutability which is the fit mirror in time of the changeless
order of eternity' and with 'the ordered succession of forms—a kind
of dance—in which the regenerative aspect is institutionalised in
marriage'. I do not wish to dispute them, but prefer to conclude by
referring to some of the sublimities of 'Epithalamion': its tone of
serene happiness; the sense of onward movement—of the procession,
of the sun and the day, of time, of the progress of the love, all marvellously interwoven and inseparable; the delineation of an idealised

but real landscape with lakes and fish and mountains) and a townscape
with streets full of processions of virgins and 'fresh boyes', markets,
a temple with organ and choristers singing anthems, feasting and
dancing and ringing of bells and bonfires lit at night and a rich chamber
with silken curtains, scented sheets and tapestry coverlets, into which
shines the moon; and the poet singing to himself (as the refrain suggests)—'So I unto my selfe alone will sing, The woods shall to me
answer and my Eccho ring'—perhaps outside his house of Kilcolman
below the hanging woods, and imagining himself at nightfall going
within, and calling on the woods no more to 'answer, nor theyr eccho
ring' as he joins his newly married bride. It is the most joyful and
musical of all English odes.

Beside it, 'Prothalamion' while infinitely and more regularly
musical—and in a stricter stanza more like the Italian *canzone*—is
undeniably impersonal, despite some personal passages in which the
poet complains of the frustration of his expectations at court where
he has made a 'long fruitlesse stay' (5–10), tells of his origins and
upbringing in London (127–9), pays tribute to an old patron, long
dead—Leicester (137–40)—and celebrates a perhaps new patron—
Essex (145ff). The chief matter of the poem, to honour the espousal
of two daughters of the Earl of Worcester to Henry Guilford and
William Petrie, is conveyed in a gracefully formal account of the
passage of the two ladies, pictured as swans, along the Thames to be
formally received by their future grooms. If this 'spousall verse' were
all we had of Spenser's work in the epithalamic convention, we would
place it very high, but it must always seem gravely formal, impersonal
and descriptive beside the intimate jubilation of 'Epithalamion'. Of
course the occasion was one of little personal importance to Spenser,
and the poem celebrates the formalities of betrothal rather than the
sublime rituals of marriage and the joys of consummated love.

The climax to this season of writing of love, sometimes in the
autobiographical convention, sometimes not, is provided by the
Four Hymnes (1596). While not autobiographical, Spenser seeks to
give them a distinct personal quality, keeping himself always in the
reader's eye. 'In Honour of Love' begins with the poet referring to
the long time his 'poor captived hart' has been subdued by love; in
lines 141–52, having described how imperious Cupid causes the pains
of love, he says

> So hast thou often done (ay me the more)
> To me thy vassal

and wonders why he still honours the capricious god who shows him
no favour and does not once 'move ruth' in the rebellious lady he
hopelessly loves, going on to suggest that perhaps the 'hard handling'
Cupid deals to lovers may make them more esteem him and their love
once they are successful. The vivid accounts in lines 218–45 (how
love may inspire and guide a man) and in lines 252–72 (how a lover
suffers: fears, imaginings, sleeplessness, envy, 'vaine surmizes', 'doubts,
daungers . . . delayes . . . woes', and the 'monster Gelosie') are seen
so clearly through a lover's eye that when Spenser concludes

> Ay me, deare Lord, that ever I might hope,
> For all the paines and woes that I endure,
> To come at length unto the wished scope
> Of my desire

the reader is ready to be convinced of the authenticity of the whole
statement. The woes of his hapless love for Rosalind in the *Calender*,
the sad statement of her worth and beauty, even though they may not
be for him, in 'Colin Clout', and the sonnets of love-longing in
Amoretti, are brought to mind.

'In Honour of Beautie' begins with conventional expression of
the poet's mood. His raging love now kindles in him 'more great
desyre' lifting him above his ordinary power to praise what he loves
and so he sings in honour of Beauty, hoping, in lines 23–8, that both
Beauty and his unreciprocating beloved will be pleased and that the lady

> . . . at length will streame
> Some deaw of grace, into my withered hart,
> After long sorrow and consuming smart.

This plea is repeated in similar terms at the end (lines 274–9). The
poet regrets in 'Of Heavenly Love' that

> Many lewd layes (ah woe is me the more)
> In praise of that mad fit, which fooles call love,
> I have in th'heat of youth made heretofore,   (8–10)

and proceeds to sing

> . . . an heavenly Hymne . . .
> Unto the god of Love, high heavens king,

following it with a hymn 'Of Heavenly Beautie' which he concludes
with an exhortation to himself to

> . . . looke at last up to that soveraine light,
> From whose pure beams al perfect beauty springs,
> That kindleth love in every godly spright,
> Even the love of God, which loathing brings
> Of this vile world . . . (295–9)

but the personal element is much less strong in the later two poems. Contemplating heavenly love and heavenly beauty, his expressed desire to rise above himself and the limitations of this world, he naturally effaces himself.

But although Spenser could make anything sound personal and original, as usual his material is part of the common stock of European Renaissance learning, in this case of course basically Platonic and Christian, as Miss Winstanley, Miss Welsford and Professor Ellrodt* have shown, with varying emphasis, mediated through the neo-Platonists and indebted to Dante, Petrarch, Bembo, Castiglione, Ebreo and Bruno. The ordinary reader will find attempts to specify indebtedness or actual borrowings unrewarding, as he will any attempt to solve the unimportant problem of whether or not Spenser meant what he wrote in the dedication to the Countesses of Cumberland and Warwick. There he implied that the two 'secular' hymns, composed 'in the greener times' of his youth, were too successful in commending the pursuit of love and beauty. When they were published in 1596 he therefore added the two 'divine' hymns 'by way of retraction'.

As *Amoretti* is remarkable among sonnet-sequences for its continuous emphasis on the lady's virtue, so the hymns 'Of Love' and 'Of Beautie' imply only virtuous desire for the virtuous and beautiful. There is nothing here really to give *'poison to . . . strong passion'* rather than *'honey to . . . honest delight'*. Cupid is not only the 'imperious boy' ('Of Love' 120) and the 'tyrant Love' (line 134) of Renaissance convention but also 'Great god of might' kindled at first from 'heavens life-giving fyre' (line 143) and then making the world harmoniously out of chaos, and again the

> . . . Lord of truth and loialtie,
> Lifting himselfe out of the lowly dust,
> On golden plumes up to the purest skie,
> Above the reach of loathly sinfull lust. (176–9)

---

* Ed. L. Winstanley, *Spenser, The Fowre Hymnes*, Cambridge 1907; E. Welsford, *Spenser: Fowre Hymnes and Epithalamion*, Oxford 1967; R. Ellrodt, *Neo-Platonism in the Poetry of Spenser*, Geneva 1960.

The consummation the lover frankly wants is as 'hurtlesse' and 'without rebuke or blame' (line 288) as the happy proper love celebrated in *The Faerie Queene* and symbolised there in the lovers of the Gardens of Adonis.

Similarly, 'Of Beautie', which invokes Cupid's mother Venus, celebrates Beauty as the 'wondrous Paterne' to 'whose perfect mould' God made the world, as the Platonic Form, and as the enduring and indestructible element in the body which the soul chooses to occupy

> For of the soule the bodie forme doth take
> For soul is forme, and doth the bodie make.
>
> Therefore where ever that thou doest behold
> A comely corpse[1], with beautie faire endewed,
> Know this for certaine, that the same doth hold
> A beauteous soule . . .
> Fit to receive the seede of vertue strewed.   (132ff.)

The subject of this poem is really Love though its title is of Beauty; reasonably enough for Spenser believes with Plato in the inseparability of love and beauty (though he makes a kind proviso that 'many a gentle mynd Dwels in deformed tabernacle drownd'). As always the love he commends is of the highest, not 'loose love without respect' but love as

> . . . a celestiall harmonie,
> Of likely harts composd of starres concent,
> Which joyne together in sweete sympathie,
> To worke ech others joy and true content.   (197–200)

There is nothing to apologise for in these two 'secular' hymns. They are not wanton celebrations or advocations of sensual love, nor merely Petrarchan sighings. Though they invoke Cupid and Venus, they derive from the Platonic dialogues, especially the *Symposium* and the *Phaedrus*, as mediated by the neo-Platonism of the Florentine Academy and so through the commentaries and original writings of the Renaissance. Informing them is a sense of the creating and ordering power of love; of its permeating and regulating power in the universe so that to love is to be a part of the harmonious order of the universe; a conviction of the uplifting and disciplining power of love, and a celebration of the spiritual perceived and desired through the beauty of the beloved object.

Yet the first two hymns, both creating some sense of religious awe

[1] *corpse* (living) body

and mystical apprehension, are 'secular'. Spenser in them does not go much further than the second stage of Plato's outline of the pilgrimage of the soul.* The second two hymns in contrast are clearly 'divine', the poet moving to adoration of the heavenly love of Christ and the heavenly beauty of the divine in a kind of Christianised Platonism. As the four poems have parallel structures the reader is very conscious immediately on passing from 'Love' and 'Beautie' to 'Heavenly Love' and 'Heavenly Beautie' of a tremendous step up. The slight triviality —or at any rate the slight feeling of incongruity or disproportion in the *quasi*-divine tone of parts of the 'secular' hymns—and the rather uneasy steps which the poet took as he wandered between Love and Beauty, Cupid, Venus and the divine, the soul, the body and the soul's beauty in the two earlier poems, are overwhelmed by the confident power of his assertions in the two later ones of God's creating love and of his continuing love for his creation. The awkwardness inevitable in any attempt to show the world made harmonious out of chaos by a personified Love having inseparable connotations of classical godling and Renaissance god—the mischievous Cupid—and to show the inspiring power of beauty by evoking the capricious classical and Rennaissance goddess Venus, vanishes the moment the poet begins to write as a delighting Christian of God's creation and ordering of the world.

How much more interesting as well as convincing is the brief account of the Creation and Fall in 'Of Heavenly Love' than the earlier parallel account in 'Of Love' of the birth of Cupid and his harmonising of 'contrary forces', and the description in 'Of Heavenly Beautie' of God's Order in earth and heaven than the vague depiction in 'Of Beautie' of the 'great workmaister's' 'wondrous Paterne'. There are many things in the two 'divine' hymns which make one wish almost that Spenser, with his understanding of the creative love of God, and the voluptuous fertility of his creative imagination had attempted a *Paradise Lost*. If there was a power which Milton lacked and Spenser possessed it was the power of diffusing a sense of lovingness.† In *Paradise Lost* we do not feel love for God or Christ or even any conviction of their loving natures or of love as the supreme activating principle, although Milton often enough tells us of the divine love. Spenser does not reduce God's stature by eschewing heroic effects—

* *Symposium*, section 210.
† Although in his own 'Hymn' on the Nativity Milton under Spenser's influence achieves something of Spenser's effects.

of which he was well capable—but is concerned to make him loving
and creative rather than majestically authoritative. The writing is
quiet and unforced and of course it is done in small compass, not in
an epic poem but in a 'hymne' or ode of praise of three hundred lines.
For the divine and sublime Spenser adopts simplicity and deliberately
vague detail: God is 'that high eternall powre . . . mov'd in it selfe by
Love'; 'eternall fount of love and grace Still flowing forth his good-
nesse unto all'; 'great Lord of Love'; Christ is

> . . . blessed well of love, O floure of grace,
> O glorious Morning starre, O Lampe of light,
>
> .   .   .
>
> Eternall King of glorie, Lord of might,
> Meeke lambe of God before all worlds behight.
>   ('Of Heavenly Love', 169ff.)

There is no attempt at awe or heroic distance, and, humanising by
using simple traditional metaphors and symbols, Spenser brings
the Creator and his Son warmly into our human horizon. His brief
account of the nativity ('encradled . . . In simple cratch, wrapt in
a wad of hay'), the youth and the passion of Christ, in three stanzas
only, shows not only masterly compression but cunning direction of
our sympathetic response:

> How with most scornefull taunts, and fell despights
> He was revyld, disgrast, and foule abused,
> How scourged, how crownd, how buffeted, how brused;
> And lastly how twixt robbers crucifyde,
> With bitter wounds through hands, through feet and syde.
>   ('Of Heavenly Love', 241ff.)

In these Hymns Spenser is better at the concrete and palpable than
at the anthropomorphosing of ideas. In 'Of Heavenly Love' Creation,
the rebellion and fall of the angels, and the nativity and passion of
Christ are all vividly and movingly delineated for the reader, however
briefly it is done. In 'Of Heavenly Beautie' the poet set himself to
visualise the unpicturable. While he convincingly presents the
'frame' or order of the 'wyde *universe*', thrillingly evokes the brilliance
of the skies and the exceeding radiance of heaven with all the hosts of
angels, he falls back on disclaimers about the ability of 'fraile wights'
to depict 'the glory of that Majestie divine, In sight of whom both Sun
and Moone are darke' when he comes to God in majesty and the
abstraction *Sapience* he sets in God's bosom. It was necessary to show

not only the loving God but the wise and all-powerful, but undeniably Spenser was more successful with the former. Spenser is thinking not so much of Plato's Wisdom as of the Wisdom of the Old Testament especially in the Book of Wisdom 'which sitteth by thy throne' (Wisdom ix. 4). Miss Welsford calls her a personification of the Eternal Law of God, persuasively recalling Hooker's First Eternal Law: 'that law, which hath been the pattern to make and is the card to guide the world by; that law which hath been of God and with God everlastingly . . . her seat is the bosom of God, her voice the harmony of the world'. Spenser makes clear that she

> . . . rules the house of God on hy,
> And manageth the ever-moving sky,
> And in the same these lower creatures all,
> Subjected to her powre imperiall
>
> ('Of Heavenly Beautie', 193ff.)

and 'Both heaven and earth obey unto her will'. Clearly Miss Welsford is right, but I would define it further: God's Wisdom, his Eternal Law, is shown in the Order of the Universe. It is that which man must look upon in awe, wonder, praise and gratitude, and it is that Order which man must always hope will be restored. Wisely, Spenser does not call upon us to worship, admire or even to see an anthropomorphic God, either here or in the final cantos of *The Faerie Queene* where Nature, God's vicar (as Chaucer, whom Spenser followed, called her), appears in place of God and representing God in the great debate with Mutabilitie. In the end, the great absolutes for Spenser become interchangeable as they are inter-related, not only the Platonic fusing of Love and Beauty, but also, and more momentously, the inter-relating of God's Love, God's Law and God's Order. For the further celebration of love we shall have to wait for Books III and IV of *The Faerie Queene*, and for further discussion of Love and Order and for Spenser's definitive statements on them we shall have to wait until Books V and VI and those final cantos 'Of Mutabilitie'.

There we shall find how much more vivid, potent and poetical Spenser's presentation is when he turns to imaginative and symbolic narrative. However personal the impulse may have been, or however convincingly he suggested that in these autobiographical or *quasi*-autobiographical poems, it is in the creation of imaginary worlds, shapes and people, in fact of his Faerie land, that Spenser most fully comes into his own, most powerfully expresses the real concerns of his mind and heart.

D

5

THE *FAERIE QUEENE*: BACKGROUND AND AIMS

Professor Sir Donald Tovey wrote in the introduction to his *Essays in Musical Analysis* 'no piece of music can be understood from *a priori* generalisations as to form, but . . . all music must be followed phrase by phrase as a process in time'. The advice may profitably be applied to the understanding of *The Faerie Queene*, which, as I have already claimed, is *cursive* not *uncial* and is much concerned with mutability and all the progressions, changes and transformations wrought by time. The poem is a monument to mutability, and the point is made by the very fact of its apparent incompleteness; at its end, we are left with the feeling that the life of Faerie land is still going on and will still go on, just as, while we are reading the poem we feel that the events have been happening as we read.

Some generalisations about form are necessary, and will help to explain the poem. It was naturally in the Augustan period that most doubt or anxiety was felt about the form of the poem. The readers of that age responded warmly to the romantic in Spenser, indeed often more warmly than their nineteenth-century successors, and they enjoyed his variety and the astonishing fertility of his imagination. But they were troubled about the poem's real standing as an epic, and the critics of the time were at pains to make excuses for its formal and structural defects. The first of them, John Hughes, Spenser's first real commentator, in the 'Remarks on the *Fairy Queen*' published in his edition of 1715, defended Spenser from the common charge, made by Rymer and Dryden among others, that the poem lacked classical unity, and that Spenser had been led astray by Boiardo, Ariosto and the Italians instead of following correctly in the steps of Homer and Virgil. Hughes's way out of the difficulty was to declare that Spenser never intended his epic to conform to the practice of Homer and Virgil, that *The Faerie Queene* should 'be considered as a Poem of a particular kind, describing in a Series of Allegorical Adventures or Episodes the most noted Virtues and Vices', and that to compare it with the 'Models of Antiquity, wou'd be like drawing a Parallel between the *Roman* and the *Gothick* Architecture. In the first there is doubtless a more natural Grandeur and Simplicity; in the latter we find great Mixtures of Beauty and Barbarism, yet assisted by the Invention of a Variety of inferior Ornaments; and tho the former is more majestick in the whole, the latter may be very surprizing and agreeable in its Parts.' Hughes's vague if adventurous simile enlarged into a persuasive, long-lasting and I believe illuminating analogy. Richard Hurd took on from Hughes in *Letters on Chivalry and Romance** the idea of *The Faerie Queene* as 'not of a classical but Gothic composition', and extended the application of the word Gothic from the structure to the ingredients of the poem, which 'derives it's METHOD, as well as the other characters of its composition from the established modes and ideas of chivalry'; the unity of *The Faerie Queene* he declared is 'not the classic Unity . . . but it is an Unity of another Sort, an unity resulting from the respect which a number of related actions have to one common purpose. In other words, It is an unity of *design*, and not of action.'

In Spenser's letter to Sir Walter Raleigh 'expounding his whole intention', which accompanied *The Faerie Queene* into print in 1590, the poet made plain not only in what illustrious company he wanted to stand but also what a mixed ancestry he had chosen for his epic poem. He makes no mention of form, his whole concern being with purpose and method. He claimed kinship with the antique poets; Homer in his choice of Agamemnon and Ulysses, and Virgil in his choice of Aeneas, as examples of 'good governours' or 'virtuous men' or both. He then pointed to Ariosto who 'comprised them both in his Orlando', and to Tasso whose Rinaldo exhibited the virtues of a private as his Godfredo those of a public man. Spenser's choice of 'the history of king Arthur' for the 'historical fiction' with which to colour his 'general end . . . to fashion a gentleman or noble person in virtuous and gentle discipline', made it clear that this was a poem on an English subject intended to resemble both the classical epics and the new

* *Works*, vol. 4, 1811.

romantic epics of Italy. The Italian epics have several elements in common with the classical epics: a vast subject of war and heroic activity; an underlying theme of heroic purpose; many deliberate reminiscences—epic similes, visits to the underworld and glimpses into and prognostications of the future; and disposal into books (though not the classical twelve, for Ariosto had forty, later forty-six, and Tasso twenty). Spenser's poem had automatically a closer kinship with the Italian than the ancient models, for his chosen subject, like theirs, came not from the heroic classical 'matter' of Greece or of Rome, but from the world of Romance.

Epic and Romance may seem superficially to be a world apart, but in fact and by descent they are near kin. The name Romance came into European literature as the representative and unique literary form of the Romance languages. Its subject-matter is adventure, war and love, its actual material derived originally from the three epic 'matters', the 'matter' of France, the 'matter' of Britain and the 'matter' of Rome the Great. Its epic origins, and especially epic gravity and the stern epic simplicities of heroic endeavour and resistance, were quickly overlaid by the qualities we now as a result think of as characteristically romantic: fabulous settings, magic, the supernatural, the pursuit of love. What it had originally shared with its progenitor—fairly straightforward narrative of heroic deeds and a fairly limited cast of characters—was eventually almost buried in romantic paraphernalia: much larger casts, much more involved and inventive if wayward narrative, and concern with a much greater variety of human emotions and motivations. Beginning as simple narrative of adventure which answered an elementary demand for a good story, it gradually became something like a protracted metaphor of human life. This development was slow and for long unconscious; only perhaps with the appearance of *The Faerie Queene* did it reach its conscious consummation in English.

The basic pattern is of quest or journey which culminates in combat. There were obvious symbolic possibilities in relation to the course of man's life, which were increasingly realised by the writers of Romance, and notably of course by Malory. The chief personage, originally as in epic outstanding for bravery and heroic prowess, came often to be the embodiment of a particular knightly virtue, such as humility, loyalty or courtesy (Sir Isumbras, Amis and Amiloun and Sir Gawain for example). The Romance world is peopled with monsters and dragons and enchanters, with giants and pagans as well as with knights and distressed ladies. It is a fanciful, fabulous world. The laws of the code of chivalry are the only laws in force. The laws of the probable, the logical, the natural, even the possible are not current there, in that world of the untrammelled imagination. Yet the fact that knights journey among woods and hills, are tempted and led astray by magic, are assailed by enemies and giants and terrible beasts, fight most desperately to overcome them and may come at the end to peace and heart's desire, relates the world of Romance imaginatively to the real world in which men journey and struggle, are tried and sometimes not found wanting, search for an ideal and sometimes achieve it, and may at the end, after many a contest, many a weakness or truancy or despair, be brought to felicity. Although all is remote, imaginary, formalised, and although the emphasis is on exciting and inventive story-telling, not on motivation or development of character in the modern sense (with occasional exceptions, most notably Malory's Lancelot), the Romance world and its people conceal only superficially the lineaments of the real world and its people.

A later development in Romance was a deepened sense of the spiritual, which Spenser in his new handling of the form carried much further. Simple magic is sometimes spiritualised, as in *Beves of Hamtoun* in the episode in which the hero, like Spenser's Red Cross Knight in Book I of *The Faerie Queene*, in his fight with a dragon is made 'whole and sound' by the water of the well into which he falls. The hero in *Guy of Warwick*, after many years of knightly action, leaves his newly married wife Felice shortly after their marriage to go as a pilgrim to the Holy Land, full of remorse for his undevout life. It was perfectly reasonable of Caxton to declare that Malory's *Morte Darthur* was 'written for our doctrine, and for to beware that we fall not to vice nor sin, but to exercise and follow virtue'. Although almost any literary work of the time was open to didactic interpretation, the Romance had become long before Spenser's time peculiarly available for instruction and moralising, and no doubt Spenser took it up happily aware of its deeper possibilities as well as of its surface charm and its suitability to his avowed purpose of fashioning a 'gentleman or noble person in virtuous and gentle discipline'.

His indebtedness to Malory has sometimes been discounted by commentators, though I believe it is considerable. His supreme hero was to have been King Arthur as a young prince before he won the throne. His knights one by one undertake their quests, as do the knights of the Round Table. Merlin appears, to foretell the marriage and progeny of Artegall and Britomart, and we are told something in passing of his doom through the 'false trains' of Nimue. Pollente's 'groome of evil guise' in Book V, Canto 2 is a reminiscence of the 'passing foul Churle' who stands on the bridge by Tintagil on behalf of his master, likewise a cruel knight. The knight in the same canto who, riding with his lady, draws his sword

> And at one stroke cropt off her head with scorn

and who is forced by Artegall to 'bear that ladies head' for the rest of his life as he journeys about the world, is the same as Sir Pedivere in *Morte Darthur* who suddenly turned and 'swapped off' his wife's head, and who was ordered by Sir Lancelot to bear the head to Guenever as a mark of his perfidy. *The Faerie Queene* has its King Rience who takes the heads of knights and shears their ladies' locks. Spenser tells us almost exactly as Malory does of the upbringing of Tristram. In the Grail story it is Sir Galahad, the most perfect knight of all, who bears a white shield with a red cross, and if the shield is not, as that of the Red Cross Knight proves to be, part of the very armour of Christ, it is that which King Evelake had received from Joseph of Arimathea. Spenser is also of course indebted to many other Romances, especially *Beves of Hamtoun, Guy of Warwick, Arthur of Little Britain* and *Amadis de Gaul* for many episodes and some characters. But above all he is indebted to the Romances for the *genre* itself at its most typical, for its pattern of journey, quest and combat, for its imagined world of fantastic adventure and for the symbolic possibilities always latent in the figuring of that world. The greatness of Spenser's achievement lies chiefly in the masterly way in which, especially in Books I and V, he made this genre continuously and movingly symbolic of men's journeying, questing and struggling, while maintaining a narrative fully romantic in colouring and tone and commanding the reader's interest in the surface of the story quite as well as did the best Romances. He showed how Romance—for all the charges levelled against it of remoteness from life—could make fantasy and adventure speak of reality with conviction, clarity and a compelling seriousness, while in no way relinquishing its more superficial charms.

Perhaps at some stage in the development of the poem, perhaps indeed in the initial stage, Spenser intended to write a series of knightly adventures in a form loosely modelled on that of Romance. Certainly in the letter to Raleigh he drafted an outline of the poem as, he claimed, it had begun and was to continue, in which one by one knights went out on quests from Gloriana's court. There are traces of such a scheme at the beginning and end of most of the books.

Before Spenser took up Romance, there had been another stage in the evolution of the form, in Italy, when it remembered its origins and tried to be epic again. Many of the epic themes had been romanticised during the great period of the flourishing of Romance between the thirteenth and the sixteenth centuries. Medieval Europe had seen the proliferation of tales, poems, ballads and romances which dealt with the wars against the infidels, and on this vogue the Italian romantic epic built, turning to one of the old epic 'matters', that of the Frankish wars with the Saracens.

Yet Boiardo's *Orlando Innamorato*, written in the 1470s, and Ariosto's 'continuation' of that unfinished poem *Orlando Furioso* (first published in 1516), are not, strictly speaking, about Charlemagne and his peers. We hear much of them, much of the infidel host, much of battle, campaign and siege, but this heroic matter is simply the framework of the poems, the persistent background situation and the unifying element which alone justifies their claim to be epic in any orthodox classical sense. For this reason I prefer not to call them by their usual name—romantic epic—but to reserve that name for another poem more aptly described by it. I prefer for the poems of Boiardo and Ariosto the name epic Romance, for the simple reason that the elements of Romance and not epic seriousness and grandeur are dominant in them. Boiardo's *Orlando Innamorato* begins with Gradasso—an Eastern king who covets two of the world's greatest treasures, Orlando's sword Durindana and Rinaldo's horse Baiardo—assembling an army for the invasion of France. The action then moves to Charlemagne's court in Paris, to which very soon there come four giant knights with a damsel, Angelica, who is promised to any knight who shall overcome her brother Argalia in tourney. At once we are off on chivalrous adventure and the pursuit of love. We are not in the epic world but in the fabulous and magical world of Romance. From time to time the champions of Christendom, Orlando, Rinaldo, Oliver, Astolfo, will meet and fight the Saracen chivalry, but it is not the stern warfare of the heroic world but the romantic opposition of chivalry to chivalry, and Boiardo employs it as a leading rein to keep some control over and to impose some unity on the fantastic adventures and the complications of love-pursuit that inexhaustibly ensure.

The same is true of Ariosto, who took up Boiardo's unfinished 'Roland in Love' and of course placed his 'Roland Mad for Love'

during the same wars of the Franks and the Saracens; but his real subject is the love of Ruggiero and Bradamante, the countless adventures,
separations and setbacks that keep them apart, and their eventual
marriage. The hero is not Charlemagne, or Orlando (the Roland of
legend and epic), or Rinaldo the brother of the heroine Bradamante,
but the infidel Ruggiero, who is destined to be baptised a Christian
and to marry Bradamante. Its real subject-matter, like that of Boiardo's
poem, is not epic at all but the purest Romance. It is in no sense, save
in length, an epic poem. It is not epic in the classical sense: not a
narrative dealing with the heroic or dedicated actions of one great
man like the *Odyssey* or the *Aeneid*. It is not epic according to W. P.
Ker's definition in *Epic and Romance*, dealing with 'the problem of
heroic character in situations that test the force of character'; nor
does it portray 'the last resistance of a man driven into a corner' as,
for example, the *Chanson de Roland* did. It is not even a poem of
'high seriousness'. There are moments of seriousness, even of devotion:
Ruggiero preparing for baptism, Charles and his peers invoking
God's aid and receiving the sacrament before battle, are gravely
presented, but the poem as a whole remains light-hearted, at times
almost flippant, and nonsense, magical nonsense, keeps breaking in.
There are occasional references to the right of the Christian cause,
and we know that God intervenes on the Christian side, but there is
no suggestion that civilisation is fighting barbarism, the forces of
light opposed to the powers of darkness. Rodomont, the great Turk,
is a fearsome antagonist, yet the hero of the poem is also a Saracen
infidel. The epic possibilities are almost everywhere deliberately
ignored. (This is the more surprising in that at the time of the writing
of the poem the infidel power of Turkey was reaching ever further
and further into the heart of Christian Europe: Vienna fell ten years
after the first publication of *Orlando Furioso*.) It is, essentially, a
romantic poem, and I think aptly to be called an epic Romance.

Yet is is something more than a Romance. It is not only a tale of
marvellous adventure in some remote or imagined country of the
long ago, inhabited by legendary figures, giants, monsters and fabulous
creatures; not simply a poem of the 'feyned nowhere', a naive excursion
into an undefined landscape, or a presentation of the impossible
quests and lives of fair knights and ladies. C. S. Lewis pointed firmly
in his chapter on Spenser in *The Allegory of Love* to the contemporary
and actual quality of much of the poem, especially the details of siege
and warfare, and to the lifelikeness of the characters. Ariosto's chief

characters are more than conventional Romance knights and ladies moving in formal patterns; they are characters of whose humanity Ariosto convinces us. They are not motivated solely by the necessities and conventions of chivalry, as in the ordinary Romance, but individuals making their own decisions, speaking and acting recognisably as autonomous human beings, not merely behaving without volition according to the tenets of the code of chivalry and speaking without much personality the sentiments of that convention. There seems indeed to be achievement of what W. P. Ker called (not in this specific connexion) 'the ideal which is not attained in the Middle Ages, but towards which many medieval writers seem to be making their way ... the recovery of the fuller life of Epic for the benefit of Romance ... Epic fullness of life within the limits of Romantic form'. *Orlando Furioso* is not an epic. It is a Romance, but a Romance of epic quality. The stories, the characters, the incidents, the marvels are romantic, but in scope and range the characters and the brimming life they live are epic: and the vast background, both geographical and situational—the war of Franks and Saracens that ranges all over Europe, from North Africa to the realm of Prester John, East, at least as far as India and China and even to the mountains of the moon where Orlando's lost wits are retrieved for him by Astolfo, is clearly epic in range and reality and romantic in improbability.

The Faerie Queene is not as plausibly set within a real situation, the Frankish wars, as the two Orlando poems. Possibly at some stage in its evolution it was to have been. The Sarazin brothers, the Souldan of Book V, several odd references in Book I to great wars on 'Briton fields... Twixt that great faery Queene and Paynim king' (I. 11. 7) and to 'that proud Paynim king, that workes her teene' (I. 12. 18), are probably remnants of it. Spenser's poem, too, is set not in a geographically convincing world but in the fabulous, vague, unsurveyed territory of Romance. Books III and IV are Ariostan in quality as well as in method, illustrating human actions rather than, as elsewhere in The Faerie Queene, allegorising them. Many incidents here are no more directly allegorical than similar ones in Romance or epic. Many of the characters are drawn clearly from life and provide examples of human behaviour, laudable or blameworthy, and are innocent of allegory. We continue to see the over-all purpose of the poem through these stories and characters, not only through explicit allegory.

Before Spenser took up the form, the Romance moved still further into the world of epic. Tasso's *Gerusalemme Liberata*, first published in 1581, just after Spenser had begun *The Faerie Queene*, has as its starting-point the same matter of Christendom's wars with the pagan world, the subject being specifically the siege and relief of Jersualem by the Christians led by Godfrey of Boulogne. But it is not an epic romance, using the epic matter as a canvas upon which to work the varied tapestry of Romance. Rather it is an epic poem adorned with the incidental devices of Romance. The epic theme is here the very foundation and the *raison d'être* of the poem, and not merely, as in Ariosto, the background situation against which the romantic adventures are set. Tasso makes the siege and battles, epic material in very truth, the real heart and purpose of his poem; and they symbolise the perennial struggle of the forces of light against the powers of darkness. It is explicitly an epic poem, but it is an epic told in the romantic way; the epic theme is played on all the instruments of Romance. There is a lady-knight Clorinda, like Ariosto's Bradamante (and Spenser's Britomart to come); an enchantress Armida, like Ariosto's Alcina (and Spenser's Acrasia); there are wizards and magicians, notably Ismen, kin to Ariosto's Atlante and Spenser's Archimago; there are disguise, single combat, mistaken identity, love and the common romantic complication of love—Erminia loves Tancred who loves Clorinda; there are dragons and strange beasts, spirits in trees and humans imprisoned in trees; magic armour and spells and magic weapons. The romantic diversions—the adventure of Tancred in the enchanted wood, the journey of Carlo and Ubaldo to Armida's enchanted realm of changeless spring to rescue their comrade Rinaldo from her spell—are magnificent, but they are subordinate to the epic and religious theme; indeed Rinaldo's truancy with Armida the enchantress is made a particular example of one of the ways—through lust—in which the powers of darkness assail and beguile mankind. And beside the devotion and spiritual fervour of Godfrey, or of Rinaldo rescued from sin praying on Mount Olivet, the romantic excursions seem indeed diversions, however much we welcome them. Because the poem is first and foremost epic, not Romance, I prefer to distinguish it from the epic Romances of Boiardo and Ariosto by reserving for it the name romantic epic.

Superior to them in epic gravity, it is inferior nevertheless in its capturing of the impression of 'epic fulness of life'. Its characters have not the vigour and humanity of those of the Orlando poems, and they are propelled in order to exemplify the religious theme. The synthesis Tasso attempted of epic seriousness, religious devotion and romantic adornment and idiom does not quite come off. In *The Faerie Queene*, I would claim, Spenser successfully achieved this difficult synthesis. He did it by founding his poem more firmly on medieval Romance, indeed by writing several related brief Romances; by adopting Ariosto's method from time to time, particularly in Books III and IV, the subject-matter of which—love and human relationships—was especially suited to the method; and by not choosing a single epic theme or action. As a result his poem has not the unity of Tasso's but a unity of a different kind, a cyclical unity depending on unity of theme, intention and imaginative atmosphere.

Spenser made use of medieval Romance as far as it would take him and avoided the danger of monotony, if each of the twelve books were drawn to the same plan, by adopting the different structure of the Italians. Ariosto's epic Romance *Orlando Furioso* successfully introduced into Romance the impression of 'epic fulness of life'; Tasso in *Gerusalemme Liberata* sought, not with complete success, to deepen, strengthen and spiritualise the epic again, bringing it back from Ariosto's brilliant, joyous, vivacious celebration of love, adventure and heroism, to a greater gravity, yet he wrote under the influence of epic Romance and produced the first great romantic epic. Spenser wished to stand in their company. I think he succeeded, writing in *The Faerie Queene* a poem romantic in form and incident yet epic in its expressly moral subject and in the impression it assuredly gives of 'epic fulness of life'. He did not try for the contemporaneity and realism of Ariosto, nor for his dash and *bravura*, though at many points he achieved them incidentally. He was as serious as Tasso, yet managed to avoid the uneasy tension in Tasso's poem between the romantic, the realistic, the epic and the symbolic. His poem is less lifelike but more true, less regular but more uniform, less crowded but more complete than *Orlando Furioso*, and more romantic, more engaging, more human but not less epic than *Gerusalemme Liberata*. Further, its extended and continuous allegory, perceptible now more now less clearly through the narrative of romantic adventure, relates to all human activity in an imagined world that clearly corresponds to the real world. Ariosto's poem is not allegory, although there are a few simple allegorical episodes such as that in Book 35 in which Astolfo sees Time throwing into Lethe pieces of paper bearing the names of the living; some are picked out by vultures, representing promoters and parasites fawning about the great, others retrieved by swans which represent historians and poets who immortalise the reputations of the illustrious. Tasso's allegory—the siege of Jerusalem allegorising the struggle between true and false, evil and good, the sexual temptation of Rinaldo by Armida allegorising the need for reason to control will—splendid though it is, remains limited in its reference in contrast with the comprehensiveness of Spenser's. Spenser does not rest all on one great epic action, like Tasso, nor does he rely, like Ariosto, on multiple story-telling alone. His story-telling, while not as efficient or marvellous as Ariosto's carries as grave a message as Tasso's religious epic, and lightly bears his moral purpose in delightful narrative. This purpose is not a confined or particular one, as Tasso's is, but a general, unrestricted one, almost limitless in its range, and closely relevant to almost all the diverseness of human motive and activity.

   Orlando Furioso and *Gerusalemme Liberata* (and indeed part of *Orlando Innamorato* translated by Robert Tofte) were done into English during the reign of Elizabeth, Ariosto's poem by Sir John Harington (1591) and Tasso's by Edward Fairfax (1600). It is some testimony to the contemporary interest in what was then called 'the heroic poem', and to the generally acknowledged primacy of the form. In this, as in all literary and artistic matters, England followed, some way behind, the lead of Italy. Boiardo's and Ariosto's epic Romances had precipitated discussion of the heroic form in Italy, and in the decade following 1580, while *The Faerie Queene* was being written, there had appeared not only the new heroic poem, Tasso's *Gerusalemme Liberata*, but also his *apologia* for the form in his *Discourse on the Art of Poetry*, published, some twenty years after its composition, in 1587. Tasso denied that there was any essential difference between the epic poem and the romantic poem as poems. He found the latter more pleasing because of the greater delightfulness of the themes treated, and because of its greater variety. He defined the heroic poem in terms that can readily be applied to *The Faerie Queene*. The subject must be historical—the Elizabethans were fully persuaded of the historicity of Arthur; Christian (for Christianity allows the introduction of both the marvellous and the true, a necessary combination, and for their reconciliation); the hero knight must have piety as well as other virtues; the material must neither be too ancient nor too modern. He found the times of Charlemagne and Arthur the best fitted for the heroic poem. In recognising no essential difference between romantic and epic poems Tasso took further earlier views on them put forward by Giraldi and Pigna (who thought of the *romanzi* as constituting a quite new *genre* and not to be criticised for not

complying with Aristotelian rules about unity) and thought to reconcile heroic and romantic by advocating, what he later put to practical
test, the combination of romantic subject-matter with all its delightful
diversity and heroic form with its essential unity.

Whether or not the story is true that Harington first translated some
of the bawdy tales of sexual sport which appear here and there in
Orlando Furioso and circulated them among the ladies of the Court
(for which misdemeanour the Queen punished him by requiring him
to leave the Court until he had translated the whole poem), his version
is accompanied by an elaborate apparatus of commentary and exegesis,
emphasising to the point of weariness, although often with his tongue
in his cheek, the high moral aim of the Italian poet. Yet he writes
seriously in the medieval way about the threefold interpretation of
literature: 'the ancient poets have indeed wrapped as it were in their
writings divers and sundry meanings, which they call the senses or
mysteries thereof. First of all for the literal sense (as it were the
outermost bark or rind) they set down in manner of an History, the
acts and notable exploits of some persons worthy memory; then in
the same fiction, as a second rind and somewhat more fine, as it were
nearer to the pith and marrow, they place the Moral sense, profitable
for the active life of man, approving virtuous actions and condemning
the contrary. Many times also under the self same words they comprehend some true understanding of natural Philosophy, or sometime
of politic government, and now and then of divinity: and these same
senses that comprehend so excellent knowledge we call the Allegory,
which Plutarch defineth to be when one thing is told, and by that
another is understood.' Harington's simple definition of allegory is
useful, but although I do not believe Ariosto intended any sustained
allegory in *Orlando Furioso* his English translator added at the end of
each of the forty-six books a 'Morall' and an 'Allegorie' in which he
sought to show that the loves, wars and adventures of Ariosto's
characters are not to be seen just as elements in Romance but made to
yield their ransom of serious moral instruction. To give just one
example: of the killing of Rodomont by Ruggiero in the last book he
wrote: 'This is the Allegorical sense thereof, that Rodomont which
is to be understood the unbridled heat and courage of youth . . . is
killed and quite vanquished by marriage, and howsoever the unruliness
of youth is excusable in divers kinds, yet after that holy state of
matrimony is entered into, all youthful wildness of all kinds must be
cast away.' This is straining for a significance with a vengeance,

but it endorses our understanding that to the Elizabethans, to use Harington's own words again, 'in verse is both goodness and sweetness, Rhubarb and Sugar-candy, the pleasant and the profitable . . . he that can mingle the sweet and wholesome, the pleasant and the profitable, he is an absolute good writer'.

Fairfax published with his version of *Gerusalemme Liberata* a translation of Tasso's own account of the allegory, but even here, in an analysis of a heroic poem that is clearly allegorical in a general sense, too minute a significance was attached in many places. Rinaldo is thus discussed: 'The *Ireful* virtue is that, which amongst all the powers of the mind, is less estranged from the nobility of the soul, inasmuch that *Plato* (doubting) seeketh whether it differeth from Reason, or no . . . But when it doth not obey Reason, but suffers itself to be carried by its own Violence, it falleth out, that it fighteth not against Concupiscence, but by Concupiscence, like a Dog that biteth not the Thieves, but the Cattle committed to his Keeping. This violent, fierce and unbridled Fury . . . is principally signified by *Rinaldo* . . . (whilst fighting against *Gernando*, he did pass the Bounds of civil Revenge, and also whilst he served *Armida*) may be noted unto us *Anger*, not governed by *Reason*; whilst he disenchanteth the Wood, entereth the City, breaketh the Enemy's Array, *Anger* directed by Reason. His Return, and Reconciliation to *Godfrey*, noteth Obedience causing the *ireful* Power to yield to the *reasonable*.'

Spenser's imaginative handling of men and women should not be submitted to this sort of interpretation, but the fact that such treatment was given to epic Romance and romantic epic alike endorses the appropriateness for his moral purpose of the forms Spenser turned to as models of what Italian writers had long been formulating and English writers slowly assimilating: a view of literature as not only uniquely able to discuss and promote virtue whether in private or public conduct, not only able to picture forth the world both delightfully and instructively, but also to *move* men to desire to be virtuous because of the persuasive force with which virtue was presented to them. Sir Philip Sidney's *Apology for Poetry* (published posthumously in 1595) is the clearest English discussion, and at times it is almost as if he is actually describing *The Faerie Queene*, although, as he died in 1586, by which time Spenser had been in Ireland, without, so far as we know, returning to England for six years, it is unlikely he ever saw any of it: '. . . it is that feigning notable images of virtues, vices, or what else, with that delightful teaching, which must be the right describing note to know a poet by.'* 'I have known men, that even with reading *Amadis de Gaule* (which God knoweth wanteth much of a perfect poesy) have found their hearts moved to the exercise of courtesy, liberality, and especially courage.'† And as for 'the Heroical' —'it doth not only teach and move to a truth, but teacheth and moveth to the most high and excellent truth . . . For as the image of each action stirreth and instructeth the mind, so the lofty image of such worthies' (as Achilles, Cyrus, Aeneas, Turnus, Tydeus and Rinaldo) 'most inflameth the mind with desire to be worthy, and informs with counsel how to be worthy.'‡ Sidney epitomises this 'best and most accomplished kind of Poetry' in an extended reference to Virgil's epic: 'Only let Aeneas be worn in the tablet of your memory, how he governeth himself in the ruin of his country; in the preserving his old father, and carrying away his religious ceremonies; in obeying the god's commandment to leave Dido, though not only all passionate kindness, but even the human consideration of virtuous gratefulness, would have craved other of him; how in storms, how in sports, how in war, how in peace, how a fugitive, how victorious, how besieged, how besieging, how to strangers, how to allies, how to enemies, how to his own; lastly, how in his inward self, and how in his outward government.'§ Spenser does it not through one epic hero but through a succession of knight-heroes, the chief characters of each book, but also through the countless other characters good and bad who throng the world of Faerie.

A distinction between Spenser's work and that of his great exemplars is that his is openly and indisputably allegorical. If there had been an Italian translator of *The Faerie Queene*, he would hardly have needed to append a 'Morall' and an 'Allegorie' as Harington and Fairfax found necessary. The allegory is inextricably inter-woven with the romantic narrative. It is only very occasionally that the allegorical strand obtrudes blatantly, as in the scene in Book I, Canto 1 in which the ugly monster, half-serpent, half-woman, already identified by name as Error, spews forth books and papers, or as in the sometimes tedious, sometimes comic presentation of the house of Alma in Book II, Canto 9; normally allegory and romantic narrative work together quietly, indistinguishably, like the heart and the lungs.

* G. Shepherd, Ed., *An Apology for Poetry*, p. 103.
† ibid., p. 114
‡ ibid., p. 119.
§ ibid., p. 119.

Another more significant distinction is that Spenser's poem is not only epic and romantic and devised for aristocratic reading, but is much more demotic in its range of material and therefore of appeal. He shared in and benefited to the full from the indivisibility and catholicity of Elizabethan culture, to which of course the plays of Shakespeare bear the most eloquent witness. Spenser has been too much regarded as a courtier-poet, one concerned to advance aristocratic ideal and behaviour, and it has been easily assumed that he wrote only for the Court. Yet his contact with the ordinary life of his day and with the sort of concerns which occupied, engrossed and amused ordinary people was firm. H. S. Bennett* and Louis B. Wright† among others have shown that literacy was well-spread and taste in reading catholic. Spenser deliberately gave his romantic epic as broad and firm a base in the ordinary life of his time as he could. I do not mean by this that he founds it upon real situations or, like Ariosto, includes convincing accounts of real actions such as siege warfare—though he gives much small detail of ordinary life—but that he founds it not only on foreign literary precedent but on things which had caught and held the imagination of the many as well as the interest of the educated. Of these the most obvious are the historical interest in the country's past, the historicity of King Arthur and his knights, the contemporary expression of these in pageants and shows, the familiarity of allegory (shown most obviously in these same pageants), and a continual recourse to simple and proverbial wisdom. These elements are almost as strong as the conventional epic and romantic ingredients in *The Faerie Queene*, quest, journey, struggle, combat, visits to the underworld, magic or supernatural events, and they are given even greater force by that other element in the poem, hitherto unmentioned, the continuous contemporary allegory. To an astonishing degree Spenser tapped the interests and tastes, both literary and in other ways imaginative, of the Elizabethan age, and not only of the Elizabethan court.

It was a sure instinct, endorsing no doubt a strong personal predilection, that led him to Romance. As Dr Sheavyn showed‡ 'Such records as we possess of the libraries of the middle and lower classes reveal a great preponderance of books of this class' (Romances).

---

* *English Books and Readers*, 2 vols., Cambridge 1952, 1965.
† *Middle-Class Culture in Elizabethan England*, London 1958.
‡ *The Literary Profession in the Elizabethan Age*, revised by J. W. Saunders, Manchester 1967.

It has often been complained of Spenser that he chose to write in an outmoded literary form, for Romance was, if not dead, certainly dying when he created what proved to be its final masterpiece. But if it was dead or dying, Spenser was one of thousands in England who did not recognise the fact. Caxton and his successor Wynkyn de Worde had established, to put it crudely, the saleability of Romance, and their Elizabethan counterparts, Copland, Purfoot, Burby and Creede, kept the market supplied, reviving fully one-half of the medieval Romances which had been in circulation before the accession of Queen Elizabeth and introducing many new romantic narratives, especially from the body of Spanish Romance. Romance stories survived at a popular level in many ballads. In the last decade of the century, Philip Henslowe bought or drew revenue from dramas founded on old Romances, among them *Huon of Bordeaux*, *Uther Pendragon*, *The Life of King Arthur* and *Tristram of Lyones*: Romance flourished also in the prose romances, in Sidney's *Arcadia*, in the romances of Greene, Lodge, Emmanuel Forde, Antony Munday, in the prose and plays of Lyly and in the plays of Greene and Peele, and most notably—and most Spenserianly—in the early comedies, and later, in the late plays of William Shakespeare. It is not surprising or unnatural, then, that Spenser should have chosen Romance as the *element* in which his great work was to live. Romance was not something archaic, rude, uncouth, anachronistic; it was the prevailing fashion. This is not to deny that it was in fact dying. It was dying, like the century. Who was to know that the seventeenth century was to witness a radical change of sensibility and of response? Those who still berate Spenser for writing in an outmoded form—and they imply that it is a form without relevance or significance—should ponder this. They should also contemplate the persistence of Romance's appeal, in its recent reappearance in, for example, the work of J. R. R. Tolkien and science-fiction.

I have written of Romance as the *element* rather than the form in which Spenser chose to write, partly because there is not really a strict *form*, like there is of epic, which can be blue-printed, partly because Spenser created his own new form out of the several proto-types and ingredients I have here briefly discussed, and partly because Romance, whatever its vehicle, is more than a form: it is an atmosphere, a world, a way of thinking and of seeing reality in terms other than the realistic. It is this to some people in all ages and all countries, but usually not to many people, except perhaps in the Elizabethan Age

in England. And even then, to most people its appeal was that of
colour, pageantry and adventurous story rather than as the ready
vehicle for symbolic presentation of the variety and complexity of
human behaviour that it was to Spenser. Yet the Elizabethan Age was
also well used to the allegorical and the symbolic, familiar in innumerable forms from inn and trade-signs, from sermons and homilies
and school-readers to the Lord Mayor's Show and all the pageants and
shows that were such a feature of Elizabeth's reign and which found
the most lavish presentation in the entertainments devised to welcome
her on her regular processions in the City and progresses in the
country. In such shows, as for example at the well-documented visit of
the Queen to the Earl of Leicester at Kenilworth in 1575,* the most
bizarre conjunction of scenes and personages would be presented.
At Kenilworth on her arrival the Queen was met by a Sibyl, then
by the porter dressed as Hercules and then by the Lady of the Lake;
on another day, on returning from the hunt she was greeted with
a complimentary dialogue between Echo and a Savage Man. On
another occasion, at Elvetham, in 1591, during the opening oration,
six virgins, 'representing the Graces and Hours, removed blocks from
Her Majesty's path, which Envy had placed there to impede Virtue's
progress'. The next afternoon the Queen went to the Great Pond at
Elvetham, where she saw Nereus with five Tritons who all swam to
the shore and greeted her, followed by Neptune and Oceanus drawing
a pinnace in which were three virgins playing music, a nymph and three
singers; and then Silvanus and his followers came out of a wood to
add their welcome. On the last morning of her three days' stay, the
Fairy Queen and her maids saluted the Queen when she rose. At her
coronation in 1559 the Queen in her procession through the city of
London had been greeted at various points by allegorical pageants.
At Gracechurch, there was a stage of three tiers, displaying Unity
and Concord, the figures representing Henry VII and his queen,
Henry VIII and Anne Boleyn, Elizabeth's parents, and, in the top tier,
Elizabeth herself. At Cornhill, a child, representing Elizabeth, sat on
the seat of Worthy Governance supported by four figures representing
virtues treading their contrary vices underfoot. At Little Conduit,
the centrepiece was a cave from which Time emerged, leading his
daughter Truth who held an English Bible in her hand, and on either
side of the cave stood a green hill, one surmounted by a green laurel
tree and a handsome gaily dressed youth, representing a flourishing

* See R. Withington, *English Pageantry*, Harvard 1918–20.

Commonwealth, the other by a withered tree and a mournful youth in rude apparel, representing a decayed Commonwealth, and a child expounded the significance in rhyme: it is the English Bible that teaches how to bring a decayed Commonwealth to good and prosperity. The Queen took her leave of the City at Temple Bar, which was decorated with images of Gogmagog the Albion and his conqueror Corineus the Briton, the companion of Brutus, legendary founder of the British race, shown together as a symbol of unity and amity because the Queen through her ancestry united the two strains.

Spenser's prodigal use of the emblematic, and his employment as carriers of it, of figures taken from such a diversity of sources—Biblical, classical, Romance, historical, quasi-historical—had full licence. His use, although of course indebted to Italian Romance-epic, went far beyond that of Ariosto or Tasso: paradoxically, it came much nearer ordinary life and the ordinary activities and common sights of his time. Perhaps it was this that Gabriel Harvey objected to when he wrote rather protestingly that Spenser had let '*Hobgoblin* run away with the Garland from *Apollo*'; he thought Spenser was being too English, too popular, too *vulgar* in both senses of the word, not classical, serious, literary enough. But Spenser's was the surer instinct. It is the very range of reference, and therefore of appeal, courtly and popular, literary and demotic, fabulous and real, which makes *The Faerie Queene* so remarkable, so Elizabethan and yet so universal. An example might be the stanza describing June in the procession of the months in the second of the Mutabilitie Cantos:

> And after her, came jolly *June*, arrayd
>   All in greene leaves, as he a Player were;
>   Yet in his time, he wrought as well as playd,
>   That by his plough-yrons mote right well appeare:
>   Upon a Crab he rode, that him did beare
>   With crooked crawling steps and uncouth pase,
>   And backward yode, as Bargemen wont to fare
>   Bending their force contrary to their face,
> Like that ungracious crew which faines demurest grace.[1]

not a piece of great writing, yet remarkable for its range of allusion; June comes dressed in green because June is the month when grass and trees and foliage are at their greenest. But there is also some reminiscence and suggestion of the savage man, all in ivy, who greeted Queen

---

[1] ?courtiers, ?religious hypocrites.

Elizabeth when she visited Kenilworth in 1575, or of Sylvanus's followers at Elvetham in 1591 all covered with ivy-leaves (and in IV. 4. 39 Sir Artegall, as the Salvage Knight, appears with his armour covered with moss and his horse with oak-leaves). The savage man usually stands for simplicity and virtue, the pastoral as opposed to the courtly, with all the implications of pastoral simplicity contrasted with court guile or corruption. June, then, arrayed like a player, is not just a player, but a worker, carrying plough-irons. His vehicle is his zodiacal sign, the crab, which prompts Spenser to a vivid comparison with the way a bargeman, no doubt a London bargeman, propels his craft, and to a further comparison, probably to the way false courtiers affect courtesies and humility.

The list of influences upon Spenser and of the many layers of meaning in *The Faerie Queene* is not yet exhausted. To the influence of real-life events, and especially to the influence of Ireland I shall refer later. Suffice it to say here that just below the surface of the romantic narrative lies an extended but not continuous layer of historical reference, and great personalities of Spenser's time may be descried from time to time in some of the characters of the poem. If Una at times represents Queen Elizabeth, Duessa stands for Mary Queen of Scots, occasionally perhaps for Queen Mary. If Elizabeth is also figured in Belphebe, so is Mary Queen of Scots in the false Florimell. Archimago and Duessa stand for the false religion of Rome, Una for the simple truth of the ideal Church of England. The giant Grantorto also represents Roman Catholicism and the enemies of England generally, and also Philip of Spain; so probably does Orgoglio. Gerioneo is certainly he, and his dreadful monster is the Inquisition. Timias is Raleigh, who worships and is rebuffed by Belphebe for his indiscretion with Amoret. Arthur's venture for Belge is clearly Leicester's campaign in the Netherlands. Artegall's and Arthur's quest on behalf of Irena (and very much more in Book V) clearly refers to Ireland and to England's (and Spenser's) mission to that unhappy land. But significations of this kind are sporadic. Even to Spenser minute and detailed allusion to historical persons was only a minor ingredient. An overdose of it would have been fatal to the poem's art and politically dangerous to the poet. It was a spice added sparingly for those of especially discriminating palate: in fact for noble readers. The modern reader loses little by ignoring it, though he misses something. It was one of the several ways in which Spenser founded his romantic narrative on the actual life of his age. Of course where there is larger and sustained reference, as in Books I and V, to the dangers of Catholic machination, the reader ignores it to his own disadvantage.

A more difficult problem is posed by the recent claim that the whole of *The Faerie Queene* is firmly based on a rigid substructure of numerical pattern. 'We find numerological significance in line-, stanza-, canto-, and book-totals; in the location of these units; and even in the number of characters mentioned in each episode. Pythagorean number symbolism, astronomical symbolism based on orbital period figures and on Ptolemaic star catalogue totals, medieval theological number symbolism: all these strands, and more besides, are worked together into what—in this respect at least—must be one of the most intricate poetic textures ever devised.'* It is claimed that Spenser's poem is more than a description or even an image of the world, that it is itself, because of its careful complex structuring on the pattern of the mathematical order of the universe, an example of the cosmic structure, and because of the interactions shown, an example in itself of the universal process, in which many complex harmonies operate simultaneously within the universal order demonstrated by number-correspondency in macrocosm and microcosm. It is an enormous claim and depends on some fiddling with arithmetic, yet Dr Fowler's analysis and commentary shed much light at many points in the poem, and those who follow him must see Spenser not only as the inspired fabler, allegorist and poet most readers have always thought him but as an intellectual artist of astounding command and dexterity.

When all is said and done, and through all the fascinating complexity, fancy and imagination, and through all the several layers of significance and reference, and in spite of the occasional difficulty of understanding or interpretation inevitable in a literary undertaking of such subtlety and scale, there is rarely or never any doubt about Spenser's central themes and purposes. He wrote in *The Faerie Queene* a unique and original kind of poem, a most successful hybrid of several ancient and more recent stocks—classical epic, epic Romance, romantic epic, Romance, allegory, pageant. In it he created a world, epic, romantic, allegorical and yet also native and Elizabethan, and peopled it with inhabitants from those worlds and from the other worlds of faerie, the English court, Ireland and Elizabethan London. In direct narrative and description as well as through symbols, allegories and types he presented his 'continued Allegory, or darke conceit' with which

* A. Fowler, *Spenser and the Numbers of Time*, London 1964, p. 4.

'many other adventures are intermedled, but rather as Accidents, than intendments'. It presented, basically, as in Romance, by means of a series of knightly quests—which often become momentous journeys, Odysseys and Aeneids—and sometimes by romance-epic narration of knightly adventures in love and war intermingled as in Ariosto, but with many a *vignette* clearly drawn from contemporary life and with many an insight drawn from personal observation, an imagined world that is a running metaphor for our own world. In it we recognise man's behaviour in a fallen but beautiful and desirable world; our own instincts good and bad; our own motivations, admirable and contemptible; our own apprehensions, with the vagueness and the uncertainties removed, of the divine possibilities of human achievement and happiness in a world that would return to God; our own understanding of the beauty of the world, the strength of love, and 'virtue in her shape how lovely'; and our accompanying awareness of mutability, of the precariousness of love and the vulnerabilty of virtue.

6

THE FAERIE QUEENE: BOOKS I–IV

It was not of *The Faerie Queene* that Dr Johnson said: 'I had rather see the portrait of a dog I know than all the allegories you can show me', but many have reacted in this way to the poem. Yet Spenser's allegories in fact portray dogs we know. We do not have to puzzle much or probe far to find the real life that is in the poem, and which is indeed its subject. To 'fashion a gentleman or noble person in virtuous and gentle discipline' was Spenser's 'generall end of all the books' of *The Faerie Queene*, and it is only fair to begin any discussion of the poem by remembering it.

Book I follows closely the conventional pattern of medieval romance, presenting a quest which after many dangers and adventures for the knight-hero culminates in a great contest or combat. Of course, as a poet of high purpose in an age of faith Spenser emphasised always the spiritual and moral implications of the life his stories fabled. So the hero in Book I, who is a sort of Everyman, is questing to overcome Satan, the great dragon who oppresses the world, and keeps in thrall the parents of the knight's companion (and, as it were, guardian angel) Una. He is a newly baptised Christian, wearing the armour of Christ, his 'mightie armes and silver shielde' which carry still 'old dints of deepe wounds . . . the cruell markes of many a bloudy fielde' although he has never borne arms before and yearns to prove 'his puissance in battell brave, Upon his foe, and his new force to learne'. This knight, although not quite the 'tall clownishe younge man' who falls on his knees before the Queen of Faeries and stays 'on the floore, unfitte through his rusticity for a better place' described in Spenser's letter to Raleigh which introduced *The Faerie Queene*, is simple and easily deceived. Spenser's purpose in Book I—to show man journeying through the world of falsehood, temptation and evil and often led astray into danger and sin despite the armour of Christ which is available to him—of course required *un homme moyen sensuel*—peccant and vulnerable—rather than a pattern of knightly virtue. Further, readers will much more readily identify themselves with such a figure, and in so doing the more easily understand Spenser's message.

The Red Cross Knight is accompanied by Una, a lovely lady on a milk-white palfrey. At their first adventure, when they take shelter from a sudden storm in a thick wood (which is the Wandering Wood which contains 'Error's' Den), she warns him of danger, but, 'full of fire and greedy hardiment', the knight ignores her warning and enters the 'darksome hole' to attack the monster 'Error', half-serpent, half-woman. Before long he is in great peril for 'Error' envelops him with her huge tail. Una urges him on to greater effort:

> . . . Now now Sir Knight, shew what ye bee,
> Add faith unto your force, and be not faint:
> Strangle her, else she sure will strangle thee.

So we have learned already, within twenty stanzas of the beginning of the poem, that the medieval Romance narrative carries a clear allegorical sense; that some of the characters of the poem will be personifications rather than persons; that this does not greatly harm our pleasure in the poem as story while it certainly asserts and makes clear the moral purpose; and that Una, as well as being a lady in a Romance whose champion is the Red Cross Knight, has also a dual function in relation to him—of warning him of dangers both physical and spiritual, and of encouraging him to sterner effort, again both physical and spiritual. She is identified for us in the rubric to Canto 2 as Truth, into *'whose stead faire falsehood steps'*.

For most of the book the knight is separated from Una and is the more helpless to recognise or withstand evil, which usually attacks him—as it often attacks man generally—through falseness of appearance in the attacker or falseness of spirit, faith or understanding in the victim. After his separation from Una in Canto 2, having been deceived by a false enchanter Archimago into thinking her licentious,

he falls almost immediately into the power of a beautiful enchantress
Duessa and into the very fault of licentiousness with her which he had
been deceived into suspecting of Una and for which he abandoned her.
Archimago and Duessa, partners in the deliberate practice of evil
by means of regular employment of deceit, repeatedly attack or
threaten the Red Cross Knight, and, to a lesser extent, Una. The
knight's dalliance with Fidessa (as Duessa calls herself falsely implying
fidelity rather than duplicity by her choice of name) is of course a
culpable truancy from his quest, and it leads him into further dangers,
from the giant Orgoglio (Pride) who overcomes and imprisons him,
and from 'Despair' who leads him to contemplate suicide. From des-
perate danger in the dungeons of Orgoglio's castle he is rescued by
Prince Arthur, and from the suicidal despair induced by his weakness
and sense of hopeless guilt after his incarceration he is sternly saved
by Una:

> Out of his hand she snatcht the cursed knife,
> And threw it to the ground, enraged rife,
> And to him said, Fie, fie, faint harted knight,
> What meanest thou by this reprochfull strife?
> Is this the battell, which thou vauntst to fight
> With that fire-mouthed Dragon, horrible and bright?
>
> Come, come away, fraile, feeble, fleshly wight,
> Ne let vaine words bewitch thy manly hart,
> Ne divelish thoughts dismay thy constant spright,
> In heavenly mercies hast thou not a part?   (I. 9. 52–3)

At this point in the story Una comes into her own, both as a positive
heroine—in the early cantos she is a romantic heroine as hapless as she
is helpless—and as the knight's spiritual mentor. She takes him to the
House of Caelia (Holiness) and her three daughters, where Fidelia
teaches him faith, Speranza gives him comfort. After he has been
disciplined by 'Amendment' who plucks out with red-hot pincers
his infected wounds, 'Penance' who whips him, 'Remorse' who pricks
and nips his heart, and 'Repentance' who washes the filthy spots of
sin from him bathing his body in 'salt water smarting sore', the third
daughter Charissa instructs hm 'in every good behest, Of love, and
rightcousnesse'. She then shows him the path to heaven, sending
'Mercy' to accompany him to the hermitage of 'Contemplation'.
Here he is led to the highest mount and given a sight of the new
Jerusalem,

> . . . that God has built
> For those to dwell in, that are chosen his,
> His chosen people purg'd from sinfull guilt,
> With pretious bloud, which cruelly was spilt
> On cursed tree, of that unspotted lam,
> That for the sinnes of all the world was kilt.   (I. 10. 57)

and is told by the holy hermit that he is destined himself eventually
to go thither:

> For thou emongst those Saints, whom thou doest see,
> Shalt be a Saint, and thine owne nations frend
> And Patrone: thou Saint *George* shalt called bee,
> Saint *George* of mery England, . . .   (I. 10. 61)

We now know why the hermit addressed the knight as 'thou man
of earth' who was to 'see the way, That never yet was seene of Faeries
Sonne' (I. 10. 52), and can understand why in the prefatory letter to
Raleigh Spenser wrote emphatically of his clownishness. This Georgos,
'man of earth' or 'husbandman', was not a fairy knight but indeed a
man of earth. He had been brought up by a ploughman who found him
—a changeling child—in a field, though he was a human and descended
from Saxon Kings. Spenser was right to make the hero of the book
of *The Faerie Queene* which dealt with spiritual quest, not a fairy knight
but a human, and right to show his human failings, his uncertain
faith, his easy lapses into sloth, lechery, pride and despair as well as
his blundering courage.

After being given his dazzling glimpse of the New Jerusalem, he
expresses a very Spenserian feeling—for the first time in the poem
—when he cries.

> O let me not . . . then turne againe
> Backe to the world, whose joyes so fruitlesse are.   (I. 10. 63)

But turn again he must, to accomplish his quest. With Una he comes
at last to her parents' kingdom, ravaged by the Dragon. He fights all
day and at evening is sorely wounded, and hurled to the ground by
his opponent, but it happened that he fell into

> a springing well,
> From which fast trickled forth a silver flood,
> Full of great vertues, and for med'cine good.   (I. 11. 29)

It is the Well of Life, which restores him, and he emerges the next morning freshly to renew the fight. Another terrible day's fighting ensues, and the Red Cross Knight, forced back by the Dragon's 'huge flames' and 'duskish smoke' 'that all the land with stench, and heaven with horror choke', slips and falls. But he falls near the Tree of Life, and the 'balme' that issues from it again saves him from death and restores his strength, so that on the third day, the fight renewed, he overcomes his appalling adversary. Una's parents, the King and Queen of Eden, give him thanks and gifts and joyfully receive their daughter, and, after a last brief unsuccessul attempt by Archimago and Duessa to incriminate the knight, the sacred betrothal rites of Una and the future St George take place, and there is great joy and feasting. The book ends with the Red Cross Knight's return to perform his promised further service for the Faerie Queene.

This romantic tale of knightly quest is also then an allegory of spiritual testing, with deliverance by God's grace, repentance, amendment and regeneration, showing the possibility of mankind's rising from a fallen state to salvation. It has also, with its dangerous journeying and terrible struggles, its visits to the underworld and its glimpse of the future, strong affinities with epic. There is another layer of meaning: the Red Cross Knight stands for the newly established Church of England, which, when companioned by Una (Truth) is able to perceive dangers or to overcome them (Error, for example), but which, when separated from her, is in constant peril from false religion, that is from Rome, figured in Archimago, Duessa, and the three pagan brothers Sansloy, Sansjoy and Sansfoy (lawless, joyless and faithless). It can be deceived by Falseness, laid low by Pride, weakened by Sloth, brought into despair; but, rescued by Grace as the knight is by Prince Arthur, and disciplined by Faith, Hope, Charity, Penance and Repentance, it can be strengthened to meet its greatest foe. Then, meeting the most violent assaults of Satan, it can be strengthened by God's grace (in the sacraments of baptism and communion represented by the water of the Well and the balm of the Tree of Life) so that it can overcome the devil: and it will be united in the end for ever with Truth, marking the final triumph of Protestantism.

But the book's chief purpose—as it is the declared purpose of the poem—is 'to fashion a gentleman or noble person in vertuous and gentle discipline', and Spenser was right to begin his exploration of what makes for virtuous life with the fundamental question—to an Elizabethan, indeed to any writer of any Christian period up to the twentieth century—of man's spiritual nature and his necessary relationship with God's word and will. For *The Faerie Queene* is above all a Christian work, founded upon an unquestioning acceptance of the primary relation of creature to Creator, and of the need for men to live in the light of and by the help of God's grace. Book I, the most openly Christian and doctrinal, a sort of Pilgrim's Progress through the fallen world of error, doubt, sin, temptation and evil, the book about the achieving of truth and holiness, is the crucial book. I do not think it is necessarily the most attractive, but it is the most successful, the most unified and the most perfect in its structure and in the relationship in it of structure to purpose and message.

Book II, more fanciful and quite different in tone and atmosphere —it is markedly more like romantic epic—is similar in structure. Again there is a quest, this time to overcome a lascivious enchantress who enthrals men and, Circe-like, turns them into beasts; again the knight-hero is accompanied by a mentor; again, when separated from his companion he runs into danger—though not, in this case, into serious temptation. If the moral purpose of Book I is to define man's necessary relations with his Maker, that of Book II is to explore man's relations with himself—the discovery of his own nature and the essential learning of self-control over his passions and desires. It is, of course, the Book 'Of Temperance'.

The hero is Sir Guyon, whose name has been derived partly from Gihon the river of temperance, one of the four rivers of Paradise identified with the cardinal virtues (Genesis ii, 10–14), partly from the names of virtuous knight-heroes of romance—Guy of Warwick, and Guy of Burgundy called in *Sir Ferumbras* the 'good Guy' and sometimes 'Gyoun'. Accompanied by a holy Palmer, he finds the victims, knight, lady and bleeding child, of an enchantress Acrasia. Her name means 'without rule', Aristotle's word for incontinence.* Book II's main lesson is the need for the man who would be virtuous to exercise self-discipline. The Palmer represents Reason, that which alone can control the passions, and the first big episode of the book presents a moving example of the terrible effects of intemperance (in this case sexual intemperance in the dead knight Mordant, and emotional intemperance—immoderate grief that leads to her death in front of Guyon and the Palmer—in the Lady Amavia). Guyon vows to avenge them, and his quest is thus to overthrow the enchantress Acrasia. She is not only like Circe, but a descendant, as it were, of Circe's descendants in Italian romantic epic: Ariosto's Alcina and

---

* *Nicomachaean Ethics* V, vii, 1–3.

Tasso's Armida. Guyon does not of course meet Acrasia until the last canto of the book, but on his long journey to her realm, the Bower of Bliss, he encounters several persons, some of whom attempt to beguile him into sexual intemperance; but mostly they represent other human passions, chiefly anger, sloth and avarice.

Much of the message of Book II is conveyed by means of opposites and by use of the Aristotelian notion of the golden mean, which is introduced early, in the account of Guyon's visit to the Castle of Medina in Canto 2, where live the three sisters Medina (the golden mean), Elissa ('too little') and Perissa ('too much'). Medina is properly self-disciplined, a virtuous and gracious lady, but her two sisters and their lovers Sansloy and Hudibras jointly stand for the excess and the deficiency of virtue—for the 'forward' and the 'froward' passions. Here Spenser is straightforwardly—not to say mechanically—Aristotelian and exemplary. The episode also presents the first of many examples of another preoccupation of Book II—discord—for Hudibras and Sansloy rush to attack the visitor Guyon, but soon fall to fighting each other. Medina makes concord, stilling for a while the scowling Elissa, the wanton Perissa and their paramours.

Canto 3 introduces some new characters, whom Guyon does not meet, although one of them, Braggadocchio, had stolen his horse while with the Palmer he had been attending to the bleeding child of the dead Amavia and Mordant. Braggadocchio and his knave Trompart are vivid *types* of braggartism, cowardice and baseness, and they reinforce the general topic of unrestraint, especially by contrast with Belphebe, a Diana-like huntress, whom they encounter. But the episode seems not to fit in the book, especially as it does not develop and none of the three characters reappears in Book II or indeed until a long time later in *The Faerie Queene*. Belphebe does not reappear until III. 5, Braggadocchio until III. 8. It marks the beginning of Spenser's adoption of Ariosto's method: starting a number of different stories and interlacing them, and sustaining many episodes through several books.

Guyon, after leaving Medina's castle, soon meets new figures of unrestraint: Furor (Wrath) himself and his mother (the 'occasion' of strife), one of their victims, Phedon, and shortly afterwards the figure of strife, Atin. Before long he encounters also a pagan knight, Pyrochles, another example of senseless fury and ungoverned passion, who attacks him violently, without cause, but is overcome by Guyon's cool, wary and disciplined management of the fight.

So far Guyon, unlike the Red Cross Knight, has not been seriously tempted or even tested. His first test comes in the form of Phaedria, a superficially beguiling damsel, but it is a minor test for he quickly realises that, if attractive physically, she is empty headed to the point of worthlessness. He is then attacked by Pyrochles' brother Cymochles. The two brothers present another example of the 'forward' and the 'froward': Pyrochles is intemperate in 'forward', active, violent ways, Cymochles in 'froward', slack, indolent ways. If Pyrochles is almost a representation of *Ira*, Anger, Cymochles is near to Sloth, opposite weaknesses. Pyrochles has excess of energy, leading him to wrong through violent intemperate action; Cymochles represents deficiency of purpose, laying himself open to wrong through lethargy and slackness. They are, like Elissa and Hudibras, Perissa and Sansloy, further instances of Spenser's use of the Aristotelian notion of virtue as the golden mean, implied by depiction of the extremes, of excess and defect, between which it forms the balance.

The attacks of Pyrochles and Cymochles again provide no serious test for Guyon who remains coolly in command of his judgement and so overcomes them. Like many characters and some episodes in this book they present types of unrestraint rather than actual temptations to the knight-hero. Even a large and important episode, like the ensuing one of Guyon's encounter with Mammon and his descent to the underworld, although involving danger does not really provide temptation, for he is immune to the offers of wealth, power and ambition. So again, in his book of temperance, Spenser extends his range beyond the sexual intemperance with which the book opens and closes and which provides the most vivid sequences, adding the deadly sin of Avarice to the Anger and Sloth already presented. Although he is not really tempted, Guyon is weakened by his three days' sojourn beneath the earth, and is rescued from some of his earlier opponents, who come to dishonour him and strip him of his arms and armour, by Prince Arthur, making an appearance to save and help the hero in danger after his emaciation in the underworld, as he had rescued the Red Cross Knight in Book I. As the Red Cross Knight was then taken to the House of Holiness, so Sir Guyon is now taken by Arthur to the House of Temperance, although he does not undergo penance and receive instruction as his predecessor had. Once again Spenser gives his hero an adventure or encounter not, it seems, for his own improvement or testing but in order to draw a clear moral for the reader.

Guyon only stays overnight at the Castle of Alma (the Soul)

which presents an over-literal allegory—which would be intolerably tedious were it not for the absurdity and quaint humour of much of its detail—of the human soul and body under constant siege by a rabble of knaves representing evil desires, vices, temptations, and the senses and the passions which, uncontrolled or put to ill use, continually threaten the virtuous man. Leaving Arthur to fight and overcome the 'rascal hordes' and their leader Maleger, Guyon goes on with the Palmer to complete his quest, passing many Odyssean dangers and temptations by sea on their way to Acrasia's realm. The Bower of Bliss seems delightful, and there are moments of fleeting temptation for Guyon, especially of sexual provocation and invitation from two naked damsels, but the Palmer rebukes 'those wandering eyes of his' and they go on, catch the enchantress Acrasia, symbol of sexual unrestraint, and her lover Verdant, destroy the Bower, and restore to human form the wild beasts that surround the Bower, men whom Acrasia turned into beasts when she had had her fill of them.

I have already shown that in Book II the hero, unlike his counterpart in Book I, is usually not involved in temptation and sin. A consequence is that we as readers are not so involved, but are often as it were invited to observe rather than to 'experience' them. Spenser displays characteristic forms of intemperance—Anger, Sloth, Avarice, Lechery (Ira, Accidia, Avaritia, Luxuria)—either in allegorical or type figures. The hero encounters these vices as he passes through the world to the eventual achievement of his quest, but the essential patterns of Book II are of journey rather than struggle, observation rather than tragic involvement. In other words the allegorical meaning is not so intrinsic or organic a part of the romantic narrative as in Book I. A further point to be noted is that although other forms of intemperance are powerfully enough presented, the dominant form, that which remains in our imagination when we think back over the course of Book II, is that of sexual intemperance. At the end we are made to concentrate on one aspect of man's struggle with temptation through the senses. There has been of course some preparation for it, for the story began, as it ends, with an example of sexual excess (Amavia's sad cautionary tale) and the encounters with Phaedria signify the mood, of empty idleness, and the lure, of relaxation into pleasure, which open the way for sexual misdemeanour, but this culminating episode is so well done by Spenser and comes so close to our own experience that even if we remember the other ways in which mankind may be tempted through the senses, many of the scenes in which they are presented seem

shadowy compared with what lingers vividly in our memory, the final
scene at the Bower of Bliss. Acrasia and her bower, the two naked
damsels sporting in the pool, the song itself—a literal translation—
come straight from Tasso's *Gerusalemme Liberata*. It is a significant
borrowing. Armida's bewitching of Rinaldo, an example of the way
in which even the truest of Christian knights may be beguiled by the
temptations of the flesh, is a superb episode but it seems at worst
irrelevant, at best over-emphatic: it draws too much attention to itself,
making us forget the siege of Jerusalem too completely. Something
of the same is true of Spenser's version, but Spenser comes better out
of the criticism than his mentor, for his poem is continuously and
inalienably romantic so that a highly romantic episode such as this
does not obtrude, and of course the episode is brief where Tasso's
spreads over several books.

     C. S. Lewis has made clear the subtle way in which Spenser conveys
the 'wrongness', the artificiality of the Bower of Bliss. It provides
another example of the importance of being able to distinguish the
true from the false: the imitation vines, the metal pretending to be
natural wood, the naked girls who pretend to be modestly abashed
when Guyon sees them to provoke him more, the pleasure in the
Bower which is not pleasure and the love which is not love. Professor
Lewis saw Book II as concerned with Health and Sickness, the
Bower showing natural desire in a state of unnaturalness, unhealthiness.
But it is not true that 'there is not a kiss or an embrace on the whole
island, only male prurience and female provocation', that the Bower
is a place of suspended lust, 'lust turning into what would now be
called skeptophilia' (*sic*). When Guyon arrives at the Bower he sees
no activity, it is true, only the half-naked Acrasia gazing at the sleeping
young man Verdant. But Spenser tells us that

> . . . she had him now layd a slombering,
> In secret shade, after long wanton joyes

and that she herself is in a state of 'languor of her late sweet toyle'.
This is not a picture of lust suspended but one of languor consequent
on excess, and it is excess that Guyon has to fight (and we must avoid)
as it was excess he set out to overcome when he engaged himself to
avenge Amavia for her sufferings at the hands of Acrasia (that is
because of sexual intemperance).

     Not unnaturally—for it is the literary topic of most permanent
interest and appeal—this subject of sexual behaviour which came to

dominate Book II soon begins to dominate the poem. When in the prefatory letter to Sir Walter Raleigh Spenser wrote that the subject of Book III is the rescuing of Amoret from the thrall of the enchanter Busirane he was trying to suggest that this book is written to the same simple and straightforward design—the quest of a single knight—as Books I and II. But it is not true. The freeing of Amoret is the climax of the book, but we spend little time with her or her knight and champion, Scudamour, and it is only by chance that the heroine Britomart meets Scudamour and takes on the quest to rescue Amoret. Written under the influence of Ariosto rather than of medieval Romance, it does not have a strongly-marked central plot the hero of which from time to time encounters characters from subordinate but related plots. A number of plots are introduced and interwoven, and many of the characters of the book carry over into Book IV, where the same process continues. The adventures are 'intermedled', as Spenser wrote in his prefatory letter. For this reason, as well as for a more important one that the subject-matter of the two books is closely related, Book III 'Of Chastitee' and Book IV 'Of Friendship' may most rewardingly, as C. S. Lewis suggested, be regarded as one book. Its subject is not a particular temptation to which man is subject, shown in a series of assaults on a knight-hero, although it does have, like the two earlier books, a dominant character in the attractive and varied personality of the lady knight Britomart.

Having shown in Book Two mankind's overcoming of Passion in various forms, and especially of base animal desire unmitigated by intellect or soul, and of sexuality in excess, in Guyon's destruction of the Bower of Bliss, Spenser goes on in Books III and IV to present many examples, some allegorical but predominantly in straightforward narrative, of all the varieties of behaviour in human relationships. In these two books we have the various love-pursuits and encounters of Timias and Belphebe, Scudamour and Amoret, Placidas and Aemylia and Amyas and Paeana; the love-complication of Satyrane who loves Florimell who loves Marinell who loves 'no woman'; the satire of the association of the false Florimell and the cowardly braggart Braggadocchio; the representation of heady lust and indulgence at Castle Joyous

> Where so loose life, and so ungentle trade
> Was used of knights and ladies seeming gent

where Malecasta, 'not to love but lust inclined', presides over her

E

aristocratic *bordello* (III. 1), and Cupid among the knights and ladies 'swimming deep in sensuall desires . . . still emongst them kindled lustfull fires'; and the representation, of lust again, in a manifest allegory, this time with no pretence of joyousness or even pleasure, at the House of Busirane. The first, Castle Joyous, is a picture of the heedless pursuit of sexual pleasure, directed at the untutored and the unthinking. It is a place which has its attractions for all of us, a world seductive to the senses, a world of protracted indulgence and titillation, and we may think a sojourn there would be delightful. But the second, the House of Busirane (Book III, Cantos 11 and 12), is a symbol of the mechanical and undelighting enslavement which is the penalty and the reality of the life of Castle Joyous, as C. S. Lewis suggested. But he set it at too specialised a level when he explained Busirane as the emblem of courtly love and the episode of his enslavement of Amoret as an illustration of human nature in the thrall of the courtly love tradition to be freed from it by the ideal of married love.

The first stanza of the third canto of Book III states most clearly what Spenser means by love, and it is also a statement of what Britomart represents and of the virtue which Books III and IV predominantly celebrate:

> Most sacred fire, that burnest mightily
> In living breasts, ykindled first above,
> Emongst th'eternall spheres and lamping sky,
> And thence pourd into men, which men call Love;
> Not that same, which doth base affections move
> In brutish minds, and filthy lust inflame,
> But that sweet fit, that doth true beauty love,
> And choseth vertue for his dearest Dame,
> Whence spring all noble deeds and never dying fame.

Britomart, who overcomes unchastity, rescues Amoret, ever loves Artegall, and is ever ready to fight on behalf of chastity, true love and integrity and to defeat baseness, selfishness, lust and dishonour, represents—or comes to represent, for there is in Spenser's early accounts of her more than a suggestion of very human passions—ideal love, serene, selfless, controlled and fructifying. She is 'sunbright chastity' but she bears little relationship to Milton's Lady in *Comus* who derives from her. She does not merely extol or defend a personal chastity, but champions, advances and represents Chastity as an active and beneficent principle. Destined by her own inclination and by the prognostication of Merlin to love Artegall and eventually to marry him, she openly seeks him throughout the books in which she appears, but there is nothing displeasing or immodest about this. Sincerity, loyalty, generosity and unselfishness are all hers, and with them a frank and lovely ardency and vitality. She is the paragon of true and healthy love, and we know that when it comes, hers will be with Artegall a glorious and proper fulfilment of all her womanly potentialities.

She derives from Ariosto's Bradamante, and not merely on account of her armour and magic lance, her golden hair and knightly feats. Her love and her constant search for her lover are modelled on Bradamante's for Ruggiero. It is only one of Spenser's many debts to the Italian poet, but it provides a good example of a fundamental difference between Ariosto and Spenser. Ariosto created in Bradamante a persuasive and delightful portrait of a passionate woman sincerely in love, and C. S. Lewis—surprisingly—found Britomart unattractively abstract in comparison. But Britomart as a lady-knight of redoubtable courage and skill is good enough as a character in a romantic tale, and we must not fall into the error of expecting her to be as 'like-life' as a heroine in a novel or even as a heroine in Ariosto, although I would claim from the early accounts of her youth and passionate lovelonging that Spenser made her convincingly real and human. But in *The Faerie Queene* what she represents is more important that what she is. This is always true in Spenser, and it points to the most significant difference between the *Orlando* and *The Faerie Queene*. Spenser's chief persons are primarily symbols rather than characters. They represent principles in human activity: Virtue, Truth, Love, Justice, Courtesy. They may not be, they are not meant to be *primarily* characterisations of human types. They are symbols of the best in humanity, or of humanity achieving the best, but they are not therefore lifeless, mere abstractions, though to make them 'real' was not the poet's chief concern. Spenser made the virtues vital, and by showing these characters in unceasing activity in a narrative poem presented the virtues as active (and attractive) principles in human life.

Britomart is the golden mean in these two books. The other chief personages take their places on either side of her. On the one side, they are in some way deficient, on the other in some way excessive in their attitudes and behaviour. Florimell and Marinell are both timorous of love: she is unhappily endowed with that sort of cool, rapt chastity that particularly arouses the lustful and flees in terror from every man, and he 'ever from fair ladies love did flie'. Belphebe, brought up in all maidenliness by Diana, seems an unhappy because an unawakened damsel until love grows in her, slowly and almost reluctantly, out of her pity for the wounded Timias. The other chief characters are examples of various excesses of passion. Belphebe's twin Amoret is in peril from too ardent a love, for she has been brought up in all womanliness by Venus and so is liable to the onslaught of Busirane, representing lust. She and her lover Scudamour have allowed passion for its own sake to dominate their feelings for each other, and he cannot break through the flames (of lust) that guard the enchanter Busirane's house. Only Britomart, Chastity itself, can go unscathed through those guarding flames to rescue Amoret (Book III, Cantos 11 and 12).

These are all 'gentle' people who can be brought to see their mistakes, but there are others who, like Grille, 'the dong-hill kinde' at the Bower of Bliss, are incapable of reformation or unwilling to be reformed. Paridell and Blandamour crudely follow their animal instincts, quite unaware of any higher potentialities, and in Book IV 'Of Friendship' are shown to be incapable even of ordinary friendship or loyalty. They live by their instincts and desires like animals, quarrel and fight each other like animals. Hellenore, used and discarded by Paridell, falls in with a troop of satyrs. We remember how reverently and gently a troop of satyrs received Una in Book I; this troop behave very differently with Hellenore, seeing her for what she is, and she complaisantly even contentedly becomes their general whore.

Spenser introduces the *fabliau* of Malbecco, Paridell and Hellenore (Book III, Cantos 9 and 10) with an apology for its wantonness but, declares that

> . . . good by paragone
> Of evill, may more notably be rad,
> As white seemes fairer, matcht with blacke attone.

This is the constant method of *The Faerie Queene*, teaching good by example of evil as well as by the rapt and passionate delineation of virtue, and nowhere is it more true than in Books III and IV.

They are the most populous of the books of the poem. They are also the most imaginative, and paradoxically at once the most symbolic and the most human and 'realistic'. Paridell and Blandamour are Elizabethan gallants and yet practised seducers of any age. Braggadocchio and Trompart are like characters from an Elizabethan play. (At times indeed the former seems to speak in the very accents of Ancient

Pistol.) Malbecco belongs anywhere in literature or in life where cuckolds and misers are to be found, from Chaucer's January to Shakespeare (Shylock's cry for his daughter and his ducats) to Molière, to the Fondlewifes of Restoration Comedy. Such characters make their impact through common human experience either from life or from literature. These are the most vivid of the base characters whose behaviour illustrates unworthiness or sin. Many lesser characters, among them Placidas and Aemylia, Amyas and Paeana, the Squire of Dames, Cambell and Triamond, Canacee and Cambine, belong to the shadowy territories of Romance in one or other of its many manifestations, and illustrate inconspicuously aspects of human strength or weakness. The fleet hyena-like beast 'that feeds on womans flesh, as others feed on gras' (III. 7. 22) which pursues Florimell, the giantess Argante who seizes Sir Satyrane (III. 7), her twin Ollyphant put to flight by Britomart (III. 11), the hairy phallic giant who seizes Amoret and who flees at the mere sight of Belphebe (IV. 7), Corflambo who incarcerates the Squire of Low Degree, (IV. 8), are typical allegorical and Romance giants and monsters here personifying Lust.

There remain, apart from the chief personages who have already been briefly discussed, several characters who belong not to life or popular literature or medieval Romance or Italian epic Romance. They do not belong, either, to the society of Faerie land. Satyrane's part in the composition is only sketched in. Half-human, half-satyr, he belongs to a sort of half-world, half-pastoral, half-romance. That part of Spenser's mind which instinctively loved and revered simple natural things created him, and having done so did not know quite what to do with him. In Book I (Canto 6) he was ranged with the simple natural beings, the lion, the fauns and satyrs who protected Una. In III. 7, having captured the monster that had pursued Florimell —whom he loves—he attacks Argante and is thrown down by her; but presumably his satyr half is still subservient to his human. In the great courtly tournament for the false Florimell in Book IV, Canto 4, among a press of knights of the calibre for the most part of Paridell and Blandamour, he has little difficulty in emerging victorious: 'Truth is strong, and trew love most of might.' But he is himself vanquished by a stranger knight in quaint disguise,

> with woody mosse bedight, and all his steed
> With oaken leaves attrapt. (IV. 3. 39)

This proves to be Sir Artegall (later the chief knight of Book V) who

is himself then defeated by another strange knight, who is in fact
Britomart with her enchanted spear. It is right that Britomart should
be victorious over all comers in a tournament arranged to determine
the worthiest knight and the paragon of ladies. Virtue is presented
actively in society, positive, creative, fruitful, and rewarding, for
Spenser's ideal is a human society founded on Truth and Holiness,
Justice, self-discipline and Love: 'and the greatest of these is Love.'

Two other characters in Books III and IV seek to live outside society
or at least are shown actively shunning it. Like Satyrane, Marinell and
Florimell are simple creatures of the natural world, but their significance, although recondite, is more easily recognisable than his.
Miss Spens provided a clue when she drew attention to their names—
Florimell suggests flowers, Marinell the sea—and T. P. Roche and
Kathleen Williams another when they referred us to Alciati's emblem
Potentia amoris which shows Cupid holding in one hand flowers, in
the other fish, to show 'the power of love' over both sea and land. It
is perhaps too simple an explanation to say that they represent Earth
and Sea, though she flees anxiously through the woods and glades and
he guards the Rich Strand beside the sea. On the narrative plane, as
has been suggested, they represent a deficiency of the great dominant
virtue of Books III and IV, since they either deny or fear love. But at
some higher, less defined level of the poet's imagination Florimell, ever
in flight, suggests the instability of human life, always changing, always
restless, attractive for the very fleetingness of its beauty, as the character
is touching for her vulnerability, Marinell a sort of Constancy, like
that of the sea which seems to be in perpetual movement in its ebb and
flow of tides and yet is in fact constant and unchanging. To Spenser
for human life to be comprehended and enjoyed man had to see its
transitoriness and mutability against the certainty and steadfastness of
God. This is what the 'Mutabilitie' Cantos explore. In one rarefied
aspect the story of Florimell and Marinell seems to introduce the
theme lightly on the narrative level. Their reconciliation is brought
about through the marriage-feast of the Thames and Medway (IV. 11),
at the house of the last of Florimell's lustful captors, Proteus. In this
great musical and decorative set-piece several purposes are achieved.
All the rivers and seas of the world, all the creatures of river and sea
real and mythical, come together joyfully to celebrate the spousals,
providing an appropriate climax to the two books which have been
concerned with love and concord. It is as if all the world joins in the
celebration, and the fact that it is a great assembly of all natural things

and creatures emphasises the doctrine of the two books that concord in love, enjoined on human beings, is the natural law of the universe. The spousals of Florimell and Marinell are celebrated almost immediately afterwards, in the third canto of the next book; a great tournament takes place, with Marinell victorious over many knights, and we are to assume that he and Florimell, reconciled with each other, are made whole of their deficiency and reconciled at last with the rest of humanity.

Book IV is the thinnest in texture of the books of *The Faerie Queene*. The matter is sometimes repetitive, sometimes seems thinly spread. There is not enough under Friendship to go round, so material that ought to be by rights—or at the least could easily have been used —in Book III is brought in: the episodes of fair ladies, Amoret especially, seized by lustful monsters; the account in IV. 10 of the Gardens of Adonis and the Temple of Venus, already the subject-matter of III. 6; and other material of disproportionate length is introduced, for example the long story of Cambell and Triamond in IV. 3, and the exceedingly long account of the tournament in IV. 2–5. Probably Spenser could have covered his theme in the related Books III and IV, Love and Friendship, in one book. The story that Raleigh influenced him into prematurely publishing a part of his great poem as an instalment in 1590 seems likely. Material prepared for but not then used in Book III Spenser could not bear to discard. Although they are closely related, there is an imbalance between them, Book III having if anything too much material and Book IV too little. Book III is an investigation into what makes for truly virtuous conduct in human love-relationships, and presents a number of examples of types of human conduct, some good, many bad, ranging from sodomy, animality, violent lust and promiscuity on the one hand and rejection and fear on the other to the golden mean, represented by Britomart, clear paragon of virtuous love. Book IV presents a number of examples of discord both allegorically—in the tournament and other contests— and in human types in the many examples of aggressive, quarrelsome, faithless and intransigent behaviour, and ends with a number of reconciliations and with a splendid set-piece—the marriage-feast of the rivers Thames and Medway—symbolic of universal Concord.

7

THE FAERIE QUEENE: BOOKS V AND VI*

So far the poem has not only investigated, defined and commended several aspects of virtue but has shown virtue being achieved. There is a change after Book IV. There is a partial return to the form of Books I and II—medieval quest-romance rather than Ariostan interwoven romantic narrative of types—but, although the leading knights remain (Sir Calidore like Britomart) or through experience, endeavour or instruction become or are destined to become (Sir Artegall like the Red Cross Knight) paragons of the virtue they exemplify or seek, Books V and VI do not conclude in the certainty of virtuous achievement that was so marked in all the earlier books.

We have seen in Book II Spenser's preoccupation with one aspect of human behaviour, the relations between the sexes, and how exploration of it dominated the two following books. Similarly, the growing preoccupation with society as a whole rather than with individual problems and duties, reflected in the populousness and diversity of Books III and IV, is carried over into Book V. We have already been shown the importance of true holiness, of self-discipline, of proper love and concord between individuals. Now we are shown another vital principle:

* Some of this material is drawn from my article 'Order, Grace and Courtesy in Spenser's World' in *Patterns of Love and Courtesy*, London 1966, and I am grateful to the editor, Professor John Lawlor, and the publishers, Edward Arnold, for permission to make use of it.

> Most sacred vertue she of all the rest,
>   Resembling God in his imperiall might;
>   Whose soveraine powre is herein most exprest,
>   That both to good and bad he dealeth right,
>   And all his workes with Justice hath bedight.   (V. Proem, 10)

Spenser's virtues are comprehensive, never rigid or narrowly defined. The temperance of Book II is self-discipline which ought to be exercised in all human activity, subduing Passion to Reason in all things. The chastity of Book III is more than chastity but active virtuous love 'in widest commonalty spread', and the friendship of Book V involves love, faith and truth, without which true concord is impossible. So the justice of Book V is considerably more than a humanly legalistic conception, and those critics who have condemned the book for its cruelty and harshness have failed to perceive the implication that the virtue it celebrates is the divinely appointed Order of the universe, which must be re-enacted in the microcosm. In the Proem to Book V Spenser declares:

> Me seemes the world is runne quite out of square,
>   From the first point of his appointed sourse,
> And being once amisse growes daily wourse and wourse.

and sadly recalls

> ... the antique use, which was of yore,
>   When good was onely for it selfe desyred,
>   And all men sought their owne, and none no more;
>   When Justice was not for most meed outhyred,
> But simple Truth did rayne, and was of all admyred.

He has moved far from the stated purpose of the prefatory letter to Raleigh—to ensample a 'good governour and a vertuous man'—far from concern with the individual to concern with the state of society. The unwary reader may well feel that he is meant to admire Artegall, as he is meant, for example, to admire Una, Britomart or the errant but ultimately virtuous Red Cross Knight and Guyon, and will be unable to do so because he is repelled by many of his deeds and particularly by those of his servant Talus. We are not meant to look upon Artegall in this way. He is not so much the virtuous champion as the instrument of Justice, journeying to re-establish the Order which God ordained and man has broken. So, having failed to reason with the communistic giant who sabotages the natural order he sets Talus to overthrow him. He attempts to subdue the Amazon Radegund who has upset the natural order in her territory, where women rule and men obey, performing menial womanly tasks. He becomes her victim and is rescued by Britomart who restores women again to man's subjection and does 'true Justice deale'; and at the climax of the book, having achieved his knightly quest to rescue Irena from the giant Grantorto, he stays temporarily to restore right order in the domain the giant had usurped. These are his chief deeds. In the course of their execution he performs many acts of common justice: he punishes the cruel knight Sanglier, slays Pollente (ruthless power and oppression) and his evil daughter Munera (corruption), deals justice between two brothers who fight over their inheritance, and helps Arthur to destroy the cruel Souldan and his tigerish wife and the guileful thief and evil-doer Malengin.

For a while the experience of the active practical man predominates here over the imagination of the contemplative poet. Spenser was in more or less direct contact with the hard and evil ways of the world for many years in Ireland, and his experience there dominates Book V. In it he portrays a world given over to disorder, cruelty, oppression and injustice, only to be regenerated by the re-imposition of divine Order, of which Artegall is the agent. Ireland was undoubtedly the original of this picture. C. S. Lewis was more able and more ready than most critics to make the imaginative journey into the background of a work of literature, necessary if we are to understand it right, yet he wrote that 'Spenser was the instrument of a detestable policy in Ireland, and in his fifth book the wickedness he had shared begins to corrupt his imagination'. But Ireland was the obvious landing-ground, base and arsenal for the invasion of England throughout the years in which the Pope and the King of Spain, sometimes alone, sometimes together, planned the subjugation of England and the restoration of the Catholic faith, as well as a constant liability, a continuous drain on English resources of wealth and manpower. The pacification of Ireland was a political and military necessity, and a necessary part of the larger struggle of Protestantism with Rome, or as Englishmen saw it, of true religion with Antichrist. Ireland had to be subdued; stern, often cruel methods had to be employed. We must temporarily adjust our notions of the distinction between justice and cruelty. In Catholic Europe this was the terrible century of the Inquisition; in Protestant England even a godly man like Thomas Cartwright could insist that everything in the Scriptures was still equally binding, and that the punishment for blasphemy, heresy and adultery as well as for murder should still be death. Ireland was hostile and threatening. Above all it was in chaos, an obvious example to an Elizabethan Englishman of the result of irreligion and the complete breakdown of order, an incarnation of chaotic evil. (That originally the responsibility for the existence of this state of affairs was England's was irrelevant to the necessity of action.)

We must remember what Spenser wrote in *A View of the Present State of Ireland*. In a dozen places the poem reminds us of the prose work, in its instances of violence and cruelty and in the picture that is gradually built up of a disordered world in which true justice does not, cannot reign; evil is at large and virtue is precarious, always in danger. Spenser believed in the need for a 'thorough' policy in Ireland. As Irenius, who stands for Spenser himself, says: 'all those evils must first be cut away by a strong hand before any good can be planted, like as the corrupt branches and unwholesome boughs are first to be pruned and the foul moss cleansed or scraped away before the tree can bring forth any good fruit'.* The aim of the policy he advocates, which Lewis ignored, Spenser set down immediately after the passage quoted: 'by the sword I meant the royal power of the Prince which ought to stretch itself forth in her chief strength to the redressing and cutting of all those evils which I before blamed, and not of the people which are evil; for evil people by good ordinances and government may be made good. . . .' Here he almost echoes the words he gave to the other speaker, Eudoxus, at the beginning of *A View*: 'But if that country of Ireland . . . be so goodly and commodious a soil as you report I wonder that no course is taken for the turning thereof to good uses, and reducing that savage nation to better government and civility.'†

Behind the advocacy, in *A View*, of a stern and thorough policy of subjugation lies a vision of a disordered people, 'this stubborn nation of the Irish', brought 'from their delight of licentious barbarism unto the love of goodness and civility'.‡ Spenser's condemnation of the violence and disorder of Irena's land of Ireland in the prose work, and by implication in Book V, implies his complementary vision of a world disposed according to God's order, in which true justice— God's not man's—will hold sway. Stanzas 39–43 in Canto 2 eloquently

* Variorum edn., p. 148.
† ibid., p. 43.
‡ ibid., p. 54.

enunciate the theory of degree, which reflects and symbolises the
Order which God intended for the world, and the first stanza of
Canto 7 also defines the inseparability of the concepts of Order and
true Justice:

> For th' hevens themselves . . .
> . . . are rul'd by righteous lore
> Of highest Jove, who doth true justice deale
> To his inferiour Gods and evermore
> Therewith containes his heavenly Common-weale.

The facts of history meant that the prose work could not show the
achievement of this Order and state of virtue as the facts of life meant
that Spenser could not show them achieved in Book V either. There is
a further implication, which from this point becomes more and more
dominant in the poem, that they cannot ever be wholly achieved in a
fallen world.

After Artegall had freed Irena

> His studie was true Justice how to deale,
> And day and night employ'd his busy paine
> How to reforme that ragged common-weale.   (V. 12. 26)

But he was recalled to Faerie Court before he could reform it thoroughly, and on his journey home he was assailed by the Blatant Beast.
(The covert allusion to Lord Grey the Lord Deputy of Ireland whom
Spenser served from 1580–2, his recall and the calumny he suffered,
is well known.) It is the first time in *The Faerie Queene* that a knight-
hero's achievement is incomplete. The Red Cross Knight killed the
dragon; Sir Guyon overthrew the Bower of Bliss and bound Acrasia;
Britomart chained Busirane and saw the destruction of his house;
and although in Book IV there is no central knight or adventure and no
great culminating contest, Paridell and Blandamour were discomfited,
Braggadocchio and false Florimell exposed, Amoret rescued from
Lust, Corflambo slain, Marinell and Florimell betrothed and a
culminating symbol of achieved Concord shown in the marriage
celebrations of the rivers Thames and Medway. These books seem
complete; they all close with the final triumph of a virtue. But now in
Book V Artegall is 'forst to stay' his course of justice before he can
thoroughly reform Irena's disordered land, and the Blatant Beast is at
large. On the personal level, too, the knight-hero cannot achieve complete fulfilment. His long foretold marriage to Britomart remains in

the future, and we only learn that it will assuredly take place—and
what that will signify—from the priest's interpretation of Britomart's
dream of the idol and the crocodile in the Temple of Isis: Britomart
is Isis, and the crocodile Artegall,

> The righteous Knight, that is thy faithfull lover,
> Like to *Osyris* in all just endever.
> For that same Crocodile *Osyris* is,
> That under *Isis* feet doth sleepe for ever:
> To show that clemence oft in things amis,
> Restraines those sterne behests, and cruell doomes of his.   (V. 7. 22)

The eventual marriage of Britomart and Artegall will also symbolise
the reconciling of judgement with clemency, law with love. But
that is and remains in the future. The time is not yet when God's
love will inform the world and God's Order in the world will again
be the expression of his loving justice.

So, like Book I, with which it has other points of similarity, Book V
both discusses a general issue—here the relation between Justice,
Order and Love—and presents the education of a particular knight,
who moves through danger and error towards a perfection, which in
this case is not achieved within the scope of the book, or indeed of the
poem, yoking them easily by means of romantic love-narrative.
Although Spenser does not write specifically of religion in Book V, he
is as much a religious crusader here as he was in Book I, for the justice
and order Artegall fights to establish are part of the divine intention for
mankind, and evil, including of course the evil power of Rome
shown in so many places in both books—Grantorto (great wrong)
is Spain and the power of Rome, Gerioneo and the Souldan Catholicism again, Belge the Protestant Netherlands despoiled by Spain—
must be extirpated before the just order can be re-established. Books
I and V are close in other respects and I believe that a draft of the
latter, although not published unti 1596, may also have been originally
written early, when the affair of Lord Grey de Wilton was near to his
actual experience, and Ireland first making its impact upon him.
They share a pattern and material reminiscent of medieval Romance,
together with a high incidence of heroic journeying and combat,
and behind them both the figure of Hercules casts a great shadow.

In Book I it is a sort of Hercules's choice that the Red Cross Knight
makes—and gets it wrong when he leaves Una and takes up with
Duessa. His descents to the underworld and his final struggle with the
dragon are clearly Herculean. So is the role of Arthur, limited though

it is to the overcoming of the giant Orgoglio and a descent to the underworld to rescue the Red Cross Knight. The felt presence of Hercules is greater in Book V, at the beginning of which Spenser declared that Sir Artegall was the peer of Hercules,

> Who all the West with equall conquest wonne,
> And monstrous tyrants with his club subdewed;
> The club of Justice dread, with kingly powre endewed.   (V. 1. 2)

His victory in Canto 1 over Sanglier ('wild boar') must be meant to remind us of Hercules's victory over the Erymanthian boar. His enslavement by Radegund (Cantos 4–7) resembles that of Hercules by Omphale, cited by Spenser (V. 5. 24), but with mistaken reference to Iole; the rapid changes of shape of Malengin, ultimately killed by Artegall's lieutenant Talus in Canto 9, recall those of Achelous, slain by Hercules; Arthur's victories over the Souldan in Canto 8 and over Gerioneo in Canto 10 resemble those of Hercules over the tyrant Diomedes and over Geryon.

The association with the classical hero helps towards a new identification of the Blatant Beast. Most writers have ignored this monster, or have underestimated its significance, taking it lightly as the grotesque companion of Envy and Detraction. No doubt Spenser originally brought it in to attack Artegall in the twelfth canto of Book V because of the experience of Lord Grey (Artegall) on his recall from Ireland in 1582 ('how ever envy list to *blatter* [my italics] against him' as most of the manuscripts of *A View* read), and at some of its appearances in Book VI it expressly represents defamation. But Hercules's last opponent, ultimately overcome, was Cerberus, many-headed dog serpent, the guardian beast of Hell, and the Blatant Beast is a monster bred of hellish race. Hundred-tongued (V. 12. 41) or thousand-tongued (VI. 1. 9), grandchild or greatgrandchild of the Gorgon, nephew of Geryon and so related to Spenser's monster Gerioneo, son of the watchdog of Hell, Cerberus, and of the monster Chimera (VI. 1. 8) or (as in VI. 6. 9–10) son of Typhon the son of Tartarus and of Echidna daughter of the Gorgon Medusa—can we be satisfied that this creature merely represents Slander, Backbiting or even Envy? Spenser is surely dealing in bigger concepts, and the spirit of Slander barking and baying as it accompanies the hags Envy and Detraction in Book V, Canto 12 becomes increasingly in Book VI the spirit of Evil.

That Sir Artegall is attacked at the end by the Beast, as well as forced to leave 'the ragged common-weale' of Irena's disordered land before he could 'reforme it thoroughly', and still denied his long foretold marriage to Britomart, leaves us with a heightened impression of virtue unachieved and mission not fully accomplished. So it is a disappointing book to many, and for other reasons also the least liked of all the books of *The Faerie Queene*. Admittedly it is in some ways a terrible book for it deals with terrible events unsparingly, but if the reader can make the necessary sympathetic transition into the mind of a typical Elizabethan who was for a long while at one of the battle-fronts, it is a powerfully fascinating one. The battles, especially with Gerioneo and Grantorto, are more stupendous than any others in the poem, and the vivid horror of these two conflicts makes the Red Cross Knight's battle with the dragon seem a quaint, naive unreal contest. The lesser incidents too, the overthrowing of oppression, the beating back of savage mobs, the punishment of bribery and extortion, which all derive from Spenser's experience in Ireland, are vividly realised. It is an iron-hard book; but it is a mistake to see it as unallevi-atedly harsh, for it has more variety than most. Many episodes, notably the encounter with Sanglier, the fight on the bridge with Pollente, the tournament in honour of the marriage of Florimell and Marinell, the scene in which Artegall, overcome by Radegund's beauty, fights scrupulously in self-defence and not in order to kill her, the complication of the falling in love with him not only of Radegund but also of her maid and love-emissary Clarinda, the peril of Britomart in Dolon's castle of trick-beds and floors, and the ruse where-by Samient is rescued from the Souldan by Artegall in disguise are among the most palpably 'Romantic' episodes in the whole poem, having origins or analogues in medieval Romance and Italian epic Romance, especially in Malory and Ariosto.

Book I established that the most important duty for the individual is rightly to distinguish God's Truth and to act in accordance with it. Book V makes the equally important claim that the chief essential in society is the re-establishment and maintenance of divine Order on earth. We can only regret—in life as well—that Book V shows only the necessary preliminary subjugation of evil and disorder, and that Spenser could not show human society thoroughly reformed and brought to good order and 'civility'.

Concern with order in society—which alone makes 'civility' possible—also permeates Book VI, which is linked as a narrative to Book V by the encounter of Sir Artegall and a knight, Sir Calidore, whose quest is to catch and subdue the Blatant Beast. In Book VI the

Beast retains its superficial function of back-biting and slander, to the distress of several knights and ladies, but it comes increasingly to represent Evil at large. Although Sir Calidore eventually succeeds in his quest and muzzles and chains it, at the end of the book it breaks free and is still loose in the world. It is true that Spenser in his final words in Book VI reverts to the superficial aspect of Evil expressed in calumny and detraction and alludes to some example in his own career, but a reading of the book leaves the conviction that the real antagonist of the virtuous knight-hero, whatever form or forms it takes— whether as slander, contempt, detraction, lies or other falseness, the cankering evil which can destroy a man or the ceaselessly destructive spirit of disorder—is Evil. We should remember the ancestry of the Blatant Beast, a hellish monster hell-born of hellish race.

If Book V, as I have suggested, presents the world as a place of Disorder, and so one without true justice, which, if it existed, would epitomise and comprise God's Order, Book VI implies a complementary picture of the world as a place in which, because God's Order has been broken and not yet restored, true Virtue cannot reign. At the end of Book V the Blatant Beast appeared as a final symbol of Evil in the world, and its reappearance in Book VI, its role as chief quarry of the hero, the fact that it breaks out into the world again at the end of that book, all assert the continuing imperfection, as well as the vulnerability of virtue and happiness. The linking of Books V and VI by the Blatant Beast and by the obvious connexion between Order and Virtue goes deeper. Calidore's quest is related to Hercules's final labour, to overcome Cerberus. Hercules was seen by Renaissance commentators as 'virtue in general',* and his vanquishing of Cerberus represented the overcoming of death; Hercules, as it were, performs a pagan harrowing of hell. It Calidore had for ever vanquished the offspring of Cerberus, the Blatant Beast, he would have conquered Evil in the world. But Calidore failed to overcome it finally. In mythology a hero can overcome death; in Spenser's mythology, which by this stage in the poem's evolution is not free but one tied to the facts of the world he knows, final success cannot be attained, however valorous and virtuous the heroes of the poem. In 'Faery land' the Beast was led in bondage by Sir Calidore, but 'now he raungeth through the world againe'.

This failure is not the only one. Calidore 'fails' when he steps forward from the covert of the wood (VI. 10. 18ff.) to get a closer

* e.g., Panofsky, *Studies in Iconology*, New York 1962, p. 157n.

glimpse of the Graces dancing on Mount Acidale, causing them to
vanish, and a third instance of setback to virtue is the destruction of
Meliboe's pastoral paradise by the Brigants in the same canto. Taken
together, and in view of the incompleteness of Artegall's achievement
in Book V, they strongly counterpoise the earlier books of *The Faerie
Queene*, which end in complete and final victory for virtue. These
'failures' present significant problems, to which I will return later; they
reinforce the view that in the last two books of *The Faerie Queene*
Spenser has moved far away, not from his intent to 'fashion a gentleman
or noble person in vertuous and gentle discipline,' for in fact Sir
Calidore of Book VI is the most assuredly virtuous and 'achieved'
of all the heroes of the poem, almost a second Arthur, but from what
seems to have been his original assumption—that virtue can be
attained and can finally triumph. It is no accident or coincidence that
in both Books V and VI a dream (Britomart's in the Temple of Isis)
or a vision (Calidore's glimpse of the dance of the Graces) promises
only future felicity in a world now run 'quite out of square'. Spenser
resolves and explains this in the Mutabilitie Cantos.

Yet Book VI is more positive and optimistic than Book V, and to
many it is the most attractive book in *The Faerie Queene*. This is
chiefly because of its subject-matter. Many of the characters and
incidents epitomise or display courtesy, and the book is indeed a book
'Of Courtesy' as Book V is a book 'Of Justice'—though both Justice,
as I have attempted to show, and Courtesy as I now claim, are used in
a much deeper and more complex sense than has usually been assumed.
Spenser shows many of the other virtues which he has displayed in the
knights and ladies of earlier books to be contained in his ideal of
courtesy. Sir Calidore loathes 'leasing, and base flattery' and loves
'simple truth and stedfast honesty' (VI. 1. 3). He is temperate and self-
controlled; he can 'his wrath full wisely guyde' and does 'him selfe
from fraile impatience refraine' (VI. 1. 30). When he spared Crudor's
life, the poet, commending him, writes:

> For nothing is more blamefull to a knight,
>   That court'sie doth as well as armes professe,
>   How ever strong and fortunate in fight,
>   Then the reproch of pride and cruelnesse.
>   In vaine he seeketh others to suppresse,
>   Who hath not learnd him selfe first to subdew.
>   .   .   .
> Who will not mercie unto others shew,
>   How can he mercy ever hope to have?   (VI. 1. 41–2)

So Calidore is brave, self-controlled, just, merciful, not blemished with pride or cruelty. He is kind (3. 15), compassionate (2. 41), considerate (3. 21) and delights in 'doing gentle deedes' (7. 1). He is also a paragon of a virtuous and pleasing lover (VI. 4-10). Through him Spenser shows that courteous conduct can influence the behaviour of others and bring them great happiness, in the conversion of sad Briana in 1. 45 and 46. Spenser shares with his master Chaucer the view that 'pitee renneth soone in gentil herte', and shows it in Calidore's sympathy with the wounded Aladine (2. 41). In short, Calidore is almost the apotheosis of the virtues Spenser has displayed in earlier books.

It is not surprising that Prince Arthur's function in Book VI is less significant than in any of the other books of *The Faerie Queene*, for his virtues and his nature repose already in Calidore. Arthur's role in this book is not to rescue the knight-hero from some appalling peril. He rescues his own squire Timias from Defetto, Decetto and Despetto in Canto 5, destroys Turpine the oppressor of Sir Calepine and many others in Cantos 6 and 7, and again rescues Timias, from the giant Disdaine, in Canto 8. Indeed the knight-hero of Book VI, unlike those of all the other books, does not even meet Prince Arthur. Is it because Calidore is his equivalent, 'the image of a brave knight, perfected in the twelve private morall vertues'? Does he not seem to be 'the perfection of all the rest', as, Spenser claims in the letter to Raleigh, Arthur was intended to be? In Book VI the knight who, though reasonably virtuous, is a prey to many temptations and perils, is not Sir Calidore but Sir Calepine; the fact that he bears the brunt of infamy, evil, slander, oppression—the dominating troubles of Book VI—leaves Calidore free to appear as a paragon and exemplar of virtue.

So in Book VI we have not so much a knight adventuring in the world and learning the hard way the virtue he is to epitomise at the end—like the Red Cross Knight and Sir Artegall—as an exemplar of loving, controlled and courteous activity. This will be disputed, for it is commonly accepted that Sir Calidore is also to a degree an errant knight, shown in his so-called 'truancy' in the pastoral world. I have already mentioned three apparent 'failures' in Book VI. They do not necessarily imply failure in the knight-hero: indeed my claim is that, like the 'failure' of Sir Artegall in Book V, they mean that it is the living world of men, man in society in a fallen world dominated by evil, that has failed and is at fault. Calidore, like Hercules, is 'virtue in general'; his chief opponent, seemingly only the Cerberean Blatant Beast, is indeed Cerberus, hellish evil at large in the world.

Spenser uses two remarkable imaginative devices to establish the point, both literary and classical in origin, not drawn from life: the pastoral world and the vision of the dance of the Graces. The pastoral world of course has always symbolised for poets special attributes of virtue and innocence. In *The Shepheardes Calender* and 'Colin Clouts Come Home Again' it stands for virtuous simplicity, simple piety, devotion to duty, innocence as opposed to sophistication, honesty opposed to deceit, Virtue opposed to Evil. In many places in *The Faerie Queene* the simplicity of natural life is contrasted with the corruption of courts and palaces, and with dens, bowers and castles where evil or corruption of various kinds is rife. Simple persons, like Sir Satyrane or Timias, noble wild beasts or savages like the Lion in Book I, and the salvage men who yet protect Una, are contrasted with sophisticates like Paridell, or with unnatural creatures like the monsters representing Lust in Books III and IV and the giants of Book V. Always the simple, virtuous and natural are celebrated; but always their vulnerability is shown. Spenser carries the idea furthest in Book VI presenting a whole pastoral world in Canto 9, a place of ordered, peaceful, fruitful, creative activity. It is not often in romantic epics, or indeed in fiction of any kind, that we see people working. Here we are clearly shown the pleasant pattern of constructive work, and we hear old Meliboe extolling its virtue and charm; which he is well qualified to do, for he knows from long experience in his youth the idle hopes, the 'wrackfull yre' and the disillusionment that attend the courtier's life, and the serene contentment of the 'lowly quiet life' he now leads.

Because it is a place of virtuous ordered activity, Calidore's sojourn in the shepherd world is no mere truancy. A temporary errancy from his quest it undeniably is, but that period of his journeying which leads him to an ideal world offering him a model of order and perfection, can hardly be a culpable truancy. Spenser as a moralist must question Calidore's stay 'Unmindfull of his vow and high beheast', but quickly supplies the disclaimer:

Ne certes mote he greatly blamed be,

.   .   .

> For who had tasted once (as oft did he)
> The happy peace, which there doth overflow,
> And prov'd the perfect pleasures, which doe grow
> Amongst poor hyndes, in hils, in woods, in dales,
> Would never more delight in painted show. (VI. 10. 3)

But contrasted with the shepherds and their ideal society are the Brigants. This 'lawlesse people' who

> . . . never usde to live by plough nor spade,
> But fed on spoile and booty, which they made
> Upon their neighbours   (VI. 10. 39)

invade and destroy the happy pastoral world

> And spoyld their houses, and them selves did murder;
> And drove away their flocks, with other much disorder.

The Brigants might well have appeared in Book V, so palpably do they stand for evil and disorder. Their dwelling is a kind of Hell, deep underground (VI. 10. 42), and they are like damned fiends (VI. 10. 43) or like fiendish dogs that fight each other fiercely over their prey (VI. 11. 17) down in the filthy darkness of their Cerberean den.

It is Spenser's most powerful picture of the vulnerability of virtue in the fallen world, and, largely because of it, we may legitimately see *The Faerie Queene* as a poem ultimately concerned with the imperfection, indeed the imperfectability, of the world. It is not, in the end, as it promised to be in the beginning, an escapist celebration of the universal triumph of virtue.

If the pastoral world provides an example of virtuous ordered life, the scene of the Graces dancing, surrounded by a hundred naked maidens and encircling a fourth 'Grace' on whom they lavish 'flowers and fragrant odours', on the Acidalian hill within the confines of that world, concentrates and clarifies the symbol. There is no enormity in the fact that the Graces dance to the piping of Colin Clout, nor that he is, here as always, the poet Edmund Spenser himself, though it has led critics to dubious interpretations of the meaning of Book VI based on Colin's relation to the Graces, not Sir Calidore's.

It is strange that few commentators have asked why the vision of the dance on Mount Acidale vanished when Sir Calidore stepped forward from the wood in order to see it more closely. C. S. Lewis interpreted the Graces, in relation to Colin Clout, as 'inspiration', the fugitive thing that enables a man to write one day and leaves him dry as a stone the next, and also as 'the mysterious source of beauty . . . a similar inspiration that comes and goes in all human activities'. Kathleen Williams sees Book VI as a great tribute to poetry itself: 'the ordering power of the book of Courtesie . . . is really the ordering power of the poet, creator of the small universe of the poem' and Mount

Acidale is 'the home of poetry where the Graces bestow their vision
... upon Colin alone, vanishing when Calidore breaks in upon them,
for they come to "whom they of them selves list so to grace".' I have
no doubt that Spenser would himself have agreed that, if the dance
of the Graces is a vision of ideal beauty and ordered perfection, such
a vision may be imaginatively rendered by poets. It is true that the
whole pastoral episode can be interpreted, as pastoral always can be
interpreted, as standing for the ordered world of art in a world otherwise disordered and often hostile and dangerous, and it is true that to
the Elizabethans poetry was held a great civilising influence upon men.
But just as in Book V the poet's concern is ultimately with something
much larger than Justice—the ostensible subject of the book—in fact
with Order, so in Book VI it is with something much more than the
civilising power of poetry, or the nature of poetic inspiration, or
indeed courtesy in the ordinary sense. The episode of the Graces is
not just a charming adornment, but an episode crucial to the understanding of the book—and the poem—however light and fanciful
its imagining. It is the symbolic core of the book, providing the key
to the poet's central preoccupation, and it is necessary to ask why the
vision vanished when Sir Calidore, that very virtuous knight, tried to
come near. It cannot be just because Calidore, unlike the Shepherd
Colin, is not a poet!

The dance of the Graces is an even more lucid example of ordered
activity and therefore symbol of virtuous order than the pastoral
community. That it vanishes from sight (and that the pastoral world
was erased) makes clear that Spenser means by it another, the most
potent, example of the precariousness of virtue, and that, however
idealised many aspects of life in Faerie land may be, by the end of the
poem he is thinking unequivocally of the real—and fallen—world.
What the Graces symbolise is not actually attainable, any more than
the pastoral ideal, in the fallen and disordered world. So a further link,
a thematic one, is forged between Books V and VI. The loss of the
pastoral world has affinities with Artegall's forced leaving of Irena's
land before he could reform it thoroughly, and the disappearance of
the vision of the Graces has affinities with Britomart's dream; in all
cases something is left incomplete, imperfect, but with a promise of
some future fulfilment. Britomart's marriage with Artegall will happen,
but not yet. Order will not yet be re-established, nor Justice and Love
yet embrace for ever in an ordered world. And the Graces may not
be seen at any time, much less all the time, dancing on Mount Acidale

nor may they be seen by everyone, nor, once seen, can they be counted on not to disappear. The time is not yet, in Book VI as in Book V, for the settled achievement of perfection and the universal triumph of virtue.

If Book VI is about Courtesy, it is about Courtesy in a much profounder sense than has been assumed. The Courtesy of Book VI, which is superficially—though none the less importantly—seen in courteous and gentle behaviour, is a heavenly thing. Sir Calidore is given a glimpse of it in the dance of the Graces, as the Red Cross Knight is given a view of the new Jerusalem, Sir Scudamour his visit to the Temple of Venus, and Britomart her auspicious dream in the Temple of Isis. It is through no fault or inadequacy in him that the vision vanishes: it is the imperfection of the world which frustrates. That the Graces represent an ideal of civil and courteous behaviour, of generosity and loving kindness, goes without saying, but they symbolise much more, and I want to suggest an actual as well as a verbal association between the Graces and Grace, the 'Charites' and Charity. Spenser has invested the classical Graces, with all their beauty and their generosity to men, with something of Christian Grace. Indeed, the maid in their midst who 'Seem'd all the rest in beauty to excell' on whom they bestow gifts and sweet flowers, who, says Spenser, is a sort of fourth Grace, having

> Divine resemblaunce, beauty soveraine rare,
> Firme Chastity, that spight ne blemish dare;
> All which she with such courtesie doth grace,
> That all her peres cannot with her compare.   (VI. 10. 27)

may be thought of as symbolising Grace itself. Spenser has complicated it, seemingly, by making the central figure also 'but a countrey lasse', and the beloved of Colin Clout. But one of the messages of Book VI, indeed of *The Faerie Queene* at large, is that virtue does not only live in courts; it may grow on lowly stalk, and may in fact most readily be found among simple people and wild animals and in the world of pastoral. Spenser will always multiply significances, and is always extending the area and the application of his symbols. It is perfectly in keeping with his practice that the maiden in the middle of the Graces should be at once a country lass, his own beloved, a fourth Grace, the poet's inspiration, and Grace itself. (On the evidence of the compliment to Eliza in 'April' of *The Shepheardes Calender*, 'She shalbe a grace, To fyll the fourth place', there may also be a delicate compliment to the Queen.) She it is in the romantic narrative 'to whom that shepheard' (Colin Clout) 'pypt alone'. This can mean—I believe it does—both that the girl is his own beloved, and that she is Virtue, the only inspiration and subject of his poetry and his constant theme and vocation. It is perfectly consistent and credible that Spenser should present virtue as something that may be glimpsed but not attained in this world.

It will be objected that Virtue and Grace are not the same, and that neither is 'Courtesy', the supposed subject of Book VI. Admittedly it looks like a long step from courtesy to virtue and on to Grace. But critics have almost completely ignored the semantics of 'Courtesy'. By the time Spenser wrote the word had long carried a profound spiritual sense. In the medieval poem *Pearl* (456–7) Mary is called 'Quene of cortasye': Chaucer quite naturally calls the son of God 'the curteis Lord Jhesu Crist' (*Parson's Tale*, 245); Langland (*Piers Plowman* B, xii, 79), Wyclif (Sermons I, 378), and many others mean by the word courtesy the special loving generosity of God and our Lord. The central virtue of Book VI is indeed the generous love of God to man which I claim Spenser celebrates so imaginatively in his Botticellian dance of the Graces. The Graces in classical literature are the generous and giving ones, who 'to men all gifts of grace do graunt' (VI. 10. 15), and in Spenser we see them giving gifts especially to the maiden they dance around. She is adored by them. She is something more than they are, their apotheosis.

There is in this fourth Grace more than a suggestion of the Christian *agape*. Christ was a pattern of love and generosity, as he was also the vehicle and the vessel of God's love to man. God gives love to men, requiring it of man again in an endless cycle of giving and receiving. In classical terms, this is precisely what the Graces signify, and in Classical and Renaissance iconography their linked dance suggests it, as Spenser knew when he described their dance in VI. 10. 24, and as his early commentator E.K. knew when he wrote the *glosse* to 'April' in *The Shepheardes Calender* about 'The Graces . . . otherwise called Charites'. The New Testament translates *agape* 'charity', and, as the Collect for Quinquagesima reads, charity is 'the bond of all virtues', that by which every virtue is made valid, the root and soil out of which all spiritual fruits grow. *Agape*, charity, is also of course a social concept. Virtue can have little meaning in isolation, but only in association or relationship between man and man. The most important of social virtues is the loving selfless generosity that, as it came first from God, binds man to man and man to God. To St Paul of course it was the greatest of virtues, and always its greatest exemplar is Jesus Christ.

Charity, love, generosity, grace, *courtesie*, virtue itself: the scene of the Graces implies all of these. Although the play of words, Graces, Grace, Charites, Charity, was not certainly in Spenser's mind, the idea of their connexion assuredly was. The connexions would be obvious to an Elizabethan reader, and so, I think, would the connexions between Books V and VI. Because Order, the Order of God, was shown not to have been successfully restored in Book V, God's Justice cannot properly exist in the world. This same Order does not reign in Book VI, though it is glimpsed in the ways of the pastoral world and in the ordered dance on Mount Acidale, and so true Courtesie, the grace and love of God, virtue itself, cannot reign on earth. This is not to say that it does not or cannot exist in individuals. Calidore refutes this, and so do many others in *The Faerie Queene*, notably of course Britomart, that loving champion of love. Book VI asserts the need, in a fallen world, for the utmost exercise and extension of it— until the second coming of Christ will restore God's Order and God's Love to his creation.

So in the final book of *The Faerie Queene*—as we have it—Spenser has reached the final truth. There is an undeniable air of finality over the book, even though the Blatant Beast is said at the end still to be at large in our world. It is almost as if Spenser has drawn a line below the end of the last adventure of the knights of Faerie land, and looks up from his romancing to think of the fallen world he knows. But it was not his last word. There were still the Mutabilitie Cantos to come.

8

THE FAERIE QUEENE: THE POETIC ACHIEVEMENT

Any brief account of *The Faerie Queene* is bound to be inadequate, unable to convey much sense of the multiplicity, diversity and imaginative force of its story and meaning. Nor can it give any idea of its poetic pleasures which have ensured that it has always had 'fit audience, though few'. Nor can it show the subtle and intricate ways in which the Romantic epic is assembled, so that the story is kept endlessly interesting while at the same time its moral purpose is effortlessly carried by the romantic narrative.

But first a word about the unity of the poem, the unity of atmosphere, tone, sensibility, emotion and purpose, though not of structure. We have seen that the primary moral purpose of fashioning 'a gentleman or noble person in virtuous and gentle discipline' remained constant, and that the method was to some extent repetitive, Books I and II and V being similar in structure—deriving from medieval Romance—and Books III and IV being closely related to each other, not least in sharing an influence from the epic Romance of Ariosto. (Book VI while closer to I, II and V in plan has also many Ariostan characteristics.) The deliberately unlocalised setting in Faerie land; the fact that some characters appear in several books (Red Cross Knight, Guyon, Archimago, Duessa, Britomart, Amoret, Belphebe, Artegall, Satyrane among others, not to mention Arthur who appears in all); the repetition of adventurings through the woods and glades of Faerie land, of joustings, of visits to the underworld; the form of the poem, which is cyclical, not linear; the development of the 'argu-

ment' of the poem which is linear as well as cyclical; the basic material
of chivalrous knightly adventure and romantic knightly journeying;
its sources in the Bible, the classics, Chaucer, medieval Romance,
Italian romantic epic, emblem literature, Elizabethan pageants, progresses and shows, Ireland and the life of his time, all of which make
their contribution to each book; the scale and shape of each book,
each having twelve cantos each averaging about fifty stanzas; even the
Spenserian stanza itself, ever changing, ever the same—all these give
the poem its peculiarly strong sense of in-turned revolving unity,
and of diversity in unity.

In a number of less obvious ways the poem is held together, as
it were subliminally, by connexions and relationships of ideas and
images. Each book has its own dominating images or *motifs* filling
out the basic structure of journey, quest, encounter, struggle, conflict,
and clarifying the especial preoccupation of each book.

If we think back over Book I, the general images we recall are of
darkness and light, of forests and great combats. The book moves
continually from light to darkness and back again; from the Wandering Wood and Archimago's dark forest-hermitage to Una in the sunny
glades with the Lion and later with the fauns and satyrs; Duessa in
the underworld visiting Night; the dark dungeons of Orgoglio's
castle; the young Arthur and Saytrane brought up in the woods;
Despair in his hollow cave 'darke . . . like a dreary grave'; the Red
Cross Knight rising freshly at dawn to renew his fight with the dragon;
and finally all the brightness and joy of the betrothal of Una, now
unveiled, fresh as dawn or springtime flowers, bright as the sun. And
in this book, more than in others, we are regularly told of night
'defacing' the sky and of bright dawn bringing new hope. By the
emphasis on wood and forest, Spenser reflects both the idea of forests
as wilderness, by which, as Servius the commentator wrote of Virgil's
forests in the sixth book of the *Aeneid*, Virgil 'signifies that in which
beastliness and passion dominate', and Dante's *selva oscura*, the forest
of sinfulness and worldliness, the wandering wood of this life. And the
book has a high proportion of great contests, of which Arthur's
slaying of Orgoglio and the Red Cross Knight's victory over the
Dragon are the chief. These prominent images of light and darkness,
of forests and of tremendous struggles reinforce the sense of Book I's
epic quality. It is a sort of *Aeneid*, its hero bound to a high duty as well
as dangerous tasks and it illustrates the nature of the Christian's
dangerous journeying through the wood of life. In the dark recesses

of the forest or in its open glades and in the apparent splendour of castles and courts, false characters are always appearing, disguises always being uncovered. In the darkness as in the glitter the knight is only too likely to be deceived by false seeming.

Book II is much less sternly 'epic', much lighter in tone. The dominant images left in our imaginations are of less dire, more fanciful, journeying, danger and combats. Guyon's journey is a sort of Odyssey, and his encounters with variants of the odyssean temptations and especially of Circe substantiate its concern with man's need to subdue the passions by reason.

In Books III and IV the images are at once more romantic and more human. Looking back over the Book 'Of Love' I think we recall chiefly the many couples in it, among them Scudamour and Amoret, Timias and Belphebe, Marinell and Florimell; and as many 'triangles', Scudamour-Amoret-Busirane, Timias-Belphebe-Amoret, Marinell-Florimell-Satyrane, Paridell-Hellenore-Malbecco. Also prominent is a haunting succession of images of flight and pursuit, and the polarisation of great houses of sexual pleasure (Castle Joyous) and sexual enslavement (Busirane's House) and the Garden of Adonis, place of happy, generous and fruitful love. In Book III, too, we note a high incidence of examples of metamorphosis. Book IV has as its dominant *motifs* the opposition of Discord and Concord: jousts, tournaments and other combats on the one hand, and betrothals, reconciliations and marriage on the other, concluding with that great image of Concord, the marriage of Thames and Medway to which come all the waters and water-gods and nymphs of the world.

The clearest images in the last two books are the gigantic images of Disorder drawn in Book V and in Book VI the fleeting images of virtue and happiness in the pastoral world and the vision of grace on Mount Acidale. Almost as strong again is the image with which both books conclude, that of the Blatant Beast, hell-born, monstrous, the restless tormenting figure of Evil-at-large, still abroad in the world.

These are vague impressions, though they help to clarify each book's message. Not vague at all is Spenser's employment of some regularly repeated features. In every book, except, significantly, the pastoral Book VI, the hero or heroes visit or sojourn at a great house or castle. Such visits are common in medieval Romance, in medieval love allegory, in Elizabethan pageantry and spectacles, where they usually have a moral significance; even Ariosto provides obvious moral lessons in Atlante's magic castle of deceit and in

Logistilla's house, representing reason and virtue. (Tasso's action, being confined to an actual place, Jerusalem, and its environs, except for Rinaldo's truancy to Armida's isle, affords no scope for similar significant buildings.) Spenser reinforces the point of his argument in each book by temporarily arresting the quick-moving narrative while the Red Cross Knight encounters Pride and the other deadly sins at the House of Pride, falls victim to the pride of the flesh in Orgoglio's castle, and is then instructed in the ways of Holiness at the House of Temperance; while Sir Guyon encounters the personification of the golden mean at Medina's House and sojourns at the House of Temperance; while Britomart—not that she is tempted, in danger or needs to be instructed—is confronted with the shallow pleasures, latent sorrows and ultimate enslavement of sexual indulgence at Malecasta's and Busirane's houses. Further, the Castle of Venus with her temple in its island-gardens enshrines an ideal virtue and beauty; Radegund's 'unnatural' regimen presents a disordered world of female rule and male subjection, and Mercilla's Court clarifies the message —of love and mercy in judgement—of Britomart's earlier dream at the Temple of Isis. Spenser does not organise too precisely; there is no rigid scheme, the houses or castles are not regularly spaced in the sequence of books, and it is not possible to say that there is any 'type' of house or castle automatically endowed with good or bad properties. Yet there is enough of a scheme—most of the houses, castles or temples mentioned occur in Cantos 4, 7, 9, 10 or 11—for the reader to perceive a definite pattern which tells him of repeating emphases in the poem and of its essentially cyclic repeating unity.

In four of the books a similar repeating significance may be found in the lavish descriptions of gardens. In Book II the Bower of Bliss provides the only example (with the exception of the brief if vivid description of the hellish Garden of Prosperine in the same book) of a garden which is not a place of virtue, however beautiful it may appear. (C. S. Lewis long ago made clear beyond dispute the careful detail with which Spenser presented the Bower as a place superficially charming to all the senses but meretricious, artificial and bad—'filling his Bower of Bliss with sweetness showered upon sweetness and yet contriving that there should be something subtly wrong throughout'.* In contrast Spenser emphasises the natural in his depictions of the Garden of Adonis in Book III, and, as the place where stands the Temple of Venus, in Book IV. Book VI. which has no symbolic

* *The Allegory of Love*, Oxford 1936, pp. 324ff.

or allegorical house or castle, has instead, in the depiction of the pastoral world and of the grassy Acidalian mount where the Graces dance, two splendid natural 'gardens' which symbolise the ordered virtuous perfection which God intended for his world.

Bowers, arbours and pavilions exist in all these gardens. In Book II Cymochles is first seen in the arbour 'framed of wanton Ivie' and— 'art striving to compaire With Nature'—garnished all within by flowers which 'bring out bounteous smels, and painted colours shew' (II. 5. 29). Phaedria's gondola is

> . . . bedecked trim
> With boughes and arbours woven cunningly,
> That like a little forest seemed outwardly,   (II. 6. 2)

a very artificial boat. Prosperine's 'thicke Arber' is set next to the tree of golden fruit but in a garden in which the herbs and fruits are all 'direfull deadly blacke with leafe and bloom' (II. 7. 5). The climax of these artificial and wanton bowers—bowers of wantonness—is the arbour-like gate to Acrasia's bower.

> With boughes and braunches, which did broad dilate
> Their clasping armes, in wanton wreathings intricate.   (II. 12. 53)

Very different are the woods on Mount Acidale

> In which all trees of honour stately stood
> And did all winter as in sommer bud,
> Spredding pavilions for the birds to bowre,   (VI. 10. 6)

and the natural arbour of Nature herself, not fashioned by craftsmen

> But th'Earth herself, of her owne motion,
> Out of her fruitfull bosome made to growe
> Most dainty trees . . .   (VII. 7. 8)

The correspondences, which are close enough for similarities to be recognised and at the same time to emphasise the differences between places of good and of bad resort, extend to the nearby streams. 'Fast beside' Cymochles's bower, a stream trickles softly down with 'murmuring wave', making a sound

> To lull him soft sleepe, that by it lay,   (II. 5. 30)

fit place for the idle wanton Cymochles. Near the Bower of Bliss is a
lavishly decorated fountain 'overwrought' . . . with 'shapes of naked
boyes', and its 'silver flood' grows into a little lake paved with jasper.
At the Bower itself the water musically falls with 'base murmure';
the pun—a common Spenserian device—is emphatically pejorative.
But below the woods of Mount Acidale

> . . . a gentle flud
> His silver waves did softly tumble downe,
> Unmard with ragged mosse or filthy mud;
> Ne mote wylde beastes, ne mote the ruder clowne
> Thereto approch, ne filth mote therein drowne:
> But Nymphes and Faeries by the bancks did sit,
> In the woods shade, which did the waters crowne,
> Keeping all noysome things away from it,
> And to the waters fall tuning their accents fit.   (VI. 10. 7)

The happy reminiscence of one of the 'Epigrams' from his earliest
work, the translation of Marot's version of Petrarch's *canzone*, must
have pleased him to make. It confirms one's view of Spenser as the
most consistent and homogeneous of poets, constant always to his
preoccupations, subject-matter and images. In the original 'epigram'
(No. 4) the vision of Muses and Nymphs sweetly in accord tuning

> . . . their voice
> Unto the gentle sounding of the waters fall

is suddenly wiped out:

> I sawe (alas!) the gaping earth devoure
> The Spring, the place, and all cleane out of sight.
> Which yet agreves my heart even to this houre.

The disappearance of the Graces and their dancing attendants more
powerfully and more poignantly makes the same point about the
vulnerability of virtue. The history of Spenser's development from
simple allegories to complex and potent symbolism is summed up in
this connexion between the fourth epigram of *A Theatre* and Book VI
of *The Faerie Queene*.

At the houses, castles and sometimes in the gardens there are often
masques, dances or processions: in Book I the procession of the seven
deadly sins at the House of Pride; in Book III the procession and the
masque at the House of Busirane; in Book IV the procession of the
rivers, seas, water gods and sea-nymphs at the marriage of the Thames
and the Medway; in Book VI the dance of the Graces, that great sym-

bol of ordered virtue, and in the Mutabilitie Cantos the procession
of the seasons, months, days and hours. (Book V, the book of Disorder
has no place for any dance or procession; nor has Book II, in which
the knight-hero has to resist the unruly and disordered passions to
which man is subject; but in the other books the ordered power of
virtue or the dreadful power of vice is often symbolised in terms of
dance or procession.)

All of these recurring *motifs* help to clarify the poet's moral concerns,
give abstract power to his exploration of them, and enable him to
provide much pleasing imaginative detail. At the same time they are
mostly conventional elements in epic and Romance literature: *locus
amoenus* or pleasance, *hortus conclusus*, or secluded garden, castle, court
and palace. Yet in many cases they give also an effect of real contemporary life; real houses, real courts and courtly ritual, real gardens.
They also emphasise again the recurring cyclic structure and purpose
of *The Faerie Queene*, and of course they strengthen the sense of the
poem's unity: they are like the 'bonders' used in dry-stone walls,
great stones placed at irregular intervals and running through the
entire thickness of the wall.

Another recurring factor in the poem is reference to Ireland or
reminiscence of it. This extends from the slightest allusion or comparison, either generalised, like the cloud of gnats molesting a shepherd
(I. 1. 23) or, specifically placed, the swarm of gnats at the 'fennes of
Allan' (II. 9. 16), to descriptions, for example, of the Red Cross Knight's
wasted appearance (I. 8. 41) or of the 'vile caytive wretches' encountered
outside Alma's castle (II. 9. 13–17) which seem to echo passages from
Spenser's own prose *View of the Present State of Ireland*. There are
also many topographical references to and extended treatment of Irish
matters and places in Book V and in the Mutabilitie Cantos. As I have
already shown (Chapter 7) Irena's land is Ireland and its disorder,
violence and cruelty Irish; many a fierce skirmish, siege, battle and
ambush in Book V, together with the hatred, treachery and guile so
often presented derives from Spenser's real-life experiences in that
'salvage Island'. And in the Mutabilitie Cantos he charmingly makes a
new myth—a second, for there is one in 'Colin Clouts Come Home
Again'— out of two Irish rivers near his estate of Kilcolman, and places
the assembly of the gods and the great debate between Nature and
the goddess Mutabilitie on the neighbouring Arlo Hill.

There are also a number of ideas, beliefs or preoccupations which
constantly recur throughout the poem, and add their contribution to

the unmistakable sense of its unity in diversity. Chief among these
are the Aristotelian notion of the golden mean, most prominently
deployed in Book II 'Of Temperaunce'; the conflict of Reason and
Passion, and the dissonance between appearance and reality, which
dominate Books II and I respectively, concerned as they are with
self-discipline and with man's need of truth; the contrast between
courtliness which often means falsehood, corruption and insincerity
and the simple virtuous ways of pastoral, shown in the lavish depictions of evil courts such as Pride's or Malecasta's and in the virtues
of simple folk, unsophisticated knights like Sir Satyrane and Timias,
and the Fauns and the Lion which gently tend Una, and chiefly of
course in the self-contained pastoral world in Book VI.

An even stronger bond is the patriotic impulse which permeates the
whole poem. Every time Arthur appears (once in each book); in the
three books in which Britomart, that virtuous British lady-knight,
is the dominant figure; whenever Belphebe—type of 'the most
excellent and glorious person of our soveraine the Queene'—appears;
and in many sidelong references to Gloriana (Elizabeth) or her court
or 'her kingdome in Faery land' and to England's fame, we are
reminded of it. From time to time there are more extended references,
especially when—surprisingly enough in view of his character—
Paridell at dinner in Malbecco's house (III. 9. 33ff.) tells of his descent
from Paris and prompts Britomart to amplify the Trojan connexion
with Britain and to prophesy the greater future glory of Troyno-
vant (new Troy). Britomart's lineage and future progeny are also
recounted by Merlin in Book III, Canto 3. A greater, and to modern
readers somewhat tedious, account of lineage and royal descent is
given in Book II, Canto 10, which is devoted to the '*chronicle of Briton
Kings*' and the '*rolls of Elfin emperours till time of Gloriane*' which
Arthur and Guyon respectively read in the chamber of Memory in
Alma's castle. But the whole Arthurian background of the poem, its
continuous allusions to English contemporary historical events and
personages, and especially Book I with its constant reference to the
Church of England in its unending war with Catholicism, and Book
V with its continual pointing at the political and military menace of
the Catholic powers in Europe, emphasise Spenser's desire—and his
powerfully successful achievement of it—to make his great poem
not only an enchanting romatic narrative, a work of moral instruction,
and an exploration of human motive, character and behaviour, but
also a profoundly national epic.

Most pervasive of all, in the end, is Spenser's preoccupation with mutability. Nearly all of his writing contains this, a commonplace of Christian thinkers and writers, but *The Faerie Queene* shows increasingly powerful expression of it. It is this element which is chiefly responsible for the grandeur of *The Faerie Queene* as a philosophical and religious poem, as well as a romantic epic and an allegory. While the early books show the achieving of their quests by the Red Cross Knight and Sir Guyon, the Dragon slain and Acrasia's Bower of Bliss destroyed, increasingly Spenser depicts Faerie land as the world since the Fall, a world governed by imperfection, sin and death. If he had written other books he could not have shown, as he did in the early books, the achievement of ideals in the Faerie world. The flux of the world, its imperfectability, its corruption and decay, the transitoriness of human life and the ultimate inadequacy of human endeavours are aspects of life of which Spenser was deeply conscious. They presented him with the great dilemma of faith, which always confronts the Christian writer who enjoys and loves life: how to reconcile the alluring variousness of the mortal world with its imperfection and instability. Chaucer made several attempts to untease the dilemma: in *The Parlement of Foules* in which he dodged the issue by inventing or 'incorporating' the parliament; and in the *contemptus mundi* of the palinode to *Troilus and Criseyde*. Spenser triumphantly made use of Chaucer's Nature and Chaucer's *débat* in the Mutabilitie Cantos, with which the poem concludes. All the paradoxes and antitheses which the poem rehearses, the perfect and the imperfect, the real and the illusory, the ideal and the actual, good and evil, fertility and sterility, sophistication and innocence, happiness and misery, are resolved in Nature's brief reply to Mutabilitie. But any element of *contemptus mundi* is largely overborne by Spenser's understanding, which is the theme of the Mutabilitie Cantos, that change is not only the sad human consequence of the Fall but that some change is an essential part of God's purpose for that fallen world. Nature herself, God's vicar in Chaucer's 'Foules' Parley', with her changing seasons and the pattern of birth, growth, death and renewal of her creatures whether animal or vegetable, stands for the very principle.

This links the Mutabilitie Cantos closely with the ideas of perpetual renewal and divinely ordained change presented in the account of the Garden of Adonis, especially in Book III, Canto 6. In Book V Spenser again rehearsed the idea of the rightness of perpetual change, *eterne in mutabilitee*, in Artegall's reply to the egalitarianising giant:

F

> What though the sea with waves continuall
> Doe eate the earth, it is no more at all:
> Ne is the earth the lesse, or loseth ought,
> For whatsoever from one place doth fall,
> Is with the tide unto an other brought:
> For there is nothing lost, that may be found, if sought.
>
> Likewise the earth is not augmented more,
> By all that dying into it doe fade.
> For of the earth they formed were of yore.
> How ever gay their blossom or their blade
> Doe flourish now, they into dust shall vade.
> What wrong then is it, if that when they die,
> They turne to that, whereof they first were made?   (V. 2. 39–40)

The puzzling series of appearances of Marinell and Florimell in Books III, IV and V has also been seen* as part of Spenser's expression of the same belief in 'the rich productive strength of nature' and in change as 'only an expression of permanence . . . Florimell lives through the individual destruction inherent in the circular motion of generation and corruption' to be reborn in what seems, every year, a miracle. In Books III and IV, apart from the great central sequence of the Garden of Adonis, there is also much stress on metamorphosis. Spenser loved and used Ovid greatly, and knew very well that although all his metamorphoses present change, they also imply permanence: it is usually to escape corruption or change that his nymphs, youths and godlings undergo metamorphosis, and so for ever preserve love, honour or chastity. Metamorphosis in itself contains the idea of 'eterne in mutabilitie' and expresses or implies that the change is in the direction of perfection. In these books, of love and concord, the poet begins his asseveration of his belief in love as the force in human affairs which alone can counter change, decay and death. The love in these books is the proper virtuous love which leads to marriage and generation, and as the poem continues Spenser extends its realm from the particular world of individual knights and ladies in Faerie land to human society in general. In Books V and VI, if God's love still governed the world, perfect Order, perfect Justice and that perfect generous Love which is God's 'courtesy', would prevail, instead of the disorder, injustice, cruelty and oppression which are rampant. But, as his poem is cyclical in structure and message, so he shows that the

* Kathleen Williams, Spenser's 'Faerie Queen', The World of Glass, London 1966, pp. 138ff.

world of humans which provides his subject-matter and inspiration, is also cyclical, bound to a cycle of change and repetition, but revolving against the great back-cloth of God's unchangingness. The poet ends with an expression of his loathing for life's mutability and of his desire for 'stedfast rest of all things', his longing for the time when

> . . . all shall rest eternally
> With him that is the God of Sabbaoth hight.

There is much in the claim of S. P. Zitner that 'the rejection of "this state of life so fickle" is not made because change is evil, but because mutability—sad or delightful—is merely a process, inferior to the state that will be revealed at "the great Sabaoth's sight"' and that 'Change is not random or erratic, but directed by the desire of all things to realise their particular perfections'.* This is why Mutabilitie's beauty—as well as her power—is emphasised so strongly (VII. 6. 28–31).

None of these elements in the poem is used simply as a device to achieve unity. Each is integral to the poet's thinking about the world, and each exists because of its intellectual and imaginative power over Spenser. Yet they all in fact contribute greatly to our sense of the poem's order and of its essential cyclical unity.

Spenser engages, persuades, and ultimately convinces, the reader by a number of techniques and skills, that Faerie land exists, and represents the real world of humanity *sub specie aeternitatis*, and that the poet's preoccupations are preoccupations of the utmost consequence to us all. Or so I think. There are those who are inimical to Romance, slightingly dismissing it as escapist or unreal. There are others for whom Spenser's firm basis of belief not only does not exist for themselves but is thought to be naive or nonsensical in anyone else. In a post-Christian post-Freudian world, Christian concerns and Platonic ideals may be dismissed as antiquated superstition no longer meeting social or spiritual need, or as paternalistic structures no longer necessary to organise or bolster human spiritual inadequacy. Yet when we look again at what Spenser's chief concerns are, we find them as vitally relevant to human happiness and to spiritual health and need as ever they were. If we leave aside the specific Christian element, we find that Spenser's concerns in *The Faerie Queene* are with the need to distinguish true from false (Book I), the need for self-control (Book II), the importance of truth, loyalty, love, concern,

---

* Ed., *The Mutabilitie Cantos*, London 1968, p. 20.

unselfishness and compassion, whether in private and personal be-
behaviour (Books III and IV) or in society as a whole (Books V and
VI). In a materialistic, unsettled, greedy, dissatisfied and sensation-
seeking period, the anguishes of which are aggravated by population
explosion, the mass media and the breakdown of many traditional
restraints—and we live in such a period in the West—there is already
some sort of move backward, away from materialism and greed, even
though it may only so far have shown itself in 'flower-people', in
'hippy' ideals, 'hippy' communes, a growth of interest in meditation
and mysticism, and slogans of the kind 'make love not war'. However
minor or recherché such things may be and however much part of
only a minority culture, they have in them elements Spenser would
recognise and approve: some of the ideals which lie behind pastoralism,
notably simple living, love and compassion.

Even on matters in which social change in the nearly four centuries
since *The Faerie Queene* was written would seem particularly to have
made Spenser irrelevant, his wisdom is timeless. To venture briefly
on to the subject of sex, for example. Although Spenser has been
charged with a puritanical attitude to sex, and with it accused of a
perverted and unhealthy interest in sex and bodily functions, the
swiftest reading of passages describing Una's love for the Red Cross
Knight, or Britomart's for Artegall, or Calidore's for Pastorella,
will show how groundless such a view is. Unquestionably he stands
for loving virtuous sexuality: in the Garden of Adonis 'franckly each
paramour his leman knowes'. Passion in love he never denies. What
concerns him as a moralist is the quality and the motivation of sexuality.
If it is impelled by love, he celebrates it, even if, like Amoret's for
Scudamour, the possibility of its destructiveness is acknowledged
(and healed). The passionate lovelonging of Britomart is elaborated
in great detail. The shy approaches to love-awareness in Timias and
Belphebe are presented with clear sympathy. But the selfish, self-
advancing or simply itching desires of Duessa, Acrasia, Malecasta,
Paridell, Hellenore, who seek only sexual gratification and whose
sexual satisfactions are brief and temporary, are vividly shown: they
are as unsatisfying and ultimately degrading as they are shallowly
compulsive. The animal associations of their couplings clearly indicate
the distinction between the highest potential and the lowest (animal)
actuality in human sexual relations. Nor does Spenser accept the
practice of sex for its own sake, now increasingly prescribed by our
society for its members. This is because he could not or would not

dissociate sexual congress, which involves the actual and symbolic giving and receiving of another's body, from ideas of loving generosity of which the Graces, ever giving and ever receiving gifts, are the symbolic presentation, and God's loving generosity (courtesy) the ultimate transcendent model. Sex for its own sake, however enjoyable (Spenser does indeed show this among the lords and ladies at Castle Joyous where '*Cupid* still emongst them kindled lustfull fires'), like the appeasing of any other hunger or like any other merely physical pleasure, is a reduced and minor activity, because it does not involve the whole of a person but simply appeases a part. What Spenser always seeks and celebrates is the enhancing, the deepening, the hallowing of human activities, not their reduction to motor actions, however pleasurable. Virtuous happiness, not pleasure, is what he prescribes and celebrates.

He draws the contrasts between different kinds of sexual response and activity, from the lowest to the highest, with clarifying power. Hellenore having eloped with her seducer Paridell has been abandoned by him ('He nould be clogd') and has fallen in happily with a troop of satyrs. Her old husband Malbecco finds her

> Embraced of a *Satyre* rough and rude,
> Who all the night did minde his joyous play:
> Nine times he heard him come aloft ere day,
> That all his hart with gealosie did swell;
> But yet that nights ensample did bewray[1],
> That not for nought his wife them loved so well,
> When one so oft a night did ring his matins bell.   (III. 10. 48)

Florimell, fleeing from the desires of the witch's son and from the lustful beast 'that feeds on womens flesh, as others feede on gras', takes refuge in a boat, only to find that her beauty arouses the lust of the fisherman:

> Beastly he threw her downe, ne car'd to spill
> Her garments gay with scales of fish, that all did fill.
>
> .   .   .
>
> She struggled strongly both with foote and hand,
> To save her honor from that villaine vilde,
>
> .   .   .
>
> Ruffled and fowly raid with filthy soyle,
> And blubbered face with teares of her faire eyes:
> Her heart nigh broken was with weary toyle,
> To save her selfe from that outrageous spoyle.   (III. 8. 26, 27, 32)

[1] *bewray* reveal

The famous description of Acrasia with her exhausted young lover Verdant in the Bower of Bliss is notably pointed by Spenser's carefully emotive description:

> Upon a bed of Roses she was layd,
>   As faint through heat, or dight to pleasant sin,
>   And was arayd, or rather disarayd,
>   All in a vele of silke and silver thin,
>   That hid no whit her alablaster skin,
>   But rather shewd more white, if more might bee:
>
> .   .   .
>
> Her snowy brest was bare to ready spoyle
>   Of hungry eies, which n'ote therewith be fild,
>   And yet through languour of her late sweet toyle,
>   Few drops, more cleare then nectar, forth distild,
>   That like pure Orient perles adowne it trild,
>   And her faire eyes sweet smyling in delight,
>   Moystened their fierie beames, with which she thrild
>   Fraile harts, yet quenched not; like starry light,
> Which, sparckling on the silent waves, does seeme more bright.
>
> The young man, sleeping by her, seemd to be
>   Some goodly swayne of honorable place,
>   That certes it great pittie was to see
>   Him his nobilitie so foule deface:
>
> .   .   .
>
> His warlike armes, the idle instruments
>   Of sleeping praise, were hong upon a tree,
>   And his brave shield, full of old moniments,
>   Was fowly ra'st[1], that none the signes might see;
>   Ne for them, ne for honour, cared hee,
>   Ne ought that did to his advauncement tend,
>   But in lewd loves, and wastfull luxuree,
>   His dayes, his goods, his bodie he did spend:
> O horrible enchantment, that him so did blend.   (II. 12. 77ff.)

In the original (1590) conclusion of Book III, Scudamour was immediately re-united, after her rescue by Britomart from Busirane's spell, with Amoret:

> . . . that most on earth him joyd,
>   His dearest love, the comfort of his dayes,
>   Whose too long absence him had sore annoyd,
>   And wearied his life with dull delayes:
>
> .   .   .

[1] *ra'st* erased

Lightly he clipt her twixt his armes twaine,
   And streightly did embrace her body bright,
   Her body, late the prison of sad paine,
   Now the sweet lodge of love and deare delight:
   But she faire lady overcommen quight
   Of huge affection, did in pleasure melt,
   And in sweete ravishment pourd out her spright:
   No word they spake, nor earthly thing they felt,
But like two senceless stocks in long embracement dwelt.

Had ye them seene, ye would have surely thought,
   That they had beene that faire *Hermaphrodite*,
   Which that rich *Romane* of white marble wrought,
   And in his costly bath caused to bee site:
   So seemd those two, as growne together quite,
   That *Britomart*, halfe envying their blesse,
   Was much empassiond in her gentle sprite,
   And to her selfe oft wisht like happinesse:
In vaine she wisht, that fate n'ould let her yet possesse.

Una, her long adventuring concluded by the Red Cross Knight's defeat of the dragon and freeing of her parents, is at last betrothed to him:

Thrise happy man the knight himselfe did hold,
   Possessed of his ladies hart and hand,
   And ever, when his eye did her behold,
His heart did seeme to melt in pleasures manifold.

Her joyous presence and sweet company
   In full content he there did long enjoy,
   Ne wicked envie, ne vile gealosy,
   His deare delights were able to annoy:
   Yet swimming in that sea of blisfull joy,
   He naught forgot, how he whilome had sworne

      .   .   .

Unto his Farie Queene back to returne:
The which he shortly did, and *Una* left to mourne.   (I. 12. 40–1)

The animal imagery—and the contemptuous comedy—of the scene of Hellenore's night with the satyr: the broken diction, strong alliteration and onomatopoeia, and the powerful picture of beauty spoiled in the scene of Florimell's struggle to avoid rape; the languorous metre and the piling up of pejorative words (*faint, sin, disarayd, spoyle, hungry, languour, toyle, ydle, fowly, lewd loves, wastfull, luxuree, horrible, enchantment*) in the Bower of Bliss, are in marked contrast with the feeling of the last two passages. In these the serenity of pace and the descriptions and images (*her body bright, the sweet lodge of love and deare delight, long embracement, blisse, happinesse, gentle sprite,* melting happiness, *joyous presence, sweet company, deare delights, blisful joy*) proclaim virtuous love and happy union and fruition.

There is nothing original or unusual about Spenser's method here. In choosing appropriate epithets, images and metaphors, as well as significant metre and diction, and in using alliteration and onomatopoeia Spenser adhered to the obvious requirements of decorum and to elementary poetic practice. What is unusual is the degree of emphasis and the amount of repetition and hyperbole. A few more examples of his practice may be shown.

In Book I, Canto 1 the Red Cross Knight enters Error's den and sees by the little light 'much like a shade' made by his glistening armour the ugly monster.

> Halfe like a serpent horribly displaide,
> But th'other halfe did womans shape retaine,
> Most lothsom, filthie, foule, and full of vile disdaine.
>
> And as she lay upon the durtie ground,
> Her huge long taile her den all overspred,
> Yet was in knots and many boughtes[1] upwound,
> Pointed with mortall sting. Of her there bred
> A thousand young ones, which she dayly fed,
> Sucking upon her poisonous dugs, eachone
> Of sundry shapes, yet all ill favored:
> Soone as that uncouth[2] light upon them shone,
> Into her mouth they crept, and suddain all were gone.

The Red Cross Knight gives her a mighty cut with his sword:

> Much daunted with that dint, her sence was dazd,
> Yet kindling rage, her selfe she gathered round,
> And all attonce her beastly body raizd
> With doubled forces high above the ground:
> Tho wrapping up her wrethed sterne arownd,
> Lept fierce upon his shield, and her huge traine
> All suddenly about his body wound,
> That hand or foot to stirre he strove in vaine.:
> God helpe the man so wrapt in *Errours* endlesse traine.

But the knight

[1] *boughtes* bonds   [2] *uncouth* strange

> . . . grypt her gorge with so great paine,
> That soone to loose her wicked bands did her constraine.

> Therewith she spewd out of her filthy maw
>   A floud of poyson horrible and blacke,
>   Full of great lumpes of flesh and gobbets[1] raw,
>   Which stunck so vildly[2], that it forst him slacke
>   His grasping hold, and from her turne him backe:
>   Her vomit full of bookes and papers was,
>   With loathly frogs and toades, which eyes did lacke,
>   And creeping sought way in the weedy gras:
> Her filthy parbreake[3] all the place defiled has.
>   (I. 1. 14, 15, 18, 19, 20)

The extracts are characteristic of Spenser's methods, often criticised for their hyperbole, repetition and over-insistent alliteration and onomatopoeia. By the austerest standards this might be a just complaint. Yet to condemn this constant practice of Spenser's is to overlook the cumulative effect he achieves. He forces the reader to see and feel only what he intends. He will not let him think of anything else or admit any more complex or ambiguous metaphoric associations. We have here to see, to feel almost, to fear, smell and recoil from a hideous monster, half-serpent, half-woman, *lothsom, filthie, foule, vile* with *poisonous dugs, beastly, filthie*. We must remember that one of Spenser's necessary tasks in this moral allegorical epic Romance was to make us *feel.** The chief way in which he succeeds, so that we feel the radiance of virtue and the vileness of evil, is by hyperbole and repetition, even, some think, to excess.

Critics have also pointed to the over-employment of weak epithets, e.g., *durtie* ground, *beastly* bodie, *huge* traine, *loathly* frogs, *filthie* parbreake. In a poem of this length, about 35,000 lines, indeed in any long narrative poem, especially one deliberately set in the epic tradition with its constant implication or implicit memory of oral delivery, and with its almost obligatory use of stock epithets, it would be absurd to expect every epithet to be lustrous with intense meaning. And in Spenser's capacious scope and leisurely flow the repeated use of obvious epithets not only makes an impressive aggregate of emotive meaning but allows the really significant epithets or descriptions to emerge with special force. The stock epithets keep the mood going

---

[1] *gobbets* lumps of flesh   [2] *vildly* vilely   [3] *parbreake* vomit
* See p. 110.

like an orchestral continuo, and the solo instruments sound above it
with heightened effect. In these extracts this is true of the muted
unemphatic

> A little glooming light, much like a shade,

the 'poisonous dugs' the straightforward

> Into her mouth they crept, and suddain all were gone,

the 'floud of poyson horrible and black' that spews forth, and the
corroborative detail (even the grass is corrupted) of 'the weedy
gras'.

I think that Spenser weakened his achieved imaginative effect by
the detail of the beast's vomit being 'full of bookes and papers'.
As the monster Error disgorges a mass of Catholic propaganda and
erroneous theology, she becomes, momentarily, only an allegorical
representation. A few lines before this Spenser had more subtly
brought the allegorical significance of this in other respects acceptably
conventional epic or Romance monster to our attention, when, describing how she had wreathed her huge long tail around the knight
so that 'hand or foot to stirr he strove in vaine', he commented in the
alexandrine—the first of many authorial moralisings in the poem—

> God helpe the man so wrapt in *Errours* endlesse traine,

thus making the Romance monster briefly a moral abstraction and
at the same instant vividly actualising the moral observation. Spenser
is not always so explicit as in these two examples, but this is early in
the poem, only eighteen or so stanzas from the opening, and he must
make sure the reader does not miss the moral signification or the
allegorical methods he is going to employ. Before long he has no need
to be so explicit, once he can be sure that the reader perceives the
moral and often allegorical significance carried by the romantic
narrative. In any case, here he swiftly re-imposes his supremacy in
imaginative narrative, as the frogs and toads 'which eyes did lacke'
vomited forth with the books and papers, seek their way in the weedy
and soiled grass, and with the monster's 'cursed spawne of serpents
small' swarm about the knight's legs. So vividly is it done that the
reader instinctively shrinks from the loathsomeness of it.

Immediately Spenser gives relief, moving into a pastoral simile:

> As gentle Shepheard in sweete even-tide,
> When ruddy *Phoebus* gins to welke[1] in west,
> High on an hill, his flocke to vewen wide,
> Markes which doe byte their hasty supper best.   (I. 1. 23)

It is another obvious device, but none the less necessary or effective. Throughout the poem, like some great symphonist, the poet is thinking about balance and variety and never allows a scene or a mood too long a dominance but achieves at the right point a switch of atmosphere or feeling, or at the least, as in the example quoted, a momentary let-up. (It is fair to acknowledge that sometimes he allows an instructive sequence, for example, the House of Alma and the listed chronicles of Briton and Elfin Knights at Alma's house, too long a run.)

Contrast of another kind, he uses as a linking device as well as to make a moral point. At the end of Canto 2 and at the beginning of Canto 3 in Book I, he gives us an image of a lady lying on the ground. In Canto 2 it is Duessa (pretending to be Fidessa) who has swooned 'with feare' at hearing Fradubio's (unknowing) denunciation of her, and who 'seeming dead' with 'eyelids blew, And dimmed sight, with pale and deadly hew' has aroused all the Red Cross Knight's (misguided) tenderness. Immediately afterwards Spenser draws a picture of Una, deserted by the Red Cross Knight:

> ... on the grasse her daintie limbes did lay
> In secret shadow, far from all mens sight;
> From her faire head her fillet[2] she undight[3],
> And laid her stole aside. Her angels face
> As the great eye of heaven shyned bright,
> And made a sunshine in the shadie place.

It is a good example of Spenser's subtle power, in an effective romantic narrative, of drawing a moral conclusion and directing the reader's attention to it; here, by the association and contrast of the dim, pale and deadly-hued false enchantress with the sunshiny beauty of the virtuous Una.

If in these examples Spenser used contrast-linking for thematic and visual effect, as well as for relief, he also uses profounder kinds of linking. Book II affords a good example of his powers in this essential aspect of technique that is little commented upon. Near the end of

---

[1] *welke* fade   [2] *fillet* headband   [3] *undight* unfastened

Canto 6 (stanza 47), after we have seen Pyrochles burning with
'implacable fire', an old man comes. He is quickly identified as Archimago. He eventually heals the burning pains inflicted on Pyrochles by
Furor. There seems no particular reason why Archimago should
re-enter the story at this point, though his magical powers are used in
the healing. But as the narrative develops it becomes apparent that
Spenser brings in Archimago here to prepare us for the underworld
scene—the Mammon sequence—that follows. This is also the reason
for the emphatic references in stanzas 49 and 50 to the 'hellish furie'
which had seized Pyrochles, in the form of internal flames caused by
Furor, 'cruell feend of hell', whose 'infernall brond' has caused a
wound that burns twice as sorely as 'flaming *Phlegeton*' burns the
damned ghosts in Hell. These references to Hell, after the Ariostan
episode of Guyon's brief sojourn with Phaedria and contest with
Cymochles—not momentous or dire; she is a charming, loose,
immodest girl whom he quickly finds tedious in her shallowness and
empty mirth—prepare the reader for the great deepening of seriousness
in the succeeding scene of Guyon's encounter with Mammon and
his descent to the underworld.

The change of tone and mood is soon established. At the beginning
of the next Canto (Canto 7, stanza 3) Sir Guyon comes to a gloomy
glade which like the Wandering Wood of Book I is so thickly over-
grown as to be cut off 'from heavens light'. That is no euphemism;
it is indeed cut off from the light of heaven. Here he finds sitting

> . . . in secret shade
> An uncouth, salvage, and uncivile wight,
> Of griesly hew, and fowle ill favour'd sight;
> His face with smoke was tand, and eyes were bleard,
> His head and beard with sout were ill bedight,
> His cole-blacke hands did seeme to have beene seard
> In smithes fire-spitting forge, and nayles like clawes appeard.
>
> His yron coate all overgrowne with rust,
>   Was underneath enveloped with gold,
>   Whose glistring glosse darkned with filthy dust,
>   Well yet appeard, to have beene of old
>   A work of rich entayle[1], and curious mould[2],
>   Woven with antickes[3] and wyld Imagery:
>   And in his lap a masse of coyne he told,
>   And turned upsidowne, to feede his eye
> And covetous desire with his huge threasury.

[1] *entayle* ornamentation   [2] *mould* shape   [3] *antickes* ancient designs

This is a subtle and temperate description, more varied and detailed than the earlier one of Error, but it is composed in exactly the same way, and with similar hyperbole, alliteration and onomatopoiea. Mammon is cleverly compounded of elements of Plutus, God of Wealth, Pluto, God of the Underworld, and Vulcan. A powerful suggestion of the symbolic is combined with a great sense of actuality: his face 'tand' with smoke; 'bleared' eyes; his sooty head and beard; the 'nayles like clawes'; and the rusted 'yron coate' its 'glistring glosse darkned with filthy dust'. Mammon comes before our eyes first as a dirty, bent all-too human smith; gradually we learn of the rusty but rich iron coat with fine chasing in gold, and the telling of his coins, and he appears as the quintessential miser: *miser* despite his riches, wretched hoarder of gold, furtive and fearful of its theft, a mean human wretch, before he reveals himself to Guyon as 'God of the World and worldlings . . . Great *Mammon*, greatest god below the skye'.

There are echoes throughout the episode of Guyon's three-day sojourn in the underworld of Christ's three days and nights in the heart of the earth (Matthew xii, 40), and of the temptation of Christ by Satan (Matthew vi, 24 and Luke iv), which deepen the gravity and significance of Guyon's sojourn. We can see why—and how success-fully—Spenser introduced the infernal subject with those premonitory chords at the end of the preceding canto: he rightly prepared the reader for a transition from an Ariostan romantic epic to deeply significant moral epic narrative.

I have shown how Spenser developed his portrait of the god Mam-mon slowly, not identifying him as a god until he had told us of his abjectness, foulness, meanness, fearfulness and misery. We are forced into dislike or hatred before we can be impressed. (Milton's Satan we are allowed to admire before we are required to hate.) This is Spenser's common practice. An earlier example was the presentation of Despair:

> That cursed man, low sitting on the ground,
> Musing full sadly in his sullein[1] mind;
> His griesic[2] lockes, long growen, and unbound,
> Disordered hong about his shoulders round,
> And hid his face; through which his hollow eyne
> Lookt deadly dull, and stared as astound.
> His raw-bone cheekes through penurie and pine[3],
> Were shronke into his jawes, as he did never dine. (I. 9. 35)

[1] *sullein* gloomy   [2] *griesie* grizzled or hideous   [3] *pine* starvation

Here a character first introduced to us as a 'cursed man' gradually evolved into a personification. In the course of the process, he attempted to lure the hero into suicide. Failing, he attempted the deed himself. And, as we leave him, this is what we see him doing, as he has done many times before, attempting to kill himself in despair, but in vain; he cannot die, and has become an animated emblem of Despair. A later example is to be found at the end of Book III, Canto 10. Malbecco, the jealous old husband of the faithless and immoral Hellenore, turns into an emblem of Jealousy, and is left for ever wakeful, for ever in pain, hating and hateful, deformed and ill yet unable to die, living on for ever miserably in a cave.

How characteristic it is of Spenser, to leave us with not so much a character as a personification, a picture, an allegorical presentation as in a Tudor pageant, show or morality-play. He employs this method because it is an exemplary teaching method. The identity of the vice or evil is not just presented to us. We meet the figure as an intriguing character in the narrative, and get to know and recognise him and his activity. Often we understand him as an abstraction or emblem before Spenser proclaims his identity, and so he is all the more persuasive because identifying him has been a mental process performed by ourselves. *We* have done a lot of the work. It is a superb justification, if justification were needed, of the use of the allegorical method in a romantic epic with a vital moral purpose. The allegory does not obtrude (as Ariosto's rare use of it does) for in the extra dimension in which Spenser works, a romance figure can easily 'zoom' into character close-up and 'fade' into moral emblem, a vivid episode end by 'freezing' into exemplary tableau. Such sequences refute the perennial complaint of critics about the incompatibility of Romance and allegory, fairyland and moralising, and also about Spenser's being 'remote from life'.

The emblematic—the encapsulating of a moralising idea or a moral lesson in a simplified image—contributes valuably to Spenser's didactic purpose. It is a peculiarly appropriate device, with its ancient lineage, long history and Christian sanction. Its recent recrudescence in the emblem-books of the sixteenth century, together with the Elizabethan passion for the emblematic shown in so many pageants, shows and moralities, encouraged the poet to use it in his moral, patriotic, Elizabethan romantic epic, itself a 'continued Allegory, or darke conceit'. A number of emblems from the emblem-books are released from the woodcut and set to move in his narrative. His chief quarry was

Alciati, numerous editions of whose *Emblemata* appeared from the first edition in 1532; there were nearly one hundred in several European languages before the end of the century. Spenser's detail of the elongated crane's neck of *Gula* (gluttony) in the procession of the deadly sins in the House of Pride (I. 4. 21) probably comes from Alciati's emblem of *Gula*, which itself was inspired by Aristotle's story* of a glutton who wished his neck as long as a crane's that he might the longer enjoy the taste of his food. Similarly, while his depiction of Duessa when she becomes Orgoglio's leman (I. 7. 16–17) has its obvious source in the words describing the Scarlet Whore of the Apocalypse in Revelation xii, 17, in his mind's eye as he wrote was Alciati's emblem, illustrating it, called *Ficta religio* (false religion). His *Occasion*, whose locks

> Grew all afore, and loosely hong unrold,
> But all behind was bald, and worne away,
> That none thereof could ever taken hold.   (II. 4. 4)

embodies a detail from Alciati's wood-cut, itself illustrating the proverbial saying about seizing opportunity 'by the forelock'. He is also in debt to Alciati for his Tantalus (II. 7. 58), his *Envie* (V. 12. 29ff.) whose 'dull eyes did seeme to looke askew', whose bones you might see through her cheeks, whose 'lips were like raw lether, pale and blew' and who feeds on 'her owne maw' and gnaws hungrily a venomous snake, and many others.† There is nothing elementary or superficial about Spenser's use of others' emblems: he wants to simplify and clarify big issues as much as he can, and this purpose the emblem —and allegory generally of course—notably serves. But this own 'emblems' are superb: Despair; Mammon; Ignaro (Ignorance) blind and slow, his head turned backwards on his neck (I. 8. 3ff.), who impedes Arthur in his search for the Red Cross Knight in Orgoglio's castle; Maleger the evil, sick leader of the besiegers of Alma's castle (in II. 11. 22); and many more. They function admirably on the moral plane, but they are also excellent characters in the narrative. Spenser is careful to humanise them as much as he can as he sets them moving. When Arthur urgently searches Orgoglio's castle and receives no answer to his calls,

* *Nicomachaean Ethics* iii, x.
† See Jane Aptekar, *Icons of Justice*, Columbia 1969, for a recent illuminating study of the iconography of Book V.

> At last with creeping crooked pace forth came
> An old old man, with beard as white as snow,
> That on a staffe his feeble steps did frame,
> And guide his wearie gate both too and fro;   (I. 8. 30)

but Ignaro is 'senceless' and 'doted' as well as blind, and answers
to every question 'he could not tell'. Our impatience grows with
Arthur's. And Maleger—surely the most un-picturable of all abstractions, this 'badly-diseased evil-doer', leader of the passions attacking
the soul—is vividly evoked in the simplest of similes drawn from
ordinary life: his 'looke' is 'pale and wan as ashes', his bodie 'leane and
meagre as a rake', his skin 'all withered like a dryed rooke'. They are
combined with skilful suggestions of the unearthly: his 'helmet light' is
'made of a dead man's skull'; he is large-limbed and broad-shouldered,
and yet

> ... of such subtile substance and unsound,
> That like a ghost he seem'd, whose grave-clothes were unbound.

It is a good example of Spenser's ability to conjure up an abstraction,
make clear its moral function and at the same time promote in us a
moral and emotional response to it, while successfully keeping our
interest in the romantic narrative.

This astonishing power of making the reader see and feel different
things at the same time in a character or episode is best shown in his
presentation of the Bower of Bliss. A brief comparison of Spenser's
depiction of Acrasia with Ariosto's Alcina and Tasso's of Armida,
which both inspired it, may serve to demonstrate his special power
in making actual. In *Orlando Furioso* (Book VII) the episode is brief.
Alcina accords a formal welcome to Ruggiero to her castle; she enter-
tains him to a sumptuous feast; he breathlessly waits in his chamber for
her to come to him; she comes secretly to his bed, and they couple
hastily. In *Gerusalemme Liberata* (Book XVI), from which Spenser
drew much detail for the Bower of Bliss sequence, the Armida episode
is equally courtly, though it takes place in a garden by a lake. In
neither case is there any suggestion of a wicked enchantresss, until
the conclusion of the episode, when Alcina is revealed in all her real
deformity (like Spenser's Duessa), and when Armida, after Rinaldo
has come to his senses and departed, destroys her palace (as Britomart
destroyed Busirane's palace). Although in these episodes both Ariosto
and Tasso had a moralising intention, they described the seduction
neutrally from a secret onlooker's viewpoint. They pointed the moral

separately after the conclusion of the episode. Characteristically, Spenser intensified the emotional force, by describing and moralising at one and the same time. (In any case, he makes the episode the climax of his book; in Ariosto and Tasso it is but an episode in a larger framework.) Spenser was frankly concerned to move his readers to realise in their own senses the power of the temptation, and so the possibility of their own succumbing to such temptation. We are required to judge at the same time as we are incited to desire Acrasia. Spenser knows, with the classical writers and the Renaissance emblematists and mythographers, that Circe, ancestress of Acrasia and her Italian siblings, is the type of self-indulgence and sensuality, able to make men, despite their angelic potentialities, into lusting beasts. In Ariosto and Tasso the enchantress is distanced and prettified as in a tapestry, and described predominantly in visual terms. She is attractive to the sight, but not arousing; the descriptions are too formal for that. We see her beauty but we do not feel its power. Spenser, brilliantly paradoxical in this, makes Acrasia very real: she sweats and sighs and dotes and devours. But her physical allure is not so much visual and aesthetic as sensual. So Spenser makes a powerful double appeal to the reader. His animal senses (already titillated, as Guyon's, by the two provocative girls at the edge of the little lake displaying their naked charms) are aroused and respond to her sexuality, while his moral sense is alerted and must (and does) reject her animal appeal.

Perhaps above all it is Spenser's vividness that is his greatest poetic virtue. Its achievement is due partly to the exaggeration and repetition of image and sound I have already referred to; partly to his use of all the senses, of touch, taste and smell as well as of sight and hearing of which good examples are the description of the Dragon (I. 11. 8), and of Duessa stripped naked (I. 8. 46ff).

But there are many other contributory factors. His similes are usually simple. He always keeps the reader in close touch with the things of ordinary life, and is careful to include the minutest detail—blood running from spurs down a horse's sides; a knight walking slowly because of the weight of his armour; a horse trampling 'dockes' or biting his 'yron rowels into frothy fome'; 'the salt brine' springing out of the 'billowes' as a ferryman rows; the shallow sea discoloured and the waves checked thus betraying the existence of a quicksand; Night's horses softly *swim* away through the black sky; the satyrs, like goats, have 'backward bent knees' and cannot kneel to worship Una as they would have wished. Obviously the poet is thinking hard and visualising clearly. It is vital for his purpose that he should make Faerie land, and all its people and actions, totally convincing.

In addition to exact detail of the *minutiae* of ordinary life, he gives accounts of ordinary human response to situations with insight, sympathy and humour. Morpheus the God of Sleep—and here Spenser is indebted to his master Chaucer—naturally sleeps very soundly. The messenger rudely thrusts and pushes to wake him up

> Whereat he gan to stretch . . .
>
> .   .   .
>
> As one then in a dreame, whose dryer braine
> Is tost with troublous sights and fancies weake,
> He mumbled soft, but would not all his silence breake. (1. 1. 42)

and falls heavily asleep again the moment the messenger's mission is completed. After the Dragon has been slain, the ordinary folk of the castle emerge to gaze and gloat. Some are fearful, some now bold and knowing. One mother, out of fear, angrily rebukes her foolhardy child, for venturing too near the Dragon's body in case there is yet some lingering life (I. 12. 11). Who ever conveyed a lover's tormented anxious longing as well as Spenser in his account of Britomart's reactions when she hears that Artegall is 'in womans bondage'?

> Sometime she feared, least some hard mishap
>   Had him misfalne in his adventurous quest;
>   Sometime least his false foe did him entrap
>   In traytrous traine, or had unwares opprest:
>   But most she did her troubled mynd molest,
>   And secretly afflict with jealous feare,
>   Least some new love had him from her possest;
>   Yet loth she was, since she no ill did heare,
> To thinke of him so ill: yet could she not forbeare.
>
> One while she blam'd her selfe; another whyle
>   She him condemn'd, as trustlesse and untrew:
>   And then, her griefe with errour to beguyle,
>   She fayn'd to count the time againe anew,
>   As if before she had not counted trew.
>   For houres but dayes; for weekes, that passed were,
>   She told but moneths, to make them seeme more few:
>   Yet when she recknd them, still drawing neare,
> Each hour did seeme a moneth, and every moneth a yeare. (V. 6. 4–6)

We find nothing like this care for human reaction and detail in presenting it in any other epic or Romance, not even in Ariosto; outside

Shakespeare, we do not find such humanness until the arrival of the novel.

A few stanzas after this Britomart sees Artegall's groom, the 'yron man' Talus coming with 'hasty speede':

> Even in the dore him meeting, she begun;
>   And where is he thy Lord, and how far hence?
>   Declare at once; and hath he lost or wun?
>   The yron man, albe he wanted sence
>   And sorrowes feeling, yet with conscience
>   Of his ill newes, did inly chill and quake,
>   And stood still mute, as one in great suspence,
>   As if that by his silence he would make
> Her rather reade his meaning, then him selfe it spake. (V. 6 .9)

And when she learns from him of Artegall's bondage to the Lady Radegund, she is angry and bitterly complains of her lover's falseness:

> A while she walkt, and chauft[1]; a while she threw
>   Her selfe uppon her bed, and did lament:
>   Yet did she not lament with loude alew[2],
> As women wont, but with deepe sighes, and singults[3] few.
>
> Like as a wayward childe, whose sounder sleepe
>   Is broken with some fearefull dreames affright,
>   With froward[4] will doth set him selfe to weepe:
>   Ne can be stild for all his nurses might,
>   But kicks, and squals, and shriekes for fell despight:
>   Now scratching her, and her loose locks misusing;
>   Now seeking darkenesse, and now seeking light;
>   Then craving sucke, and then the sucke refusing.
> Such was this Ladies fit, in her loves fond accusing. (V. 6. 13–14)

How accurately seen and humorously described this is. Is there another epic or Romance heroine presented so graphically and movingly?

It will be apparent from many of these extracts that the detail given by Spenser is almost like that of a film scenario, so closely is the scene observed, movements, gestures, facial expressions and 'business' described. This skill of the great narrative artist is always used in the furtherance of his compelling moral concern. Although Britomart's passion seems at first sight too unbridled for a virtuous heroine, it is justified by Spenser's need to make her more than a paragon—a believable woman too. For, as I have said earlier, she is the one true and supreme hero of the poem. Taking his cue in this from Ariosto's

[1] *chauft* fumed   [2] *alew* howling   [3] *singults* sobs   [4] *froward* perverse

Bradamante, Spenser has made her the heroine of his narrative, and
a credible passionate loving woman. But she is also the heroine, as
it were, of his moral, for the ultimate message of *The Faerie Queene*
is of the creative power, the renewing force and the immortalising
vitality of love, which is what she symbolises.

I am convinced of the poem's completeness, despite the fact that
there are only six and not the promised twelve books, and despite the
'Mutabilitie' fragment, which has always been taken to be part of an
unfinished seventh book 'Of Constancie'. It is difficult to imagine any
conceivable development beyond the conclusion of Book VI, with its
almost ideal hero Sir Calidore; or any narrative continuation which
could legitimately show the adventures and perfecting of another
knight, superior to Calidore or more significant; or any lacunae in the
poem as a whole. Spenser has shown us man overcoming error and
falseness, and establishing a proper relationship with God's will:
man mastering the passions and so achieving self-discipline; the proper
way of love between man and man and man and woman; he has
implied an ideal of ordered God-fearing and God-loving society,
and shown the central importance of love in the whole conduct of
life: love of God, love of others, love of God's order in a just society,
love in society.

He has gone further even than that, for he altered his focal depth
towards the end in order to sharpen the image of the real world—
disordered, imperfect and mutable—seen against the steady glow of
God's perfection, love and unchangingness. There could be no book
'of Constancie' once Spenser had expressed his consciousness of the
imperfection of the world, symbolised in the disorder of Book V,
in the destruction of the ideal pastoral world and the vanishing of the
dance of the Graces in Book VI, and in the Blatant Beast which pursued
its evil way through both books and was reported at the very end to
be ranging 'through the world againe'. The most he could do was to
think (in Book V) of a future time when Love and Justice would be
united (Britomart and Artegall); to give us glimpses of perfect order
and grace (the pastoral world and the dance on Mount Acidale in Book
VI); and, in a characteristic symbolic set-piece, the most masterly
of them all, in the Mutabilitie Cantos—which could well be called the
Cantos of Constancie—to show us how we may be reconciled to the
imperfection of the world and its inconstancy by reflecting that change
is itself an aspect of renewal (and therefore of permanence), and, in

the fallen world, a part of God's purpose, and that the time will come

> ... when no more *Change* shall be,
> But stedfast rest of all things firmely stayd
> Upon the pillours of Eternity ...
>
> .   .   .
>
> But thenceforth all shall rest eternally
> With Him that is the God of Sabbaoth[1] hight: (VII. 8. 2)

Thus, with hope and confidence, he brings his great work to an end. He has fashioned 'a gentleman or noble person in vertuous and gentle discipline'; depicted the faults and perils that beset mankind in the world and shown how they may be overcome in the journey of life; honoured Elizabeth's England and demonstrated the triumph of Protestantism; related man's whole life and activity to God's purpose; and above all celebrated human love as a part of the divine love which alone can certify the perfection all idealists, moralists and artists seek. It should be emphasised that an ideal—the Christian ideal—of selfless service to others permeates the entire narrative of knightly adventure. In its greatest exemplars, Arthur (whose *only* function is to serve others), Britomart and Calidore, the Christian activities of love, generosity and succour are clearly demonstrated.

And it has all been done in a romantic and epic narrative which yet never loses contact with the real world as the poet knew it—and as we ourselves know it—for Spenser's world is universal, however fabulous, remote and fanciful it may seem. Spenser comprehensively explores man's impulses, motives, fears, hopes, desires, dismays, dreams, joys, in a way that no other epic or Romance quite does, and presents them so humanly and vividly that we believe in the fantastic fictions which carry them, and easily relate them to the world we ourselves live in.

The Faerie Queene is the most human of epics. Yet it has often been found extravagantly remote from life, and not epic at all. I hope I have to some extent controverted both views. It is, I think, the most comprehensive of epics. Many elements contribute to its greatness: Spenser's imagination and poetic vision; his metrical mastery, his music, and his narrative and dramatic skill; his genius for world-creating and myth-making; and his ability to make the reader 'experience' the poem almost as he experiences things in life. (C. S. Lewis

[1] *God of Sabbaoth* God of rest, and of hosts

wrote that *The Faerie Queene* was not 'like life' but the experience of
reading it was like the experience of living.)

The lines from F. R. Leavis which I quoted at the beginning were
not, of course, written of Spenser or *The Faerie Queene*. They might
well have been. The great poet and his greatest poem marvellously
illustrate that continuity with the past—Biblical, literary, imaginative,
human—which Leavis demanded. I do not think the great critic admires
Spenser. I do not think he sees *The Faerie Queene* as having its life
in the present. Yet it markedly had its ample life in its own present
day of Elizabethan England, and only a little imaginative effort is
needed to see how valid are the experiences it offers today.

Spenser's ultimate and enduring greatness as a moral poet lies here:
on every subject of crucial human concern—faith, trust, discipline,
friendship, sex, love, generosity, pity, truth, justice, responsibility—
he writes of what our consciences (and our common sense) recognise
to be true.

SELECTED BIBLIOGRAPHY

EDITIONS
(No manuscripts of Spenser's poetry exist)

The Faerie Queene, 2 volumes, Ed. J. C. Smith, Oxford 1909 and reprints.
Minor Poems, Ed. E. de Selincourt, Oxford 1910 and reprints.
The Poetical Works of Edmund Spenser, Ed. E. de Selincourt, Oxford 1912 and reprints. (The good text of the 1909 and 1910 Oxford editions cited)
The Works of Edmund Spenser, a Variorum edition, 11 volumes, Baltimore 1932 onwards, Eds. E. Greenlaw, C. G. Osgood, F. M. Padelford and others, including *Prose Works* (1949), *Life* (1945) and *Index* (1963).
The Complete Poetical Works of Edmund Spenser, Ed. R. E. N. Dodge, Boston 1908 and reprints. (Lightly annotated edition)

CRITICAL STUDIES AND COMMENTARIES

(a) *Spenser's poetry in general*

W. Nelson, *The Poetry of Edmund Spenser*, New York and London 1963. (The best modern book on Spenser's work as a whole, but less concerned with poetry and techniques than with ideas)
W. L. Renwick, *Edmund Spenser*, London 1925 and reprints. (Still the best brief introduction)

(b) *'The Faerie Queene'*

P. J. Alpers, *The Poetry of 'The Faerie Queene'*, Princeton 1967.
H. Berger, *The Allegorical Temper*, New Haven and Oxford 1957. (*Book II*)
L. Bradner, *Edmund Spenser and 'The Faerie Queene'*, Chicago 1948.
A. C. Hamilton, *The Structure of Allegory in 'The Faerie Queene'*, Oxford 1961.
G. Hough, *A Preface to 'The Faerie Queene'*, London 1962.
C. S. Lewis, *The Allegory of Love*, Oxford 1936 and reprint. (Final chapter revelatory on Spenser)
M. P. Parker, *The Allegory of 'The Faerie Queene'*, Oxford 1960.
T. P. Roche, *The Kindly Flame*, Princeton 1964. (*Books III and IV*)

J. Spens, *Spenser's 'Faerie Queene'*, London 1934.
K. Williams, *Spenser's 'Faerie Queene': The World of Glass*, London 1966.

(c) *Minor poems*

A. K. Hieatt; *Short Time's Endless Monument'*, New York 1960. (A study of 'Epithalamion', The first book of the numerological wave)
J. J. Higginson, *Spenser's 'Shepheardes Calender' in Relation to Contemporary Affairs*, New York 1912.
M. Stein, *Studies in Spenser's 'Complaints'*, Oxford 1934.
E. Welsford, *Spenser: 'Four Hymnes' and 'Epithalamion'*, Oxford 1967.

Three recent useful introductions are:
K. W. Gransden, *Spenser: 'The Faerie Queene'*, Macmillan Critical Commentaries, London 1969.
R. Sale, *Reading Spenser: An Introduction to 'The Faerie Queene'*, New York 1968.
E. A. F. Watson, *Spenser*, Literature in Perspective Series, London 1967.

BACKGROUND AND OTHER LEARNED STUDIES

D. Bush, *Mythology and the Renaissance Tradition in English Poetry*, New York 1957. (Valuable study of his mythology in ch. 5)
R. Ellrodt, *Neoplatonism in the Poetry of Spenser*, Geneva 1960. (Important discussion of Spenser's philosophical ideas)
N. Frye, *Anatomy of Criticism*, Princeton 1957.
C. S. Lewis, *Studies in Medieval and Renaissance Literature*, Cambridge 1966.
H. G. Lotspeich, *Classical Mythology in the Poetry of Edmund Spenser*, New York 1965. (A useful short dictionary)
R. Tuve, *Allegorical Imagery*, Princeton 1966.

BIBLIOGRAPHY

D. F. Atkinson, *Edmund Spenser: a Bibliographical Supplement*, Baltimore 1937. (Brings Carpenter up to 1937)
F. I. Carpenter, *A Reference Guide to Edmund Spenser*, Chicago 1923.
A. E. Dyson, Ed., *English Poetry: Select Bibliographical Guides*, Oxford 1971. (Chapter on Spenser, and Bibliography by P. C. Bayley)
W. R. McNeir and F. Provost, *Annotated Bibliography of Edmund Spenser, 1937–1960*. Pittsburgh and Louvain 1962. (Changes method, but brings Atkinson up to 1960)
K. Williams, *The Present State of Spenser Studies*, University of Texas Studies in English, 1965.

COLLECTIONS OF ESSAYS

P. J. Alpers, Ed., *Elizabethan Poetry: Modern Essays in Criticism*, London 1967.
P. J. Alpers, Ed., *Spenser*, in Penguin Criticism series, London 1970.
R. M. Cummings, Ed., *Spenser: The Critical Heritage*, London 1971.
W. R. Mueller and D. C. Allen, Eds., *That Soueraine Light*, Baltimore 1952.
W. R. Mueller, Ed., *Spenser's Critics*, Syracuse 1959.
W. Nelson, Ed., *Form and Convention in the Poetry of Edmund Spenser*, New York and London 1961.

There are recent editions of:
Ariosto, *Orlando Furioso*, Sir John Harrington's English version, Ed. G. Hough, Arundel 1962.
Tasso, *Gerusalemme Liberata*, Edward Fairfax's English version, Ed., R. Weiss, Arundel 1962.

INDEX